9/10 – Skunks, "creature
cycles" –
9/17 – Lakesho. Drive –
– (Chi

Norbert Blei

DOOR STEPS

Linda Jenewein

DOOR STEPS

THE DAYS, THE SEASONS

NORBERT BLEI

THE ELLIS PRESS
PEORIA, ILLINOIS

First Edition

Portions of *The Seasons* originally appeared in *The Milwaukee Journal,* the *Door County Advocate,* and the *Chicago Tribune.*

Special thanks to Alice D'Alessio for her assistance in typing, and to Bruce Mielke for photographing the sketchbooks of Charles Paterson and for end paper picture.

Dust jacket painting and sketch of Norbert Blei by Charles Peterson, Ephraim, used by permission of the artist. Interior art consists of pencil drawings done especially for *Door Steps* by Charles Peterson, and pencil sketches borrowed from his sketchbooks. All are reproduced by permission of the artist.

Published by The Ellis Press, P.O. Box 1443, Peoria, Illinois 61655, David R. Pichaske, editor.
Typesetting by Ty-Comp, Peoria, Illinois.
Printing by DJ Graphics, Peoria, and M & D Printing, Henry, Illinois.

ISBN 0-933180-44-6

DOOR STEPS

I have attempted many journals in the past, and continue to record my observations in a variety of notebooks, but never have I kept a journal so consistently, so religiously, as the daybook that is the heart of Door Steps.

I am a walker. Country or city, whatever the season, early each morning in Door I am on the road briefly, only to return to it again at odd hours of the afternoon and night. I can't explain the attraction or the movement. It's an unconscious act at best, for I am often surprised to find myself there. It is my river, my mountain, my path. Upon entering, I lose myself. Walking becomes a meditation.

Distance is of no concern to me. I plan nothing. I may walk as far east as the lake or as far west as the fields. Actually, my walks tend to be brief, and they end the moment I turn back. Then my feet are on the earth again. Then the everyday world returns, and I am anxious to get back to my desk and begin.

My pace, if it can be described at all, is rather leisurely. I am certainly not on the road for exercise. Brisk walking for physical fitness is not my style. I would rather slowly experience the peace of the fields and fall over dead in my footsteps, than suffer a heart attack jogging and recall only the trees flashing by. Health is beyond the physical.

My joy is to walk and not know I am walking. To be absorbed.

My intention in Door Steps *was somewhat deliberate: to record something each day for an entire year, something of the natural presence of this place—even other places where I happened to find myself. To record something that affected me, often just* one *thing, yet stimulus enough to go even beyond the initial impression which set my mind wandering, to hold it all in words. Even "the walk" was sacrificed at times to other ways of knowing.*

This is a book of entries, then, impressions, little stories, little poems, little pieces of the day and night that add up to a year in a man's life.

As a writer I found keeping a journal a good discipline, and one I wanted to sharpen. To make something of each day. To let no day of an entire year go unrecorded. A minimal goal, perhaps, yet more of a challenge than I ever imagined. The longer entries seemed to take less time, while the shorter entries grew more and more time consuming. The temptation, the real world pressures and obligations to miss an entry, to let a day or two or three slide by, became quite seductive at times. Sometimes the entries seemed too internal, too intense, too superficial, too simple, too dark, too vague, too uneventful, but I would not force a form, seriousness, or beauty on them if the mood of the day did not dictate so. So I persisted. Or it *persisted: the*

1

*journal, or journey, continued, day after day after day. I continued the
journey.*

*I imagined myself (in another setting, years from now) or a reader in
some distant city wondering, "What's November 8th like in Door
County?" And that kept me going.*

*And an extraordinary journey it was, for me. The danger in achieving
one's dreams, satiating one's desires, falling in love with a place, is the
inevitable loss of innocence. Even a landscape as beautiful as Door's fades
after a while. Many city people, having retired here, come to learn this the
hard way. It's primarily the visitor who retains the stars in his eyes. His
addiction requires an annual hype of vacation here, and the economy of the
entire Door peninsula is now based on tourism and land values, on* dream.

*The dream dissolves, though, in the reality of living here. A stand of
birch trees becomes commonplace. Sunsets across quiet waters are
expected. Birds, flowers, stars lose their initial attraction. One grows weary
of winter. A sameness of seasons sets in.*

*Door began to die for me once I had permanently settled in. I will never
see it again quite the way I first imagined and experienced it. I know its
drawbacks too well now, and witness its inevitable destruction in the hands
and hearts of men, as each day they reduce natural mysteries to the realities
of the marketplace.*

*It has been a difficult love affair at best. Door is an easy place to hate
when you suspect the insular culture, the greediness of men, the isolated
setting, are all at least partially responsible at times for your own
unhappiness. And the more this preys on a man's mind, the more it helps to
destroy the innocent relationship to nature he once revered here, the more
he loses touch with himself. I call it being "outside" as opposed to being in.*

Much of Door Steps *deals with this dilemma. It is an attempt to get back
in, to see and feel and know the world as it is, and in so doing to save the
day, to save myself.*

*Keeping a diary worked remarkably well. There were times I could not
wait to get outdoors, to discover what was waiting for me to see, to record,
to rush "outside" only to be quickly absorbed, to go immediately "in."
There were days when the abundance of impressions made recording them
overwhelming. And there were experiences so singular in impact as to
immediately become poem. Many of my later entries, in fact, were honed to
just that. The landscape was sharpening me. I was prepared for only the
elemental.*

And then it was over. The year's end.

What I discovered most poignantly in Door Steps *was the absence of this
daily commitment after the final entry was made. I recall, in particular,
awakening one morning, the magic of hoarfrost on the branches of trees, on
every plant along the road and in the fields, and being saddened in the
realization I would no longer be putting it down in words.*

Walking the road this morning at sunrise, I am reminded again of all this,

2

the journal I once kept, the days, the seasons, feeling "outside" now instead of in. I hear a fishing tug chugging through Death's Door, a rooster opening the day with his call . . . connections . . . to the earth, the water, the sky.

I've been "outside" far too much lately. It would be good to go back in. My walks these days hold me only momentarily. Then the outside world rushes in. I think it would be satisfying, perhaps even necessary, to record another year in Door some time. But I suspect I never will. I grow increasingly unsettled with this place. And I have not found the words either out or back into it yet.

The Days

Initiation

Whoever you are, go out into the evening,
leaving your room, of which you know each bit;
your house is the last before the infinite,
whoever you are.
Then with your eyes that wearily
scarce lift themselves from the worn-out door-stone
slowly you raise a shadowy black tree
and fix it on the sky: slender, alone.
And you have made the world (and it shall grow
and ripen as a word, unspoken, still).
When you have grasped its meaning with your will,
then tenderly your eyes will let it go . . .

—Rainer Maria Rilke

to Christopher
Bridget,
and Barbara

and the woman who loved roses

January 1   *Stone Awakening*

Gray. An absence of mind. Deadly morning. White wrinkled sheets.
Warmth in the nest of a feather comforter. View from the upstairs bedroom
window: sharp black trees, a black iron fence of spears.
To read awhile the story begun last night just before sleep?
Dreams? Mia, what was she telling me? The traveling dream . . . lost . . .
loss, loss.
"Skarda" . . . to work on her once more.
Eggs or French toast? Must go for fresh milk. Food turning. Christmas
stolen.
Stolen woman. Herb bread, herb bread love. Ah, the smell of it.
Dog, bird, fish, plants. Life on the inside.
Morning of gray birds at the feeder, gray seed, new gray year.
Candlelight in the coop. Incense, pinon from the Southwest. Tobacco
smoke. Water colors for each child.
To read the January 1st entry in Derleth's *Village Daybook:*
  "I rose in the grey dawn this morning to put things in order."
Then a letter. To do, to begin all things today to last throughout the year.
This book—the idea of all this from the preface of *New Heaven, New Earth*
by Oates. Turning the Rainbow Calendar, ordering a new book, rethinking
the first novel, to continue writing the story of "Skarda" . . . tarot, major
arcana, star, sun, moon.
A call from my mother and father in Chicago: that love which goes
unexpressed except in anxious questions of no meaning, save that our voices
can be heard and felt.
A lunch of herb bread, cheese, wine.

An afternoon walk behind the coop, through woods and fields . . . leaves, mud, branches cracking underfoot . . . a knoll, a ring of juniper, branches swollen in blight, a mound of discarded cornstalks from Matt's garden, rusty barbed wire, strands and strands and strands of it tied and shaped in a large O. Blackberry thorns piercing my calves . . . bright green moss at my feet. Charley's abandoned farmhouse, chicken coop. Wheel ruts in the weeds where men have secretly pulled in with their pickups to steal the stone from old stone fences. Life underground . . . snakes? insects? fox asleep in their burrows? I flush a grouse near the stone fence.

Stone . . . gray, rust-marked, crumbling, shelled, split, white, smooth, rough, round, flat, layered, spilling, clunking underfoot as I climb. Weathered posts of an old barbed wire fence lean, dead, buried in stone on both sides. Charley building his side, Matt building his . . . farming stone . . . 1920's? "Good fences make good neighbors" . . . a harvest of stone . . . a religion of stone. Stone boat . . . stone speech . . . stone worship . . . stone men . . . stone women . . . stone sky . . . stone star . . . stone earth . . . stone sleep.

January 2   Dust of Snow and Dreams

Cold gray. The faintest dust of snow gathering in the brittle cups of leaf cover, branches, on the blue shingles of the roof. Through the trees, a blue-gray ribbon of sky edged in light. The tops of trees nod in the wind. A limb squeaks. Underfoot, the frozen earth crust shatters with each step. A woodpecker drills. The garden rows are crystalized in frost. The leaves of cornstalks rattle in the wind. What is still green, frozen now in place, is dead.

January 3   Rendezvous

Good dreaming now, but not for keeping. Fragmentation and fear await me in the day. Rendezvous in a rural landscape of guilt and love . . . running, stark naked, stone, bone, barren fields. The incompleteness of moment, season, man. Peace in the night of a Ryder moon, a sky whale. The singular loss of motion. Tarot. Starwalker singing of Buffy St. Marie. Nin. Miller. Watts. Progoff. Singer. 3 and 6. Light. Shiny black. Chili. Cinema of night. But mostly her laughter in the right places.

Clarity of sky. Blue. Yellow sun. Winter without snow. Yet for the last time, a day, an afternoon of birds in free feathered flight, weeds rattling in a south flowing wind, woods of many winding pathways, none of which lead to any darkness. Warm wooliness of love peeling away passion to the skin, to handfuls of hair, openings of liquid warmth. Stiffness, resiliency. Strength in sway, in give . . . limb in the wind. Love laughter. Sounds over words. Resonance. Sunflakes falling.

Echoes. Not in the natural world, for this is a setting absent of echoes. Echoes of the human heart . . . the writer's way of hearing. A writer's voice having somehow become theirs. That kind of love, of knowing. Reading that in the feelings of others, others who have been moved enough to speak acknowledgment, praise, thankfulness for the words, the feelings that are theirs and the writer has somehow given back to them. Clothing the forest with words. Clothing the backroads, the fields, the winter, the night in holiness. Spangling the people with earth's starry wonder. This is us—in my eyes. The preciousness of silent human hearts. A man alone under a string of colored Christmas lights. A farm widow staring down the trees that hold his name, his history, their love beyond the windowpane. Love it all for what it is. What we are in the midst of time, in the sap of maple trees, the bark of white birch, the bird gathered in the feathers of itself, asleep in the center-deep, evergreen, fir tree night.

Blowing, drifting snow. An unconscious desire to be vanquished by it all, to leave no traces. A howl from the blind heavens to uproot these staggering footsteps and carry one away in white. The earth covering its history quickly, layering it. The wind working it in shallow wells around trees, swirls, and dreaming drifts. The weed, the twig, the rock struggling in prayerful presence: this is what I am, still.

From behind window glass, transformations outer, inner—a way of the natural world lost to me, a new, nether world gained, not to be approached or, certainly, loved. Not yet. In time. I am becoming what I must. No control. When it is over . . . the clearing, the blue sky, the sun. Then to acquaint myself once again with the cold deadliness of white, of drift, of depth, of an emptiness beyond glass. And try to love.

Inside, candles burn and lick the night away. I grow older by the images in this season. And there is a comfort to the warmth inside that any man who reads his blood despises.

The clearing, the sky, the sun. Nothing but the wind. The storm's center passing. The self-assuredness of snow: come, do with me what you will. There is no end to the conjurer within me. I am all things, forever in your vision. Forever until spring. And then again.

I push a door open, into it. I punch holes, ankle deep and more. I am not prepared, not yet, to love a single flake. I want a woman and the sun and the nakedness of green, earth smudges and the prodding and language of sharp stones and hot sand on skin.

Snow and an orange snowplow/Snow and dripping black motor oil/Snow and a red woolen cap/Snow exchanging white for skylight blue, late afternoon . . . dusk moaning darkness . . . mouthful of night.

A web of evening grosbeaks at the morning feeder. A circle of sunflower seed. A circle of smoke-colored feathers, of night, of day lilies, of olives, of snow. Creaking birch branches. A flutter of feathers as I toss more seed. A scatter of wings hanging in bobbing bushes and branches. The eye of the bird sees its life in the husk of a seed. Sees death? Never knowing it. Only

flight, the knowledge of air, of
altitude, of turning, of drifting,
of setting down, lifting up,
swooping down again. Dark
feathers of a dying night. And
then light . . . the sense of wings
sculpting the air. A sublime
emptiness in sustenance, procre-
ation, flight.

January 9   *Sky*

Rising in the 6:30 a.m. darkness of a January morning. A branch of lilac
bush outside the bedroom window nods with snow, the only light. View
from the downstairs kitchen window: gray, black, white. The sky graying
lighter in the approach of dawn. The black mass of trees slowly defining
themselves into bark, into branches, into movement as the sky opens into
them. The light of snow, radiant in itself, reflective, till that moment is
reached when each is the light of the other . . . with the sky then moving on
to yet other changes in the day.
A slash of orange in the horizon.
Orange thinning out to yellow, to sunlight struggling with light falling snow
and a gathering of gray storm clouds.
The purity of sun then lost in the morning's progression of cloud cover,
muted light in a solid, pale gray sky. The snow-covered earth fixed for the
day in its own glow.
Afternoon, falling light, sky thinned gray to fissures of yellow with a
sudden unmasking of turquoise blue. Spreading, Unfolding. Closing.
Lingering. Sky woman, seductive in her unravelings. Turquoise to violet,
yellow to rose to the softest pink slipping down, drawing the whole day, the
entire sky into itself. Leaving the wind, the emptiness, the snow, the
emerging light.

Light snow . . . dream sifting, real/unreal, throughout the day. In a van somewhere out West, Ross is driving. No color. White, perhaps, but not snow, not the light falling of it as it does this day. Whiteness, though, and a woman beside me in the back of the van, which is dark. Vision comes, when it does, through the windshield and in the mind of the dreamer and the dream, opening up to whatever landscape, sometimes Southwest, sometimes Midwest. Her hair is black. We are discussing the past as if it were now. She is a girl I loved twenty years ago, and age, once again, is no age at all. We are what we were and what we are in the moment. She laughs and touches me. I am aroused by her. We sense the wanting of each other, while outside, past the windshield, are first fields, then mountains, then city. A huge building is going up. The top two floors are solid glass. Ross comments that that will be the place to take lunch, that that will be the view. The snow whirls lightly in the afternoon.

A call from V brings the heavens back in focus, the times, the signs in the stars. "You need flexibility," I'm reminded. "Constant change."

In Tarot, the Fool was V's card.

That's very good, I say.

"Yeah [laughter], me walking off a cliff."

One day, all seasons. Temperature climbing to the upper 40's in the night. Rain falling on snow. One could almost expect the sound of a whippoorwill, all the voices of spring. By morning, rain has washed most of the snow away. The roads—water above ice in some stretches. Within a single hour: rain, fog, wind, snow, sun. Then the falling temperatures again, the barometer at 29, the wind from the northwest, howling through the trees, bending birches and maples, the trunks of them, first one way, then back, then down again. Branches snapping. Electric wires humming. Lights flickering. Cold air finding the tiniest crevice of the coop. First hands, then feet of ice.

After lunch, tossing cans of compost on the crusted earth, last summer's garden. Halves of yellow Florida grapefruit, and bright orange rinds fall upon the earth like broken moons and suns.

A piece of last night's dream, white ceramic and silver. A vessel? A sculpture? A white base moving into a crescent, the arc of it on top, ceramic and silver, and each end of it, like the hair of the Hopi Indian woman's head, shaped solid in silver.

The menacing wind blowing into late afternoon. Unsettling. Unrelenting.

Retrieving all that was good in the day, casting it now full of foreboding, a touch of terror, a scream caught in a throat of ice.

January 12   Milkweed Dream

And the wind lessens somewhere along the night. The blackness of the sky glows, star-webbed, sparkling, pulsing. A crystal laughter as infinite as the mind of a man asleep. Dreaming. The clarity of the inner terrain in such hours. The face, familiar. The dream-story-line near enough to touch. I have it, extend a hand to it, a floating in milkweed-seed dream. I carry it gently without breathing. Shelter it from the slightest draft. Save it for words in the waking . . . The day assumes itself in sun. I open to light to retrieve the dream images preserved. Gone.

January 13   Circle Snow

Mildness in the woods. A slow melt of snow around each tree and rock. Islands of leafy earth emerging. Circular, always circular, as if the very form of air, of wind, of fire, of water, of sun . . . circles within circles. Rain circles. Snow circles. Wind circles. Moving amongst them now. The tree, the rock radiating boundaries of warmth toward the hardpacked snow. Unshackling themselves till the ground yields, the patches of snow disappear in a circle of themselves. The earth loose—then the circling of new snow before day's end.

January 14   The Solitary Walker

A walk with someone else beside you, in front of you, behind you, qualifies your steps, your direction, your meaning and mood. Though the walk to the lake may be familiar, it is never the same. Time of day and weather conditions, though unmentioned, immediately affect the walkers. What one sees, though it be familiar, is also not the same. A walk, to be most meaningful, most meditative, most astonishing, must be solitary. Talk destroys quiet perspective. Thinking, the mind in a muster of images or memories to be talked out, diminishes reflection and surprise over the most mundane rock, weed, bird, tree, or farm in the landscape that seeks the solitary walker's attention. The delicacy of both sound and silence are lost to walkers. The walker alone becomes these.

January 15   Cold Rain

Winter rain. A madness of its own. The steady drumming on the roof of the coop precludes a January of the mind with a sound of spring. Welcome enough for the moment. But sinister in a teasing way. How can the earth be green tomorrow? How can there be blossom? The song of birds? The sun warming the moisture away? Nature in opposition to itself. Meaning enough in that. Those things within us so diametrically opposed. Rain falling into snow, opening it, honeycombing it, reducing it, transforming it to what it was. Is. Come night, the miracle of ice.

January 16   Faceless Woman

A piece of a dream lost some nights ago, only to reappear today, somewhere between thinking, some vacant area of the mind, some silence in the mildness of another rainy winter day: "first face, then form." A fragment associated perhaps with a dream of watercolor painting. I am about to do a woman's face, which I always begin with an oval outline, filling the space, finding what I hope will be a beautiful face to match the form. But the meaning, the "instruction" as it were, was to first find the face . . . the form will follow. There was the watercolor of the faceless woman I did before Christmas, complete but for the emptiness of eyes, nose, mouth. Studying it for days, I discovered she was quite beautiful that way. The form appeared so complete in itself that one either never realized the face was missing, or imagined the face was there.

January 17   Watercolored Landscape

Walking the wet road with the children early in the morning to meet the schoolbus. The trees, field, old orchard, road ahead wrapped in thick and thin fog. The trees appear pliable enough to take in one's hand and bend, twist, knot, even wave. The children disappear and reappear. The dog drifts in and out of reality, its pink tongue alive like the petal of a rose. In the

14

distance, the sound of the schoolbus lumbering its way down the road. First, the headlights aglow, casting light back upon themselves. Then the wet, black grill. Then the wash of yellow, soft. Nearing the stop, the red blinking lights begin. And I stand and watch and wait for it to disappear once again in fog, a carnival of my youth, a neon street in an October, Chicago rain . . . red light, yellow light, white light . . . red, yellow, white, red, laughing red . . . clown's nose, stoplight, train lantern, vigil candle, woman's passion, all heightened in fog . . . red beyond red, light beyond light . . . disappearing, rolling into, snatched by fog. The light that remains in the eyes. Then the field, bronzed. Burnished trees. Weeds vibrating like welding rods. The dog, golden, dead still, against the ghostly air. A hawk drops from a tree, treading a sky that swallows its wings.

January 18   *Sightings*

Like looking through a window past the trees, seeing a road, a car going by. Silence. Then the road again. Missing the trees, the leaves upon the earth, the eastern stone groupings I have assembled. Days, times, moments of the physical, the civilized—be it road, car, or telephone—too solid, too real, to break through and enter. The mind chatters. Time is either time past or time future. A busybodiness that takes precedence over other-mindedness. A cloudy sky rather than the clouds themselves; birch trees, maple trees, beech trees, rather than bark, surface roots, a woodpecker's hole. Desire rather than passion that opens no-mindedness and the blessing of fire. . . .

January 19   *Creature Comforts*

Life in these wintry wooden walls makes itself known now, for the first time this year. All life, before now, has been outside of me: a chickadee peeping, twirling on a branch; a squirrel skittering along the ground; the wind; the rain; a dog's bark. But now, inside, between these walls near my desk, the tentative scratching begins. A creature small, possibly furry, rolling over in my mind's eye, stretching the merest of legs, the tiniest of claws. Grasping wood, pushing itself off in movements marked by inconstancy: upward scratching followed by long moments of stillness. Scratch. Stillness. Laterally now. Silence. Up again. Steadily up to the ceiling. Silence. Then a long, almost fluttering sound over and across and beyond the top of my head, coming to a kind of final rest. A retreat, perhaps, to a far corner. Nestled there in a world of wooden darkness and perhaps a pillow of

15

milkweed seed, claws curled in, creature tight. The tiniest of hearts pulsing into a deepening night.

January 20   *Night Bird*

Night. Blue-black ink and a lemon slice of a moon. A curved splinter. A crystal crescent balanced on my head. Eyebrow, lady night. Venus off the lower point. The stars rain down. The makings of a man leap up. I am an arm of a child picking up brush, splashing paints, making a universe of the darkest light that speaks to me in wings, settles the fire, and lifts me above . . . my bodyweight flesh, then liquid, then ice, then feathered: the shiniest, blackest of birds coursing through bone.

January 21   *Ice Light*

Into the sun, 4:35 p.m., a winter's afternoon. Field fragile in last summer's weeds, stems unbending, threads of glass. Wheel ruts coated, thick and thin, in ice. Walking solid ice lends a seeing to the soles of feet. Thin ice, the brittleness of a windowpane shattering because I want it to, long for the childhood sound of cracking, of water, under crushing heels. The sun diffusing a descent above the woods, sucking the sky, an inhalation, a yellow glow into an orange mouth, swallowing woods, illuminating skeletal branches like sparrow bones, exhaling an after-breath of sky far to the east . . . opal, magenta, a memory of blue, and a moon transparent as a sigh.

For the past few mornings, seconds, minutes more of morning light upon awakening. A door of night ajar, the crack widening. This morning, leaden sky holding back, weighing down the early light, compressing it, loosening it, filtering light in snow. The earth transformed again. A snowrise lighting the trunks of trees, the highest branches, the sky itself. This will be a day of hollowness in the heart, a body fused with wind, a head crocheted in snowflakes, hands burning in ice.

Cold. Neither bitter nor sweet. No taste at all. Freezing. Below freezing. Words . . . not c-o-l-d. Cold is a door slammed shut in anger. Cold is denial: something you need but can't have. A cold shoulder is closer to cold than ice cold. Feelings persist while I walk this cold afternoon in a sun that may have lost its fire but not its warmth. Wind, in this weather, tunes a silver deafness to the ears. Legs, in their walking, move lighter, sharp as the blades of knives. Toes and fingers, so far removed, whimper a pointed pain of tacks. The torso is flesh, wrapped in wool, hardening into glass. The face, a porcelain death mask but for the warmth of tears. The breath blossoms, blossoms, blossoms alive.

A day lost . . . but is time ever wasted? The story, "Skarda," is taking forever to write. Does it want to be written? Do I want to write it? Why is the process so slow, so painful in the agony of lost time? Often only a word a day. Sometimes a sentence, a paragraph, a few pages. Not like other stories that take hold and run themselves through me in days. Still, I have decided to watch it, do it, be aware of the process of how this story wants its own life . . . a forward, backward movement. The frustration is in myself, wanting, needing it all to end, knowing the work that waits in the wings, desiring to get on with it—yet the story of "Skarda" will not be done with me, with what it must become. Frustration, then, and an edge of fear . . . fear of all the time it's taking and that the story may prove inconsequential, not what I envisioned, not what I started out to tell. So I see the time evaporate through these very fingers, losing "Skarda" every day in a few words or sentences or nothing, making other words that become letters, that become poems, that becomes entries such as this. Words, too, that never even find life on paper, remain instead part of all this which is me, the writer, wanting to, needing to say things about what I am, what this is, what I see . . . wasting it all in a mind of dream-state, unable to grasp the scheme of it to make it into something now. And the guilt, then, eating myself alive, because the time is now, this moment, and the act is denied, incomplete, unsustaining. And standing outside in the blue snow, the fading light of afternoon, aware hours and hours have passed, my whole body crippled by unfulfilled desire. And I would drag my body, or be dragged, toward the light in the house leaving an erratic trail in the snow that will be covered by morning, when I will step out once again, sure-footed, to this coop, put on the light, turn up the heat, and make whatever it is that will be made, or refuses to be made, in the time of day. For even in time wasted, I suspect (don't I know?), the living, the dreaming, the making, the loving goes on. The completion will come later (as it often does) and will it not be stronger? Incredible? More unique? As in the hours now gone in this day, have there not been flashes of stories and poems and books ahead? And has not love visited this door? And has there not been the mind's release, the body's river-flow? And outside, though a camera's lens recorded winter, the images of flesh spoke sun, felt fire, flowed and merged past the need of any man wanting to put a measure to it in words.

January 25   *Snow Still*

What is noticeable is not so much the new fallen snow this day, the first significant snowfall this year. The evergreens, yes, are graced in fluffiness. The fenceposts, the birdhouses, the railings are capped in a white wonder slightly humorous in the new dimension it creates. The fresh snowcover of the earth brings a familiar softness to one's vision, wading into the white as one wades into water from a sandy beach. Still, all this speaks of a familiarity: I have reflected upon this scene before. What is really lost, however, is the sound, the sight, the significance of animal life. Deer tracks, but no deer. Some winter birds, but no wild color, no real song. An occasional squirrel. The prints of mice. All of which deepens the mystery, heightens the surprise when early this morning, alongside the garage, quietly, in undulatory movements, a white ermine appeared, turning the freshly fallen snow even whiter. A gladness, a holiness invades the human presence, silenced, comforted in the surprise and cunning dumbness of one's own creatureness.

January 26 — Shadow Mouse

What will it be now? The moonlight last night casting shadows of the trees on the palest of yellow snow, as if all the words were felled at my feet? Or the same shadows this morning in a warmer light, a touch of gold, tree shadowing life of its own, prone position, moving in arcs across the snow? Or the mouse, this afternoon, the mouse who must live in this coop of mine, off on a mission of food, returning from a nearby field? I watch his antics on top the snow, tracking it in minute steps, carrying his weight somewhat above him like a bird . . . then losing the balance and sinking, only to shoot up again by leaps, breathe a second's rest . . . such a moving target for the hawk . . . the mouse must carry the shadow wings of the hawk within . . . leaping again for life, falling into snow, engineered for the dark hole and warm security of this coop which lies just ahead. The mouse now out of range of my vision, I stand still and wait, wondering of its entrance way. Silence. And then moments later, the scratching of that black, beady-eyed shadow that knows the dark maze of these wooden walls . . . home free.

January 27 — Chickadee

The first time this year, that plaintive call. First a high note, followed immediately, run into, a note of a slightly lower register: Wphewwww, Wheooooooo. A sound I somehow associate with the earliest call of spring, usually heard for the first time in mid-February. In a winter-world of no melody, of mostly jay chatterings, crow calls, a matter-of-fact sort of winter bird chatter, this sound of the chickadee always strikes me as the nearest to song one can ever expect to hear in the heart of winter.

19

A day of the chickadee. Later in the winter morning, near the lilac bushes, a chickadee seemingly stuck in snow, possibly dying, and being attacked by blue jays. I reach down with a gloved hand and retrieve a weightless ball of gray, black and white feathers. The thin, black wiry feet, motionless. The eyes closed. Then one lid opens . . . the tiniest flicker of life imaginable in the black pin-prick of an eye. Turning the bird over in hand, I notice a ball of snow frozen to its breast. Not a bird dying, I feel, but a bird in trouble with snow frozen to a ball of ice upon its breast. The bird possibly floundering in snow, helpless, unable to maintain balance, or certainly flight, and so a target for attack, its wings iced in place.

Inside the house, bird in a box, the moments of thaw pass . . . the snowball melts free from the feathered breast, and the bird takes flight around the kitchen, coming to rest above the cabinets.

I hover above it with a gloved hand once again, fearing now it will fear my approach and take to flight, endless flight, from room to room. Instead, it seems to welcome my fingers cradling its suspicious flight indoors. Returning it to the box, I give it seed, cover it, let it rest a while more. Before the final freedom of the out of doors, I move it first from the kitchen warmth to the cool back porch to condition its reawakening to winter flight. Sometime later the box is opened out of doors, and the bird flies instantly to a branch halfway up a tall maple tree.

I isolate the bird momentarily in my eye, keeping it distinct from the many of its kind at the feeder, in the trees, on the wing.

A distraction, no more than a second or two, and I discover that chickadees frolic everywhere. And the difference, which was manifested in trouble, in fear, in danger, is suddenly rendered commonplace in flight, in flock, in birds everywhere.

January 28   *Winter Sleep*

It did not make the morning any easier or any more difficult. But the image of a woman, left over from dream, still hung about me . . . nameless as she must be, unapproachable, as she was . . . haunting, as I desired the reality. Her hair entangled me through my brisk walk down the road. Her hands pulled me on top of her. For hours we struggled in the white morning, denying our names, our flesh, our consumation. All day there was an anger of unfulfillment about me. It was a winter dream of an autumn reality that would not go away. I wrote words to dismiss her. I talked out loud to silence the sound of lovemaking. I went to sleep longing for nightmares.

A solid gray band of cloud cover in the east this early morning, so like a mountain range, so like the Southwest. The forms round and moving into peaks. Above, a delicate robin's egg blue sky with a dusting of white. All of this in constant flux, all but the clouds, steadfastly gray and mountain reaching. Behind them, though, the blue and white, taking on the merest cast of yellow. A yellow deepening, spreading . . . then the fire, igniting all along the cloud-rim mountain range, intensifying the running line in both directions like a fuse. Silence. A rooster crows on a faraway farm. The sun emerges behind the peaks. The light comes down like a curtain on the woods behind me. I turn till it touches my eyes.

January 30   *How the Day Dissolves Itself*

A day of sun, of snow covered earth, no wind . . . everything to engage a willing mind. In invitation, though, I refuse. The outer world of hope, of dreams, of a book to be fulfilled, appears whisked away from me after years of expectation, faith in one publisher. So I stand outside it all, a victim of my own turmoil, doubts, depressions, frustrations. I should seek solace within the landscape, as I have done so many times before. But so much of my writer's life here has been a turning into that, under similar circumstances, that I almost fear it will not hold me anymore. The spirit grows thinner in such times. I grow almost heavier, more fruitful, more real within my own anger, like the mushroom, *coprinus,* that slowly digests itself.

January 31   *A Writer's Season*

There are days, times, even like today where there is too much sun. When one, so contrary to my usual desires, wishes secretly for the worst in weather. Wishes for sleet, for heavy snow, for a wind that tears through things, bringing trees down and branches crashing on the roof. A winter that is winter. A time of denial . . . so hard for me to voice. For in those circumstances of prison-white, I fight with a passion for my want of freedom. Ah, the paradox of this man's soul; wanting to breathe when he is choking; desiring to choke when he can breathe. Knowing, though, that what comes when freedom is denied in outer realities, is a rambling through the mind, a running over of life imagined, heightened, let loose upon paper in words or paints, and suddenly I am alive in a region unknown, whatever season waits outside my window. This is a season to itself, mostly unvisited by other men, visible because it is invisible, strengthened through denial.

February 1   *The Way In with Words*

The "going in" today was one of words. Finding the one, the right, the special, the revealing, the holy—that kind of word which would be entrance. Beginning a new novel today . . . trying to find the opening in all the words, the images of the previous days, "names" of times, of people, of experiences which would lead me on. Words, a word, not to be found out of doors. A tree, a bird, a plant . . . none of that would do. Those might be called to answer for later. The need for now, for begging, was something entirely inside, unspoken, waiting to be known. And the word to me was manifested first in feeling. Feeling, soon clarified, refined to something like "desire," which became the word, the first word, and the telling of the tale, unfolding in places far removed from here, where snow and cold enwrap the day . . . far away as Budapest in spring.

February 2 *Hoarfrost*

Morning sun. 7:15 a.m. through the downstairs window, through the trees, coming across the field—evidence of wonder. Making coffee. Hurrying through it. A feeling that it must be now . . . there is something happening out there this very instant, and in five minutes, ten minutes at most, it will be gone. Making my way down the road, past the woods, toward the clearing. The sun—there, just south of Carlson's outbuildings. But not the sun only: the wonder of this morning is the thin, illuminating skin of hoarfrost on every limb, every weed in the snowy field. How, with the early orange sun lingering on every particle . . . the limbs of an old apple tree, the branch of birch, the tiniest tasseled weed in the field . . . all, all of it, a diamond dust this morning, particles sparkling in the air with light, like winter fireflies. Even a strangeness of warmth to a morning just above zero. The sun holds us all suspended in a radiant stillness till we evaporate in translucence. And far, far off, the plaintive spring-like call of a chickadee transforms the notes to crystal. A life frozen, perfectly in fire in itself.

February 3 *Ice Shanty*

Walking the sharp afternoon, an hour or so before sunset, the light already cutting the trees in darkness halfway down the trunks, the face and the ears catching the slight but bitter wind while passing the open fields. Down to the lake, covered now with snow . . . and in the distance, four ice shanties. Smoke rolls upwards from the tiny chimneys and spreads in the late light of sky. Inside, men sit around an open hole of blue, tied to the water under ice, lost in the oldest of prayers. Walking above it all, I see and feel and know the sweep and force of wet flesh stirring a muddy lake bottom that might possibly read spring to scale and fin and shell, though the clear and cloudy heaven I trod, to fish steering beneath me, remains a constancy, a limit to their leaping, a ceiling of ice.

February 4 *Jay*

Delicacy of hoarfrost in a morning partly blue-silver light. Delicacy of snow determinedly, indetermindedly falling, covering a road clear, but now holding the thinnest, first layer of snow. Now a dog's bark rips an opening in the muslin field. Then a jay hits a branch, bending it, and on the upswing, the body, the throat, the beak, the very soul of bird spews out a racous caw . . . once, twice, three times, pumping sound and energy like a spring within itself, an undulation to wake and break the day.

February 5 — Skywalker

Winter moon, winter sky, winter night. A brevity and crystalline clarity to it all. Stars and moon and sky seem most perfectly in place, where it all must be, and our knowing, seeing, loving this, is of no concern. Too much perfection, though, brings a sense of weariness to this mind. The brittle cold itself makes quick and anxious skywatchers of us all. What I need to linger there is something like the shroud of mist, the coat of hoarfrost, the ominous movement of strange clouds across a changing sky. Or, in last night's sky, a nimbus of the moon, dulling the sharp direction of perfect yellow light, diffusing it, mellowing it, spreading the spill in mute tones . . . softening the moon itself, the sky, the earth, the trees, and the very man himself, gazing, melting into snow, into moon, into sky.

February 6 — Running Man, Still

A day, once again, of sun, beguiling to the point of "almost like spring," "almost like summer" were it not for the edge of cold and the time of year. The kind of light . . . light enough, just so, to speak of green and flowery things . . . to suggest a man, any man, running away from things. Running to beach, running to woman, running to dreams. A longing for foolishness prevails. Just to forget about things in this light. And turning from it, knowing that it cannot deliver and is, in fact, false is all the harder. Taking up the work that must be done. Living the life, part hurt, part "as it has to be for now," part joy.

February 7 — Frost Upon the Pane

Of nights, of winter, sometimes not made for sleep or dream. Night of anguish, of a restlessness, of wanting too hard to die the death of day. Struggling to reconstruct the silence, the meaninglessness of words. To stop the mind. To stop the mind. To worry the illusive patterns of frost upon the pane. To climb that slope, reach the apex which harbors moonlight, only to slide down again in milky darkness, eyes alive, body whole, mind afire.

24

February 8   *Days Alike*

Though nothing ever appears entirely alike or the same, there are days
which seem to repeat themselves if only in moments. The essence of the very
same moment: sunrise, hoarfrost on the fields and trees. Then the light
awakening the sparkle in the world: I was here yesterday, or the day before?
The pulsing, tiny specks of sunlight setting off frost in fields, weeds,
branches, trees. Taken into all this, letting go in a light of fields that lifts
and carries one away into another morning, fleetingly recalled . . . so much
the way of another day.

February 9   *Judgment*

This afternoon, in sun, so much like summer. How the sun settles in a
southwestern descent over the woods, cutting in ever so slightly through the
eastern-most window of the coop. The sun has little to do with the dream of
last night, but both the dream and the sun linger. A boyhood friend has
killed someone, and I am present at the trial: prosecutor, defender, jury and
judge. The sorrow of all this is lifted, though, by the possibility of a
woman, C., coming to visit me in the city that night. I am looking forward
to her visit, making love to her. But the excitement of her mingles with the
crime of my friend, J.C., who, though saved from the death sentence, must
spend a good part of his life in prison. It's this conflict of feelings, sorrow
and desire, which most permeate the dream, my awakening, my entire day.
And now, just moments before sunset, I feel a part of me is lost beyond
redeeming. A part of me sadly alive.

February 10   *Dog*

A dog, knowing its way in winter, knowing a groundcover of snow hides
nothing from its nose. Sniffing in it. Frolicking in it. Running, head low,
down a line of fresh tracks—rabbit, deer, dog—wherever it leads. Tossing
up snoutfuls of snow. My dog today, unmindful of me at the window,
stealthily crossing the road from the woods, balancing in its mouth what
looks like a branch. Carrying it, in a dog's own kind of secrecy, to a place
near a tree, very close to me. Not a branch at all, I see, but a deer's leg, left
over, no doubt, by some local marksman/carver during last November's
hunt. The dog dropping the deer leg upon the snow, making it in its own
mind as a private place. First digging in long stretches, an appropriate

hollow, scattering snow, then leaves, and frozen earth. Nudging the hoof and bone in place. Satisfied as to size, the innate protecting of it—from me? From others of its kind? A motion now of head instead of paws. Angling the nose to the ground, rooting, as it were, earth and leaves and finally, snow. A non-stop frenzy of covering every possible hint of smell, sight of frozen blood, fur, and bone. Such a keenness of animal mind far beyond my own divining. Domesticated though the dog may be, I rejoice as witness within myself of the essence of the animal never lost.

February 11   *Animal Remembering*

Dog worrying its deer bone again. Resurrecting it from its hiding place, not to sit and gnaw, but to carry it again to yet another secret hiding place. Behind my coop now I hear a rustling of leaves, a banging of bone against my wooden building, beneath my back window. I observe the dog bury the bone once more. Cover it with the same precise movements of snow with its snout. Then walk a few steps away. Turn. Look back to see if everything is as it was. It is. Nothing has changed. Satisfied in secrecy, the dog moves into its fur, its muscle, its steps, its self. Its own head of day's light and forgetfulness, remembrance of a kind in its nose, its teeth.

February 12   *Recurring Image*

Left over from last night's call, another time of love. She remains all through the night, in and out the dawning hours, my wake-up tossings in bed. Why now? Again? Why reawake a restlessness buried in winters of snow, new memories, fresh dreams? Through the upstairs window, looking east, the wash of rose across the sky. I seek more of the same. New memories of her.

February 13   *A Writer's Numbered Winters*

Awakening to new snow falling outside the bedroom window this morning. Watching its freshness momentarily, its magic, its delight, its memory of childhood snows and visions of early morning sidewalk depths of such non-trespassing, I would move to the street, following the wheel ruts of cars to

26

school. The joy within that doing. The joy that turned to quieter times of just some years ago in a sudden acquaintance of Wisconsin wintering. There was joy here too, at first, followed by the growing realization of what a lock snow had upon the land, how my comings and going were dramatically restricted. A remembrance of all that which swept swiftly through my mind this morning. Yet this winter, this year, for some reason, a difference: not quite the unrestricted joy of childhood, but neither the isolation, the feeling of imprisonment the last few years. Perhaps the mildness of this winter?

Possibly. That, and a growing acceptance of my own work as a writer. No longer really wanting/caring to be anywhere but at my desk this morning. That, and an intimation, at best, that my winters here are numbered. Some inexplicable knowing that I will some day soon make it out of here. There will be sun, yes. And so this new snow this morning no longer contains me.

February 14   All My Walks

The walk again. All my walks. The mindlessness in such moments. How the thinking process ceases in the first few steps. How the eyes sweep into woods and fields, swallowing images of light, of form, of movement . . . not to dwell upon them, but only to absorb, to make part of the tissue—a synthesis of peace.

February 15   Shadowed Love

There are those things in the outside world, the knowledge of them affecting the very atmosphere of day, of self. Knowledge of lives lived/loved in the shadows for which there can be no expression. It tempers one's day in melancholy, self-disgust, confusion, loneliness, yet turns, ever turns toward the other in feelings so deep, could I write them, they might spell c-o-u-r-a-g-e, and could I say them, they would sound "love." It is very still this afternoon of yellow winter light. All the clarity of what you have been and done to my life rests there.

Coming home last night through the fast falling snow: flakes growing in my eyes, the play of light on the road ahead. Landscape shifting as the road, the trees, the fences, farms and fields are transformed in a unison of white. The beams of the headlights, straight, in time appear to cross, appear to turn back upon themselves, back upon the driver, eyes dancing in a whirl of flakes so big they blind, then occupy the very eye till all inside the skull is a ball of glass turned upside down, snow drifting in its own light.

A throbbing pain behind the left ear beginning last night, just before Paul Schroeder's visit. Extending throughout the night, all through a restless sleep. Tension, a delayed reaction of a whirlwind of thoughts and feelings filling my head to the bursting point. The capacity for quiet courage in a human being so rare. And the mantle of protection I feel, affecting me, since then, in periodic flashes of conscience . . . but then suppressing this again. All of it building in the subconscious, till my head, all last night, all day today, is swollen with pain and begs relief. (A fragment of a dream last night; the actual tapping of something like a blister, a boil . . . the relief in the draining process.) I wish for some of that this moment. A call to Ross and Arlene in Santa Fe this morning. Their voices through the wires of my phone upon my desk, inside this coop . . . 10 below zero outside . . . I see the desert mountain landscape outside their adobe. The warmth. The sun. My longing to be there with them overflows the friendship of the moment, speaking in a voice unheard: sadness, love, and joy.

The pain continuing to cut into my day, I abandon the scene of home and work and head into the countryside. Everywhere, in the way light rests upon the terrain so familiar to me from here to Baileys Harbor . . . everywhere I read the light of spring. And in this, a surcease to pain.

Back in the coop, late afternoon. The pain rising and falling . . . a tidal rhythm of the new moon? I try to make words. They still come, though the pain checks a certain momentum in their flow. I despise the command illness takes upon the human body. I wish to dismiss pain. To never give it the benefit of reality in my consciousness. The scene outside my window helps. But then, in the distance, the ugly roar of engines. Closer, till finally the noisy whine seems transformed into the very pain I feel. A trail-ride of snowmobilers rips through the landscape. The window rattles. I know the crack of glass.

The prism hanging in my east window of the coop, a gift sometime ago from one whom I have shared a spectrum of feelings. Through most of the year, it cast rainbows of various intensities upon these cedar walls and ceiling. For some months now, as the sun began its winter journey far south of my window, the crystal has hung alone in its own clear light, a rainbow unto itself at times. I would walk up to it at various moments of the day or week in blind and dark season, peering into the center of it, capturing a scene outside the window, so multifaceted in trees, or field, or stone, or sky. I worship the centering, circular force of it, the way it gathers whatever I focus upon, centering it in a hard, true manner, a color not unlike ice. Two days ago, though, a little after 8 in the morning, I caught what I thought was the faintest glimmer of the prism speaking in rainbows once again. This morning, at 8:15, there was no doubt. The sun is returning. Five vivid splashes of separate rainbows glazed my ceiling right above where I now sit. And each day now there will be more. Till a morning, weeks or months away, when the sun will rise due east of the prism, and this room will hold, for only minutes, more rainbow than anyone can imagine. My face, my hands, my very self: the rainbow man.

The fall, a metaphor for man, especially in winter. Three times already have I lost my balance. This afternoon makes four, all of them unexpected, some of them followed by anger, often accompanied by pain. Yet sometimes, like this fall this afternoon, laughter seems more appropriate. Why, after all, must a man be running in snow? Where was there, really, to go in such a hurry? What was driving me on? The mail? The cold? Nevertheless, the feet slip, a footing is lost, the man totters, falls, tumbles. The knees striking snow and pavement first, followed by frantic hands, useless as they lose

themselves on snow. Pain, next. The knees. A quick look to see if clothing has been torn upon the pavement. Standing, shaking, brushing off the snow, rubbing the hurt knees with the hand momentarily. Then the laughter. An old, old laughter . . . perhaps the clown, who has understood for ages the meaningless of such motion in the acts of man.

February 20   *The White Peninsula*

The silence of this life in the country every night and during large parts of the day, especially in winter, becomes so common, so casual, that only the harshest, the most strident, the most unusual of noises awakens one from this comfortable lethargy. It is almost as if a balance of nature, sounds most natural, has been reached within the ear. Which is why early this morning, 6:30 a.m., the far away sound . . . a hum? . . . coming closer to where I lay in bed . . . closer . . . rivets my attention to the ceiling, then to the window, the sky. Suddenly the steady whirring sound passes overhead, diminishing once more. A single-engine plane, flying this bleak winter landscape unaccustomed to any air traffic at all. The mind goes up to it . . . the sound, the plane, the pilot. With him I see the white peninsula, the islands, the blue waters of the lake. On the ground, snowbirds . . . a harbinger of spring.

February 21   *Thaw*

With the temperatures reaching the upper 40's today, the sight, the feeling, the smell of winter's first thaw. The snow itself, honeycombing, giving way to an almost sullenness of pockmarked, raw earth. As if the patches of saturated dead leaves, the black exposed twigs, the wet stones, were caught unaware by forces, though freeing, in revelations of stark decay, too early for the complexities and afterlife of spring. Killdeer invade the road's thawed edge.

February 22   *Being There*

The sighting of deer in the woods . . . an early sign, too, that there is movement about. An anxiousness of animals moving out of the cedar swamps in the mildness of winter. I see their fresh tracks in the morning; the dog does it crazed zig-zag dance, the nose sniffing out the trail across the road into the ditch deep into the woods wherever it leads. I like, best of all, coming upon the stillness of a doe standing a few yards ahead of me. Not leaping for cover, not yet. Merely standing. Being there. Being there as if to wonder what my presence means in its midst. What creature? What stillness—legs, arms, head—standing there? A standoff of unexplainable wonder in the nature of each other. A heartbeat, a blink of an eye, a separation of entities once again.

February 23   *The Foghorn, Death's Door, &*
The Red Gas Pump

The morning outside my bedroom window, a light wet snow teetering precariously on the branches of pine, maple, birch. Dressing. Stepping out hurriedly before it disappears. There is a momentariness to snow, so light, so wet, so fleeting in this time of year. The spongy new covering of white squishes under my feet. Every step leaves a gray imprint, quickly filled with water. On the road, a vista of woods and farms and fields. They sky a thick smoky gray. Everything about this morning world is white deepening to gray, softly beautiful and same in its color. No sound save the foghorn off Death's Door. A solemnness of the eye floats above the landscape . . . blinking alive only once at a red gas gump in a distant farmyard, all undulating in gray and white.

February 24   *Wintering*

Images from the TV screen filtering in, commercial messages laced with settings of winter: snowcovered bridges, trees, boughs laden with snow, snowmen, cross country skiers. Mostly, though, a Whittier's

"Snowbound" subliminal message. The purity and peace of it all. And the soul, the heart, the memory reads and holds this. A time of *good* snow: family, fire, friends—all felt. And then looking out one's own window in this mildest of winter times, one feels a loss of the intensity of that kind of season. A snowbound discomfort (inner white peace and pleasure) somehow denied.

February 25   The Snow Speaks the Cold Blue

More images, these of the road. An afternoon and a night's drive to Green Bay and back. The winter pleasures of a solitary driver. Snowbirds again, flocks of them. A swirling sky, part sun, part cloud, part threat of snow. Barn roofs melting. Snowfences with little to hold onto. The angle of the sun on the highway speaks memories of the same route in spring. One *sees* that, in spite of snow. And returning late at night, winter is a vivid presence once again—far stronger than daylight. The snow speaks the cold blue of a winter night. Houses tucked away in woods and snow fields, windows lit and mute in condensation; chimneys smoking the thin, clear air. People gathering themselves in tiny steps toward sleep. I like best riding slightly above frozen creeks, seeing the snow's light flowing there.

February 26   A Feel for Cold

Staring into morning with a clarity of sky so blue, sun so yellow brimming over into orange. Hours of this. Low temperatures, but indications of a melt-off. A lazy appearance of scattered clouds. Another hour . . . the evidence of wind, swaying the thinnest branches at first, but soon finding its voice, swaying whole trunks of trees, scattering a few dry leaves across the snow like frantic field mice. An absence of sun then. A feel for cold seeping around the windows, snaking its way across the floor. A light snow begins to fall. The wind crescendos from a hum to a moan. The body is chilled. The sky transforms itself to solid white. The snow whirls upon the earth. This night will be a lingering conversation in ice.

It is a bookstore again, a crowded city, perhaps Paris, though the language I speak and hear is English. A feeling that there is much to be gained by my managing/owning this establishment. I am needed, definitely, if this place is to succeed. People surround me with the intention of convincing me of something I must do. (Their faces, now, are all gone; but I know them, trust them.) I walk away with one of them. A woman. We stand off to the side of both the crowd of friends assembled to convince me, and also the bookstore (press?) immediately beyond them. I begin by telling this woman how successful the venture can be, if I should concentrate on it. How I know it will succeed, and the people (buyers) will listen to me, flock to me. And in their enthusiasm, mine too will increase. All my energies will be focused on this, all my *creative* energies—which is precisely why I must decline. Why I cannot see the promise through. I am utterly convincing to myself (to her) that in order for me to succeed in my own way (and there is no glimpse here of the material) I must not direct my forces in so commercial a venture, even though some good for others would come of it. She believes me. It is understood the decision has been made. I am to be what I am: a writer.

The night tightening into a freeze of well below zero. Walking to the house from the coop the trees creak in the wind. A branch snaps and falls the way a bone might be snapped in the fingers of one's hand. The snow squeaks underfoot. A tightening, tightening, tightening toward some final breaking point. Later at night, preparing for bed, all the lights in the house extinguished, I peer through those clear openings above and around the thick frost of the window glass. Even the moon has drawn its light to a sharpness, a clarity that pierces everything it sets upon. Shadows cut the snow in sharp slashes. There is a dull brilliancy to stone that appears to burst. All night long the house converses in timbers, siding, shingles cracking in the zero air.

A month of such variables in mood, weather, dream, love, the very act of writing, that I am glad it has almost ended. A new novel begun, another in the process of being rewritten. A new story complete. Four book reviews written. Numerous poems. Some watercolors. The daily persistency of this very entry I now write. The overflow of correspondence. Elation, depression, the deepening bond, joy and sadness that effect me, mentally, then physically—erupting in day after day of pain manifested in the head, and finally relieved by antibiotics. Living, too, with the frustration, depression, despair over the Door book and the same old gut-wrenching experience of writer in conflict with an undependable/untrustworthy publisher. Knowing that I have lost two years over the book because of a publisher who can afford to play games of his own choosing with no regard or little understanding of a writer's life. Living/swallowing all that again in this month. Then this morning driving into town, driving in sun, some clouds, freezing temperatures. Driving in the anticipation that the mail might save me. A bright sunny day to work oneself into. Less than a mile away from this (this landscape, weather, feeling of promise) suddenly entering—as if one crossed a border, opened a door, scaled a wall— suddenly entering a landscape of whirling gray light snow, buffeting wind. Entering, re-entering, a region of the mind marked as always in foreboding, darkness, uncertainty . . . that familiar borderline staked out in solitary fenceposts akin to madness and the dreary terrain of an emptiness close to death. And the mind, this mind, switching quickly from the comfort of sun to the loss of it as I move under clouds that cover this final February landscape reassured in doubt.

March 1   One Walks Aware

The frigid air mass remains, hangs in here, coats the landscape, the house, the people in a piercing silence that somehow screams . . . part pain, part searing wind, part pressure, internalized. The barometer records the highest air pressure I recall in some time: 30.5. It began its climb to that peak yesterday, and it has remained there throughout the day. There is a dizziness to one's steps in such delicacy of air and ice. One walks, fully aware that he is treading upon panes of glass shattering all around him in an absence of blood but a knowing pain that slices in the sharpest, glinting steel.

March 2   Double Vision

Another day of intimations of spring. The light, mostly the light, touching nearer and nearer north each moment, hitting these woods, these very favorite birch and maple trees, these fields, fences, birdhouses, paths, buildings in such a semblance of warmth, in such an angle of memory that clearly moves the man, the mind's eye to spring and thoughts of summer. That line of difference, though, that is weather, temperature, snow on the ground, shrill wind, frosted windows, and a high of 10 degrees above zero. That unspoken desire, invisible images separating wanting from not wanting, summer/spring, here/there. The mind alive in two places.

March 3   Orange

Sun on the east window turning the frost on the pane orange . . . the orange inside the orange-skin, the orange inside a pumpkin, a summer squash, a muskmelon, a carrot. An inside-softer orange spreading over and into the ice fronds, working a South American jungle light upon a Wisconsin winter window, illuminating the very inside of the man, the writer who steps into it all this morning desiring a path tendered in tiger lilies.

March 4   Sun Set

Yesterday's sunset, 5:30 p.m. Rushing out of the coop, down the road, over the other road and into the field to make my approach, to say goodbye as it hung momentarily, O, the huge full-circle redness of it in the branches of distant trees, the sun itself bringing the trees, the horizon, the sky closer. Slipping, sinking, bursting pearl gray sky with watercolor washes of red-orange, cadmium yellow, cerulean blue . . . the blue itself only a moment's depth before thinning, all the colors thinning, spreading to lighter hues, reds/yellows/blues, then disappearing into the thinness of gray, cloud and sky, all of it color-free, dull but for the far eastern sky slightly alive in the palest pink. Then all gray and gone. All in a slow but final explosion of deepening darkness . . . blues, blues, darker blues . . . Night.

March 5   Fish Tugs

A short journey to Sand Bay this brilliantly white noon, the sun directly overhead bearing down on woods and fields, straight with barely a shadow. The fishing tugs, Hope, Faith II, Betty, rest in a patchwork of cracked ice. Lake Michigan, still, so still in a summer's blue. Two ducks at rest in the water. The shore, an artist's conception of cliffs molded in ice. Cold, clear water lapping underneath. There is nothing to do. Stones of summer dream in a light much older than this instance. The world is water and ice. And I stand upon the edge, invisible in such shimmering light.

March 6   Told in White

A slow, slow filtering of new snow, a mist, a soft, soft spring rain, if it were spring. Not yet. Not quite yet. A persistency in winter's lingering. A reminder, ever so slow, that one is dying for the day to be told in white. No thoughts of green, of earth, of colored bird. White, white, white, covering the man's black jacket, settling on his eyelids in wet-white blindness, covering his steps, dissolving the man, the mind in white. Only white.

March 7   Dog

Dog in the warm snow, nuzzling it, running nose down, backend waving, tail high. Running it nosedown to a stop . . . a stick . . . a tree. Raising the snowy head, turning it in the wonder of who is enjoying it all? Who is enjoying it more than the dog in the warmth of snow? And again, nosedown, surfacing two feet downfield with a twig. Or burrowing into a coon's hole, fox den; pawing out snow, leaves, earth in a frenzy. Sticking the nose, then the whole head in. Pulling out. Raising the head, the anxious mouth, the wet teeth, the humorous pink tongue. Nothing in its eyes but pleasure. Energy and the warm snow. Dropping down into it then in the sun, on a bed of a knoll. Comfort me in fur and warm snow and the sun burning along the length of me. Head over paw. Head rising momentarily at the overhead flutter of a bird: dog ears, dog vision, dog tired. Returning the furry head to paw. Closing the eyes. The sun settling the beast in us all. In snow. In a light beyond silence. Dog sigh . . . poof of snow upon the black nose. To know the nothing of the padded paw. This, this dog.

March 8   *Hoar Frost and Syrup*

Morning again. Light snow. Hoar frost. A crispness of winter's edge yet a warmth in the steady progression of a spring-like sun. The fields are laughing in diamond dust. There is a happiness about the earth today, a loosening, a giving-up, a sense of seasons changing. Even the snow, thick in the wheel-ruts snaking down the road's edge into the field, curves into a smile, awaiting the separation of itself in sun. Further in the countryside, farmers tap their maple trees in accordance with an old knowing of the time. The sap runs sweet and clear.

March 9   *Along the Day*

A day I hardly realize has ended. Work here in the coop has been so long, and so intense, that I am almost unaware of time's progression outside. I believe I saw sun outside my window in the early hours. I recall a rainbow from the crystal across my page. There was warmth enough for melting, for the earth was visible and wet around the base of trees. A nuthatch made its customary headfirst progression down the trunk of a maple out front. Chickadees occasionally dropped from trees. A mole was spotted in his full-speed animated patter across the floor of snow. Somewhere along the day, I lost the sun. Sudden flurries. Beckoning storm. Inconstancy of time . . . mind of man . . . me in March.

March 10   *Tracking*

Following a tiny tunnel through the snow, occasional breakthroughs where the creature (mole? mouse?) raised its head . . . following from near the garage, where my path to the coop begins, running parallel. At the cement apron before the cedar door, the creature trail follows the concrete apron wall past the right angle, the tunnel then turning into tiny footprints, then disappearing beneath the front of the coop. Checking the back, I see the trail again leading from/into the northeast corner (I know the creature's patter above me, across my ceiling) and am curious to just how it wends, where it leads. A snow tunnel again, past trees, directly into a fort of sticks my children and a friend built years ago. In . . . and then out of there again, deeper north through/under the woods/snow . . . past beech, birch, maple, ironwood . . . into the hollow of a maple. Then around (deep under snow) and further north once more. Till suddenly stopping. Did it turn and retrace its pathway tunnel here? Is it yet submerged beneath the snow? I probe with a stick . . . nothing. Did a bird descend and carry it away? No trace of feather, fur, or anxious struggling. I retreat, leaving the mystery alone. And all day, unto the darkness, sit at the desk, awaiting the scratching sounds of the creature overhead. It does not return again.

March 11   *Being It*

Opposites. Black and white. Dual nature. Tao: thoughts of that today. The books, writing, always pulling me in, leading me back, pointing to other directions, new and old terrain. I like revisiting, reenvisioning ideas/feelings I have known before, possibly expressed . . . and here they are again, looking for the writer to make them into words in another new way. The harmony of opposites. The Tao. The I Ching. Ying/yang, male/female . . . two fish, black and white, head to tail, swimming into one. Foreground/background. These black trees all around me. The white snow. Distinctly the same. Sky and earth. Sun and moon. Earth, thunder, fire, mist, heaven, wind, water, mountain. Whatever it is, I am.

Sounds . . . still harsh, still with the bite of winter to them. The jays gathering each morning in the tops of trees, hearing me step outside, the door banging behind me . . . the raucous chorus of cries as they signal each other and me that it is the moment, the morning hour, for seed to be spread on the open feeder. Their cries cloud above me, swirling the thin blue sky. I leave them then, to drop carefully from the branches, always with a studied distance between me and them. I leave to occupy the road, granting them a space of some security, unhampered by the presence of the man with seed, who fades further and further away down the road still listening to their cries, occasionally spotting a jay at the far end of the woods, still signaling the time of seed over a vast field. And sometimes spotting, far in the distance, high over the field, yet another jay who has heard the message, breaking high above on a singular, wing-flapping mission straight to the heart of seed.

Snow melting along the edge of the road by day, turning to ice overnight. And next morning—the satisfaction, childhood joy, discovery and remembrance of "cracking" ice. Ah, the destructive sound of it as each foot comes down solidly cracking, smashing, shattering. How the hollowness of it, the clearness of the road's surface underneath lit by sun, responds to the pressure of my footsteps. How to explain the delight? Is it the pure sound itself? A sound echoing from one's wintertime as a child, rich with a morning of ice formed over small puddles and depressions? I recall instances back then, in the city, of putting a heel through it all, releasing water, then standing back, jumping, creating a pumping action, and delighting in the gush of water over ice. There was the quick flight of running into a slide over ice as well. Swoosh! Doing this again and again to "polish" the ice, to make it quicker. All this returns to me this morning, man-like/child-like, pounding my heels into the ice. Crackling . . . thinking . . . a goblet of the thinnest, finest crystal, dropped to the hollowest depths of a well, that kind of sound. Destruction? Perhaps—in youth. But now, confirmation. Releasing the music contained within ice that awaits a man's winter morning sojourn into spontaneity.

March 14   *Moons*

The water moon. The dream of a still, blue body of water no bigger than a pond. It is daylight, the suggestion of afternoon, alternate waves of mist . . . but the blue of the water, like the bluest of eyes, is constant. And then the appearance of a perfect round white moon upon the water, in the water. Even in the dreaming mind I am aware of a Japanese haiku which has caught this experience. Aware, too, that it cannot be held, taken, made real. Its reality is the image upon water. Then, still delighting in the appearance of the water moon, I begin to see others the same size, but many more of them, moons, moons, moons, floating by, and I am reminded, perhaps, of a watercolor I once painted of many suns. And why only one? I thought, both in the dream and the execution of the painting. Why not a sky full of suns? And that thought persists as moons upon the water float by, rippling gently before me. Then, upon the other shore, just before the dream disappears, I see a pile of cut logs and study the wooden circles of them, thinking again in terms of moons, and how the reflection of the cut logs upon the water's surface may be the many moons I see. But the circles of the logs are a woodsy warm color, not unlike the sun, while the moons remain round and white as china plates.

March 15 *Upon Leaving*

Part of the emptiness of the day, the departure. Knowing of the journey of another, from this day still touched in winter, blowing cold, to a land of sun, mountains, spaces I love Where, especially today, I want to be. In afternoon, near 3 p.m., the wind takes on a steady drone but all I hear is the sound of jet engines heading over a snow-patched Midwest—over rivers, plains, mountains—into the desert Southwest. All afternoon I hear the plane's whine outside my window. I see its descent in darkness over the lights of Santa Fe, into a spring warmth of Albuquerque. Dead leaves on a maple tree shudder in the cold wind outside my window.

March 16 *Bare Bones and Mud*

A time of March melting, snow in lessening degrees of depth, everywhere getting thinner, honeycombed, transparent, transforming into water. The bare bones of earth sticking through again: rocks, twigs, leaves, moss, husks of sunflower seeds, animal shit. Winter in transition. A definite ugliness upon the earth marked by moisture, dampness, puddles of gray water still holding a layer of ice beneath. There are more and louder bird cries. There is a sudden release of odor upon the landscape, a wet woodsiness, a pungency of raw earth. I breathe deeply and listen to the mud suck the soles of my boots in the ditches along the road.

A feeling, for days now, that winter has departed, and I have not really known it in the usual way. (As I type this very message, two pickup trucks drive past my window towing fishing shanties that have been on Europe Lake all winter. It is time to get off the ice.) No, I have not really been caught walking in a terrifying snowstorm. I did not, this winter, trudge thigh-deep in snow through the woods to cut our Christmas tree. I did not skate upon the lake. Did not toboggan down Hill 17 in Peninsula State Park. Never once touched my cross-country skis. Never found it impossible to back down my drive or manuever through deep or drifting snow into town. Never once felt the fear of total isolation (deep snow, no plows, nowhere to go) I have faced almost every winter here. Nor did I find it necessary to take the ladder to the roof, make my careful ascent, and spend hours, day after day up there, chopping ice from the edge of the roof, chopping channels to let the backed-up melting water flow, or shoveling deep piles of freshly fallen snow. And this is all quite remarkable. Almost as if the winter and I came to some kind of an agreement that I had much writing to do, and desired a mild peace of a winter which I could almost ignore. And so it has been granted me. Perhaps, at times, it *was* worse than I thought. But I did not think much about it, and maybe that made it all seem less than the snows of yesteryear. And there were those few instances, recorded here and there since January, if I recall, when yes, admittedly, I did wish again for the darkness of white death. A contradiction within my psyche. A desire to know a separateness, an isolation beyond redemption. And in that sacred time—an afternoon, a night, a day or two—savor the light, the warmth, a man finds inside himself.

March 18   *A Certain Faith*

It has happened once or twice already this month. It has begun to happen. The day, so promising of mildness, melting, sun, blue sky . . . it pulls me right out of this chair. It beguiles. It makes a man question his work, his worth. It says: "What is going on out here is more important than anything one can possibly imagine." Often in the past I have listened to it. I have abandoned the inside for being out there. So far this March, though, I am in control. I close myself from that world. I have been swept briefly away only momentarily, going for my mail, going to town, and suddenly finding myself unconsciously moving into the backroads to see what transpires there in the movement of fields out of snow, birds, wild animals, a farmer walking a muddy pasture looking across to the sky, knowing he has nothing to say of these matters, only witnessing with a certain faith.

March 19   *South Wind*

The first real south wind I can remember this year. Though it blows slightly
cold in the early hours, it moves the waters, moves the ice on lakes, rivers,
ponds, marshes. It scatters the flight of birds, twirls the last clinging leaves,
oak, beech, maple, on tiny branches on the tops of trees. It neither whistles
nor moans. There's a welcome wail about it. By afternoon it sprinkles a
warmth almost like rain. Tomorrow, the first day of spring. The first purple
finch at the feeder today. The first common housefly awakens in the coop,
droning on and on, up and down the warm windowpane. I catch it in my
hand, feel the tickling buzz, and open the small window behind me and
release it to the wind.

March 20   *Spring*

The melting continuing. The snow now almost completely gone. From
yesterday to today outside my desk window, I am amazed again to realize
just how much of it has vanished from afternoon to next day. Only in the
small hollows do patches, shaped like continents, still exist . . . off to my
left, South America in snow. Before me, the bareness of the dead earth once
again. Dead but for clumps of weeds, already green. Dead but for scabs of
the greenest moss. Dead but for the song—though not the sight—of a single
robin, somewhere in the back woods. On the tips of the maple trees across
the road, huge ravens swing, sway, call out a raucous chorus across the
field. Everything seems alive, despite the polished blackness of their wings
taking flight, lifting it all to whatever meaning in their circles, in their cries.

March 21   *Wanting Wildness*

A first walk, first this new spring. Past the coop, down the path leading to
my grapevines and the garden. A sponginess to the earth. The ground itself
suspended in this moment of early sun, suspended between a film of frost
and the soft giving-way to mud. Looking at the vines, a feeling of forlornness touches me through them—unpruned, wild, ragged, abandoned. I have
not been attentive to their needs the past few years. I am torn between the
responsible gardener with hands and heart of trimness, and the
irresponsibility of the natural in me, in them, in all of it: Go at it in your
own way, given the setting and the circumstance of season and the elements.
I really do not care to impose myself. Domestic though the roots may be I

planted years ago, I want only wildness now. The hope that years from now strangers may come upon this knot of vines, twisting upon trellis, tied to weeds, wandering around branches, extending beyond the stone fence, and remark in their discovery: "Wild grapes!"

March 22   *Black Angels*

The morning after a day of dying, clear enough, bright enough. I rise and walk upon the land, catching the handle of the door to here in reverence, marvelling how there can still be hope. Writers, to move at all, must move continually in ignorance, dumb (or is it numb?) to the days before. Though there was nothing in the nature of the day, yesterday, to forsee the darkness on the rise, one does have a penchant for black angels, November hearts, gray waters. There are no metaphors as real as rejection, unpaid bills, time diminished, love in assorted disguises. Another one of those days when No is on everyone's lips twice as loud as the trees and earth, which may whisper yes in March. A time of tallies, when totaling up seems forced upon the hand and mind. I owe this, and this, and this, plus this, plus that, and this from before, plus a reasonable estimate of this still coming, and that on the way . . . which equals: gnawing reminders of what all this costs, trying to make feelings out of words. Yet today, I must touch laughter . . . the truly hard part. All this spreads the blackness, deepens the despair which never seems so wasted as in times like these, when things seem to need to all "add up." And the totals are staggering. The cause and effects, infinite. The guilt—not to be eased by a thousand priests in black cassocks in a thousand dark confessional boxes. Her life should be cut free from mine. She should not be expected to bear this anymore, though what we share is still mystery, shadowed in dependency and uncertainty, which adds up to weakness in both our natures. The need, the wish, the will to write . . . to be free of needs . . . to grow stronger, stranger, and more solitary in other landscapes. A feeling, here too, I've lived—and failed. So the attempt last night to rid the darkness of the day (the meanness of the night of sleep) with alcohol—a limited reprieve. A wanting to talk it through, cut the threads, find the clearing—but the words, even with liquid additives, will not make themselves free. I am choked with verbs, numbed with adverbs. The dream of "get-aways" again. If not that, the final get-away to put this anguish all in place. Thinking of the lady, and what I've put her through I oves and friendships, won and lost. I scatter the last half of night away, reading/ finishing the *Letters of Anne Sexton* till dawn. Madness, she says, is quiet; not hysteria. And she is correct. A purge, perhaps. I rise and walk upon the land, and catch the handle of the door to here . . . in reverence.

Robins and new snow and a 6 a.m. gray sky and snow on the road melting in another hour, a fickle sun, the air both cold and warm. A day trying to define itself, as even I this morning, suffering from too many people last night, a day, a dinner, and a late night shared with good friend, R, and his wife (that, the best part) while the partying for 3 hours with local acquaintances inevitably turned to the lowest level of stimulation: gossip, story upon story, and O the weariness of it all. I wanted either the solitary night myself, or good talk, good friends from Chicago—R, to whom at times I can bare this ragged soul. We need a day of warm-up to arrive at this. And always, it seems, the time for the midnight hour of confrontation here in the woods slips by like the moon last night—a vague suggestion of light behind swiftly moving clouds.

March 24   *Fool's Snow*

Yesterday determined itself indeed in snow. A soft filtering in the early hours, continuing till night. The warm, wet snow of spring—fool's snow, I once heard it called. Outlining the sides of tree trunks and branches like an etching. A condition of constancy/inconstancy (ah, the mind of this man), calling itself permanent/impermanent. Am I this? My presence imposing a transformation of the "thing?" Or am I that? Visible/invisible? Of no matter but the moment? I sing in snow, speak in water, to whisper again in air.

March 25   *The Land Extends Itself*

The earth pushing through again, once more rescuing its own vision. Snow blind, mute. The land extends itself, stretches yet another day in sun. The matting of weeds and leaves and vines, dead, left over . . . yet a presence to be recognized. See me. Feel me. Hear the stone once more unbend itself in light. The earth undresses in muddy shadows.

March 26   *Circle Light*

The floating world, the rising sun, the delicacy of a woman this day, remembered. The pathway toward the water. Mist and morning frost. The sun, almost imperceptible in form, though the circle is there in the mist. Brass, gold, a yellowing of light, turning, spreading from circle, from form, to glow. Such radiance awaits my steps hovering just above the path, the way, the road. Standstill in silent light. A raven disappears in gold atop a tree. In the far mist-filled forest, a woodpecker accentuates the day. Further still, the foghorn tunes the distance of light on waters most mystifying. This is her day. Ascend. The light and the eye and the spirit soar. Blur. Stones drop their weight in dance. Branches twirl and disappear. I walk backwards as the day lifts higher, all of it wending with me in hosannas of such perfect light toward her.

March 27   *Shaman*

Reviewing yesterday's time—after sunrise. Tuning this room, the consciousness both in and out, to a level of religious celebration—prayer, the beseechment of the gods in the great circle of earth sky, and those in these very fingertips. Calling on the ritual—self-created—to manifest itself, to build a bond with the eye, the touch, to Red Man, Eastern Sage . . . the woman in a faraway room with the knife on her mind. The fetish (Zuni) of the turquoise toad—first. Placing it in a glass jar on the eastern windowsill, beneath the crystal. The turquoise toad, perfectly centered, facing east—its eyes glancing upward to the sun. I keep the transit, turning the glass-jarred toad to the sun's sweep. I light some pinon in the adobe incense burner—the scent of New Mexico, the pueblos, drifting through the coop. I rummage through books of poetry to find an appropriate prayer, settling for Simic's, "The Bird": *I give her my sleep/She dyes it red/I give her my breath,/She turns it into rustling leaves.* Then proceed to write the day, beginning with the third part of the novel's revision, tossing the I Ching . . . Hexagram 41, Sun . . . "Loss and gain, filling and emptying—each occurs at the proper time." The morning mail simply states: "Hold that toad fetish at noon (11:45 a.m.). You know the magic . . . what to pray for—thanks." At 11:40 I fire more incense, pinon. I stare through the eastern window, just above the turquoise toad, still tracing the sun. Ceremoniously, I fix my left eye to gaze through the crystal's center, into the immediate woods, far field, and sky. I multiply it all in many facets. I move it all in a patterned circle in my eye. I bring it to rest upon the dark stone with the river vein of light flowing down its black side. Again, all is magnified. At 11:45 I remove the turquoise toad, hold it in my left hand, and stand, feeling it pulse in my hand. I attempt to begin, once more, something like a prayer, though I do not chant, and I do not dance. Watercolors, though, are on my mind. And so I begin with black ink on white paper . . . sumi, most likely, singing somewhere inside me. The hair in deft and flowing strokes. To shape the head, the face, the eyes, the mouth . . . black and white, black and white . . . remembrance of a China doll dream many months ago. She flows freely, perfectly in black ink . . . images begin to multiply . . . the sun . . . the bird . . . the rainbow . . . calligraphy . . . Indian . . . West . . . East . . . coming together blue, cerulean blue for the bird overhead . . . making, then taking away the face . . . not right . . . not yet . . . again . . . no . . . again . . . yes . . . colors mingling now in a wash . . . the black defined by white, heightened by color. . . . The mind of the celebrant lost in the Zen of all this, but aware, so religiously aware that while his hands are alive here, they touch her there. Communion in color. Soul. Grace. Silver earrings. Moon. Words, now, to pull the painting in the true ways. In Chinese calligraphy I shape the message of *rainbow*. In Zuni, I add the rainbow word again—A-mi-to-lan-ne. And for bird, for flight, for airiness of soul, the saying for the Master of the Upper regions: ". . . for thou fliest through the skies without tiring . . . ." In all this, a journeying, a love. I descend in time lost to find the painting aglow, alive. All the while, in my left hand, I clutch the throbbing turquoise toad.

March 28   *Separate from Footsteps*

Fuzziness. The mind, wool gathering. Seeing nothing. Neither the weather, the people, the time. One's own self, separate from footsteps, touch, sound. An aftermath of dream? Poor sleep. The body/mind wanting to reconnect again with a sleep of death. The words do not flow today. The weight of a life buried in doubts, economical, artistic, personal, physical, mental . . . the rack and ruin of a weary soul. Wanting but not having; having but not wanting. These past three months have emptied me far more than I ever realized. Yet the fire was good all of February. I want that back again, soon. Mood swing. Waiting here, though, waning, is a form of suffering most intense, aware as I am, of what I can do, how I can dream, when all the spirit is the moment's presence, and I sing and soar and love and know the meaning of us.

March 29   Snatches of Spring

The progress of the seasons, though dramatic in thunder, lightning, hot sun, colored leaves, snow, is still a process almost beyond man's measuring of time. Neither the month, the day, the time of season really accounts for the slow rebirth/change nature undergoes in its own way. The wet snow, spring snow, false snow of only a week ago, again has left the earth, all but a few patches in the deepest woods. Wet earth, robins, chipmunks, skunks . . . once again the land stirs, smells of rotting leaves, shows evidence of low ground cover working in various shades of green. The sun, the earth, advances toward another clime. Yet I do not hope so much, so hard, for more—for June or July—while this is still March, the end of it. I prepare myself in ways, for nature's undoing once again: snow, certainly, sometime again soon. Cold weather. Raw wind. I'll take my spring in snatches now . . . bird, plant, scent, warm air. The unevenness of things is what I've come to respect. "Finally spring" (should it come at all) is the mere evenness of things. A constancy of sorts—days, weeks, months—to be upset by the stirring, foreshadowing, of nature's slow changes once again.

March 30   Simply 6:30 A.M.

Simply a walk the opposite way this morning, west, down the road, across Timberline, into the field toward Gust Klenke's beehives. Simply 6:30 a.m., the sun shining, the air clear, crisp, smelling like spring, feeling like fresh mountain stream water. Simply a walk. One man, one dog, and the sounds of crows, jays, robins, and from some distance behind me, the sound of Lake Michigan's waters crashing on the shore. Earth, once again webbed in an icy tracery. A sponginess to my footsteps. The stone fence yawns, the pine trees hum. The fields shimmer, gold, bronze, in the sweeping sunlight. Simply this: walking toward and into it, saddened only in the knowledge of having to turn back and face the familiar, when the light, this simple walking moment, is the wonder that lies ahead.

March 31   *So Much Light*

The first visit to Mud Lake this year. Cedar waxings on the way. Good sign. The road, muddy, inaccessible to the usual places. A few more days of drying in the wet-land place. The place of golden dry weeds, almost as high as a man. Rocks. The comfort of old cedar logs. Ducks on the water. Silence. The warmth of a body nearby. Words chew up the morning. Good words. But in those moments of pure silence we live and love and breathe. Breaking weed stalks at the joint. Looking through them. Tasting them. Filling them with breath. Catching the mystery of water through the rush of weeds. So much purity. So much light. So much faith in the darkness of the still waters. Hands clasped.

April 1   *Fire on the Land*

A feeling, a desire, the earth be done with snow till winter comes again. A feeling there is fire beneath the ground I walk. A blackness of earth burning. Roots branding their way into soil. Stone bubbling. Insects stirring dark tempests. A boiling and a simmering all day as the sun processes the heat, keeps the slow but constant sprouting, greening in check. Placing both hands upon the firmament. The field, burning.

April 2   *The Edge of Morning*

Mornings now when I can smell the warm sun upon my hands and face yet feel a cool steeliness in the wind. One is held on edge: is it this? or is it that? It is both. It is one. And the mornings, in moments like these, are mornings most like my walks in April, out along the arroyo in New mexico. And ah, how this air, this warmth, invokes that space.

April 3   *White, White, White*

Just when the feeling for the very word of it seems lost beyond recall, snow again. To wake to a sky overcast in gray—November once again. *That* feeling of forlornness. But surely, in April, the revelation of the day will come in rain. By noon, rain indeed—mixed with the vague suggestion of snow. One, two, three o'clock in the afternoon, all the trees, up and down their trunks facing east, are streaked in snow. The earth, once more, beyond redemption. And the fields careen by their own volition, leveling, rushing into horizon, infinitely white, white, white.

April 4   *Inside*

Interior weather today. Loneliness and the inner landscape. Family gone: wife and daughter to Chicago for Easter. My son to France. The father sits here in the woods, still in quiet pursuit of himself after all these years. And much of the day (a beautiful one out there of sun and warm temperatures) fighting the fog of last night's dream. It is rare when I awake in tears. I am driving a red van in a strange city. I lose control, not fearing my own life, yet witnessing the possible death, certain injury of others flying into my path. Screams (my own? theirs?) God, how many have I killed? Am killing? Maiming? At a court? Hospital? I stand/stood viewing the people I have injured. Some come toward me in anger. Others, quiet acceptance. A few, perhaps, show some sympathy, though I will have none of it. One, without a leg. Others, broken limbs, bruises: I am clearly being accused. The guilt rushes over me. I shout, mumble, scream, pray: "I am sorry, I am sorry, I am sorry!" but the tears are unending. I am on my knees. I am crying and at the same time re-experiencing myself in the vehicle, unable to take control. It will not steer in the direction I want it to. The bodies and faces of people are at my mercy, a mercy itself I have no strength to control. Waking, the dream is not of the nature I usually forget. It haunts me all day. I fear the journey of my wife and daughter by car. I fear my son's trip to Chicago by bus, and then his flight to France. I fear myself upon the road today, tomorrow, next week. Who were these people I was mowing down? Why had I lost control? What is the Jungian message? Guilt? Guilt above all, that feeling so overwhelming in the dream. I was injuring people (strangers?) I loved. I could not help to hurt them. And I was to know and feel the guilt (how long?) in the heightened sadness that the act which brought hurt to others was a power beyond my nature to control, call back. I could do nothing but ask forgiveness, live the guilt, and place judgment far beyond myself and those I had no reason to cause suffering and pain.

April 5   *Silver*

A day out there of such sun and scent of spring beyond dreaming, though dreaming itself continues to pursue me, encapsulating me from that which awaits outside. The hours before bed last night spent fighting off an almost childish fear of night and darkness. Turning to books, but unable to concentrate. Turning to the mindlessness of TV, held there by colored images, music, song, till 1 in the morning. Flirting with the idea of drinking heavily, but denying myself even that temporary balm for fear of even greater demons in my present psychic state. Retiring, finally, after 1 a.m. to the darkness of whatever waits upstairs. Through the windows of night I see but take no comfort in the clarity of the heavens: the stars, the moon, the stillness of the silver light. In bed I read another hour or so, still fighting sleep . . . dream . . . death. When finally I turn off the light, I lie flat on my face, hearing water rush through the heating pipes, the dog downstairs, turning, wheezing in sleep, the bird ruffling feathers in its cage, the house creaking. I sleep in an awkward state of consciousness (part of me will not give up) and dream/see/know my body prone, hovering over an abyss, a depth the approximate size of me, beginning with layers of wrinkled white cloth, fading into depths of black unknown, unexplored. I am suspended yet aware that were I too reach alongside of me, I would grasp something secure. (A conscious knowledge of the bed?) But most amazingly (am I frightened? do I wonder? do I know?) all around my body waves of energy pulse—silver? yellow? white?—while all in my mind is stuck a chant-like phrase: electric magnetic field, electric magnetic field, electric magnetic field. There is no noise. But the power is visibly understood. Then I am awake again (or feel awake) for at least another hour. And then, near morning, one more dream. I am pulling plates, printing, with artist and friend, Ross Lewallen in some room very far away. And the first print we pull—a grid of approximately eight equal squares—is perfect in itself, its art, and we share this joy. Some of the squares are gold in color and filled with images (forgotten, but some of them red) while the upper left-hand corner square (and at least two or three others) are prisms, actual crystals, radiating with such light we are forced to partially shield our eyes. We are pleased in our work. And again, we *know*.

April 6   *Dream Rain*

The dreams subside. The restlessness, anxiety, terror, telling—whatever it might be called—passes. And the dreamer returns to the daily-ness of life and the solidness of sleep undisturbed. Holding, though, retaining the fragmented images, the messages, the language of dreams to be either worked out in his own life or ignored, left alone to be forgotten or reassembled on other nights, in other directions. The heaviness of the mind, confusion of the body, fogginess of the spirit, slowly dissipates through the day, a day, strangely enough, of fresh water, the first spring rain. A gentleness to it, yet a persistency in trying to reassert itself upon the earth. Fields washed in golden browns. Barns painted black. A shininess to trees, branches, the water of the bay itself. Seagulls glistening on a barn roof. Bursts of yellow meadowlarks. Stone fences washed smooth.

A good part of the day spent on the road, driving to and from Sheboygan. A meeting there with R.K. to discuss a book (monograph) based upon the life and work of the Wisconsin primitive artist Fred Smith. Lunch and a long conversation with friend, Nancy Ellrodt. Through it all, the dreariness of the weather persists. The drive down, I remain mostly outside the weather pattern of heavy falling rain, wrapped within the confines of the car, the radio, smoke, and my thermos of coffee. Cocooned in such a way with my own thoughts of books to read and write, people I miss, places—in and out of the country—I want to see. Some exhileration as long as I am *moving* again, the first time since the beginning of this year, and the first time on this route toward Chicago since last November. A feeling, too, of oppression, rainy day depression. I reflect, both departing and returning, just what a creature of the sun I am. How much happier this journey would be, were the skies open and blue, the sun shining. On the return, though, somewhere north of Manitowoc, my mind, myself, all my feelings are fixed to a landscape undergoing incredible transformations in light. From a vista, an arc, from left to right, I witness rolling patches of misty gold light fading into wooly gray clumps of rain/fog, then light again, then gray, a veritable necklace of atmospheric wonder. The land heaves in water, light . . . burnished fields, ebony earth, barns and outbuildings porcelainized. I remember, too, an apple orchard near Egg Harbor, the trees just pruned, the tentacled branches grasping water, grasping light, grasping sky, alive in a glowing red fleshiness of bark . . . translucent, thirsty, thin.

April 8   *Water Song*

The third day of rain. This more unrelenting than the day before. No hint of anymore than rain to this. Gray sky, wind, the ever falling rain. Entrapment. But for the singular sound of freedom to be found here in the coop—the sound of rain. Its rhythm, its voice. How the wind affects the patter. A song heard for the first time this year. It lifts the day considerably in its growing darkness.

April 9   *Night Music*

Night rain, night wind, the darkest of spring music, the deadliest of nights.
Blue-black trees bending, branches crazed. *Where do the birds hide?* The
earth tosses. The wind's voice uncurls the bark of white birch trees, berates
fence posts in a whine through barbed wire, sends stones clacking upon
themselves, snaps branches in mid-heaven, strumming others in their
descent and muffled drum fall, flows steadily, high-pitched across the
fields, fragmenting itself through the woods in a chorus of voices, rattling
my midnight window transformed to feathery drumbeats, water washing
the windowpane.

April 11   *Falling*

Day of a dark dream again last night. How it does affect my waking time.
Befuddled. Mind in a fog all morning and afternoon. People falling from a
great height. My watching them. Once more, unable to act. A building. The
top of a building giving way. People plunging to death, I am either on the
ground or on another floor across the way, watching. A relationship
(possibly) to the Tarot card of the burning tower. One of the cards used in
the recent short story of mine, "Skarda," a card discussed yesterday with
O. A disassociation of self all day today . . . as if the body is scattering itself
beneath the leaden sky. It is all I can do to move it forward, place it here
before the typewriter. Attach my fingers. Make them work.

April 12   *The Light of Trees*

The trees in early morning: traceries of snow illuminating each branch in the
softest brush stroke of a Sumi master. The dark and light airiness of it all.
Trees turning above the earth line. A spatial movement of a world whirling
again in white.

April 13   *What Green There Is*

What green there is on the earth's floor (the snow again vanishing by late
yesterday afternoon) . . . what green there is grows greener still—moss,

lichen, patches of leafy grass—though the temperature hovers once more near freezing, and the air is raw, and the slightest anticipation of spring in a man's soul as inconstant as the snow which fell yesterday morning and disappeared in yesterday's afternoon.

April 14   *The Absence of Sun*

I have not seen or felt the sun in more than a week, and the absence of such light stirs the restlessness in me, makes me brother zombie to the leafless tree, the cold stone, the woods impenetratable in entanglements of deadly branches and dumb bark.

April 15   *The Undoing*

To see, to know the slow certainty of it. The gradualness of spring. The time itself, almost something to be worked out of the atmosphere. Also the raw wind. The tightness of the earth. The knots of trees and limbs and fields. All of it, awaiting a process of unloosening. An undoing. An inhalation of sun, an exhalation of green.

April 16   *Back to Here*

5:20 a.m. The sunrise. A robin in the tallest maple tree . . . fiery breast to sun. The fuzzy new growth of sumac trees, curved in the light like soft antlers. In such a newness of the day I stand and forget myself. Such a freshness to such an hour. Everything else fades. I can't recall just where I stand, how long, or how I made my way back to here. Though I do recall the light awaiting me here, the prism scattering rainbows on ceiling and walls . . . the spider drifting across the window glass.

April 17   *So Inside*

A long day, opening again at 5 a.m. with an uncertain sky that hinted snow but resolved itself in light rain. And then that too, passing into sun. The light in the gold weeds of Mud Lake, the wind, the pond, the mallard ducks, the sound of frogs. Mittened hands. Sweater. Neither the day nor the people certain. Is it warm? Is it cold? By late afternoon, warmth overwhelms. The coop itself fills with sun. The air outside is squeaky clean. A sweetness to everything. At 5 p.m. two blue herons pass directly overhead in a sweep of wings that seems to lift the very ground. I return to the house, the setting sun flashes on the back windows and sets the whole north wall on fire. If this be the ecstasy of a pyromaniac, I understand. Night. 8 p.m. I sit here still, loving the light on these keys, the quiet but for distant howling dogs . . . the darkness of these windows that reflect me so inside.

April 18   *Day Dream*

The first warm day. Shirtsleeves. A day made of soft wind, soft sky, soft sun. A daydream day. In the very air, both the reality and promise of elsewhere. As if what is real and pleasurable in the immediate has the purest clarification in other landscapes lived, or other places yet to come.

The dream last night of Charley's farm. Alone in the kitchen there with a woman, my feeling of sanctuary suddenly destroyed by her realization that someone is coming. Man enters. The three of us seem uncomfortable, conversation failing to resolve the obvious. Soon others enter. The house grows full. The scene shifts to a country lane behind the house (no reality) where woman and I are walking. At the end of the road, near the house, another woman stands waiting. I fully realize she is aware of us, aware in the manner of acceptance. The scene shifts again to yet another country road. Woman and I are walking. The trees, the air, the roadside is filled with birds, beautifully colored, and as large as men. On a tree near us, a cluster of these man-like birds grasp the trunk and branches. Their feathers are brown and yellow. Their faces, human. Woman has a name for them, knows precisely what they're called. The name (forgotten) strikes me as very humorous. I walk some feet ahead, then, (lured or in chase?) of two magnificent white birds which hover, angel-like, three feet off the ground. S-shaped, their backs float away from me. Their plummage is something like lace, swirls of white frosting, angel hair, filagree, silken white cords. Their faces, again, human. I am delighted to have discovered them. I know their name. Woman does too. Together we feel a sense of serenity amidst the beauty of the white birds.

A hawk sighted as I lay in bed this morning, a hawk over the tops of maple trees and down the road. A spring day of birds, flowers, earth, fish moving in to spawn. Crocuses—yellow, purple, blue, white—have appeared in front of the house. The hawk returns in my morning walk. Swallows descend toward the houses I placed years ago along the road and down the stone fence line. I rake leaves to bury in the garden for compost. Garlic, from last year, is up. Onions. Carrots remain buried under straw in a wint of cold storage. The earth smells sweet. I prune the grapevines. Such a stir within this world, blind but to white root, speechless but to sun. Within me, the darkest blood whirls. Planted, I rise.

Love upon the earth's floor this spring. Woods, warmth, a quiet circle-clearing of grass envisioning green. Hawk, stone, logging lane, warbler, the intimation of unicorn. The white bird of dream only nights before— transformed, bodily human, alive, plummage shed. Bird of high noon wheeling out of the circle of trees into open sky. While a small unicorn observes, rests, in a close field. . . .

> The second characteristic of the Unicorn which recommends him to mankind's love is his purity. He is pure because he is rare, distant, untouched. He is not rare from biological in- adaptibility or geographical accident. He is rare because it is the expression and fulfillment of his nature. He could not bear being common, seen, and we could not bear having him so. He is pure and this necessitates his distance from the world. His vulnerability is an expression of his purity. We love him be- cause he is taken and defeated not by strength but by another purity. We love him for his innocence, and whitness is the proper coat for innocence to wear.
> —Welleran Poltarnees

The bird of white, of spring, of flesh and human form . . . aground again, dislodging a unicorn underfoot, holding it firm in hand, passing it to me. I hold the wooden image, silver-gray, smelling of earth, of innocence.

April 22   *Sun Sight*

Early evening. Sunset. Sky, blue to gray to violet. The sun, yellow-orange, as far north across the fields now, as Harvey Olson's farm. Attempting to hold even one second of the sun's color in my eye, knowing the moment I think I hold is already gone, the sun already a blood-red orange, the light diffused as high as the birch tree tops. Another moment and there is nothing left to tell. The sun is setting. I am here.

April 23   *Night Images*

Blue night.
Moon illuminating the bedroom walls, the sheets, these hands, white.
Night of sharp, flashing silver knives.
Night of loss.
Morning, my eyes still wet.

Rapid changes. I think back to the evening of the 22nd, walking the road, first east toward the lake, then west toward the bay. Somewhere just past the house, heading west, the sudden feeling of walking into a wall of atmosphere steeped in memory. On the one side (east), cold air; and on the other, warmth. I walk back and forth several times just to know and remember and feel the intangible presence of air. The possibility of two extremes existing in the same space. Like yesterday's early morning spring and the afternoon's snow. Or this morning's snow . . . and this afternoon's rain.

The branch outside my window now, beaded, jeweled, sprakling in cold raindrops left from an hour ago.

A hawk swoops by.

I will not see the sun.

This is November, and I am very cold.

April 25   *The Secret Gestures*

The garden: the path past my coop, muddy now in April. May flowers bloom along the way. Everywhere upon the earth, darker shades of green emerge, visible mostly to the near passing eye. In the panorama of a field, the distances, the horizon, there remains the color and texture of fall. Only close up, upon one's knees, is the obviousness of spring visible in the tiniest leaf. Secret transformation, secret self: the doing and undoing before my eyes. Though not as dramatic as thunder, lightning, storm, I love the small, solitary, secret gestures that happen overnight. As if in darkness comes green.

April 26   *Gardening*

I go there expecting something new every day, this garden again, this landmark of spirit which draws me from now till the first covering of snow. (Yet even in winter I find myself there inspecting the dry sunflower stalks.) This morning I am amazed once more at the persistency of weeds and quack grass, at their stubbornness, their force. In the early years of gardening I looked upon such events in anger and dismay, while now I smile, a loser's smile. An understanding with the earth, a pact: "I respect your need to leave no space free . . . grow, tangle, turn to seed. But allow me, somewhere in the midst of this, the taste of corn, tomato, green pepper, and summer squash.'' I prefer the earth always impose its wonder upon me. None of my doing—weeds or wild blackberries. All wonder. All harvest. All Eden.

April 27   Manure

The farmer, Gordie Nelson, spread a wagon load of manure on the garden yesterday. How the garden calls again today—but now by odor. Manure and earth, the earth russet now in its new covering, an inexpressible joy. How to explain the quiet satisfaction while gagging? While observing how evenly the manure has been spread? How good one feels about it, replenishing the earth this way? How clean-smelling the occasion of cowshit upon the garden? How certain we are in the act of natural fertilizing that manure and earth will mix with rain providing a summer's richness of the tastiest green beans, the ripest tomatoes, the strongest onions? A kingdom of fruit and vegetables partially due to a farmer-friend's milk cows, a barnyard pile of shit steaming through winter, preserved for just such a day in spring.

April 28   Daylight Saving Time

In the early morning, still asleep, the loss of an hour—daylight saving time. The loss or gain of time, something I've never understood. Never by minutes or hours, certainly. Age . . . yes. Memories . . . for sure. The future? No. The Past? What occupies most of a writer's imagination: the loss or gain of time? Possibly. The loss or gain of light? That I seem to understand. That I feel. More daylight. Less night. Opposites. I seem to accept the "later" morning light at this time. It's the longer evening light I must adjust to. For reasons I've never quite probed, I dislike the tendency of daylight to hang on forever. I *want* the night to fall in blackness (stars? storm? whatever) immediately after my work is done and I go into the house for supper. A comfort in that. As if—now, the light is finally gone. That is

61

done. And with darkness, supper, society and family . . . and finally, sleep. When light lingers, an uncomfortableness gnaws away at me. I should be *going* somewhere, *doing* something, to occupy the excess time. Though it isn't time at all, but light. In another month or so I will have adapted. And I will love the way light lingers into the evening. Love the setting sun at 8 p.m. and beyond, drive toward the bay to watch it float, then sink into the waters. I will love all the time I will seem to have gained in a summer's day already full. It's only *now* . . . the soul still somewhere between the privacy of winter and the visibility of spring, when I seem to choose the latter. And come fall, the turning back of time, I will remember again the sudden depression, being overwhelmed by night's fall . . . too soon, too soon. Death and all the winter nights to come.

April 29   *Night Rain*

The spring rain that somehow stole its way over the sleeping house last night. The gentleness of raindrops on the roof. Rising at 5 a.m. in the very dim, gray light of day . . . small puddles on the gravel drive . . . fat black robin silhouettes drinking, bathing, waiting for their own shadows upon the dark, rich, wormful earth.

April 30   *Floating World*

Wet world, floating world. From late yesterday afternoon till early this morning, the moisture persists. But such a cleansing about the earth, such a new-washed smell. And such a color of green around the house, along the road, working itself up through wet, brassy-colored fields. To walk amidst this wet wonder, joyfully, though a slight rain falls, is to clean one's self. Sharpen sight. Sharpen sound. Sharpen smell . . . wet, olive bark of the poplar tree . . . meadowlarks bulleting in low flight among the small pines in Charley's fields, their captivating cry of one long note, high-pitched then diminishing to nothingness . . . the scent of cedar trees near Carlsons' . . . once again the woods engulf me as I give way to the freshly washed, glistening pines. A raven cutting across the tops of trees, calling all the way, settling in a rocking fashion atop a tall maple. A green and gray world of the highest tones, radiating a wet light. By morning, this morning, all the trees, the branches, the sounds of birds, are set free in fog. The floating world returns with me suspended. Gulls, some distance away upon the lake, yet in the closeness of this morning's way, somewhere just beyond my shoulder. Nothing is attached. We hover, all. The fog horn wails . . . praise the airy gods.

May 1   *Sun and Moon*

Full sun, full moon. Beginning with the sunset, riding down from a narrow strip of gray, clouded sky. The lower lip of the sun permeating sky and earth with a wash of intense orange. Standing in the field, alert, facing it, my dog, a nimbus all around its fur. Feeling the sun spread across my face and hands, my entire body blind with light. The dog disappears in a soft, silent burst of flame. Seconds only. I turn to witness the tall white birch behind me, branches and trunk glowing in the color of prairie rose. I walk back in the diminishment of light, still turning every other step in belief and disbelief. Then late night, the full moon. And greater manifestations yet the next day: sunrise and still the full moon in the sky. Reaching, touching, holding one in each hand: the great high-wire act, the consummate juggler. In the distance, a pair of pileated woodpeckers descends and applauds the performance.

May 2   *Spreading the Sun*

Some minutes before sunrise, 5:45 a.m., standing between the grapevines and the garden, overlooking Charley's field, spying the first, tiniest blood-red curvature, watching the form grow, spread through branches of distant woods, rise. The unexplainable excitement, satisfaction, in witnessing the ball of sun caught, as it were, but not caught in the intricacy of branches. The moment, brief. The spectacle, divine. Orange-red burning ball caught in the black wicker of trees. The East. Zen. This. And then it is done for me. The sun dispersed, I turn back, shoes darkening with dew. Raucous, jungle sounds assault my ear: birds crying, cawing, chirping, pecking. Swallows above me, a duet of woodpeckers, each at opposite ends of a far woods. Crows, unseen but heard. Jays heading toward my feeder in chorus. Robins chirping and hopping a tree at a time. Meadowlarks strafing the fields in their shrill dying sounds. A trio of gulls overhead, moving inland from the lake in cries of crazy joy, shot from the sun it seems, spreading the morning light under wings.

SPRING

May 3   *Roto-tilling*

In the garden now, late afternoon, perfect spring, perfect weather. Warm enough for short sleeves. My daughter, home from school, has gone down to the small lake at the end of the road for her first swim this year. *That* kind of day. After writing since 5 a.m., I use this late afternoon to catch up on chores. At 4 p.m., I resurrect the old roto-tiller left to me by Charley, upon his death. I pull it from the cellar, gas it up, pull the contraption once, twice, delighting in its rattle-trap firing, its coming-to-life for yet another season. The garden—covered with manure, piles of dead leaves, last year's rotting cornstalks—the garden needs a working, a turning over. And this is my calling: man and the runaway/falling-apart machine that somehow only I seem to be able to control. I do not look forward to this time. Difficult to explain. My wife, already anticipating how many hours it will take me to turn over the huge garden (and at so late a time of day) cautions me not to get too carried away, not to kill myself, not to feel I have to do the whole thing at once—which is my usual way. Compulsion? Passion? I like the completion of every act involving me. I hate to leave things for another time. Into the garden then. I've promised to make *huevos rancheros* for supper, so perhaps I will quit around then. Maybe I will work only an hour or so. Yet once I see and feel the tines turn over the first swatch of earth, turn under the new manure and leaves and compost . . . once I feel the drive of the machine pulling me (the two of us engaged in a battle of forces: it pulling me while I hold it back, trying to control the depth of the bite, the edge of the garden, the direction of the row) once this is set in my conscious/unconscious mind, I tend to go with the earth itself, under, over, deep . . . losing all track of time and other things. "I think you meditate with that machine," says my wife, I think she may be right, though machinery and I are seldom in harmony. (I still have a chain saw, brand new, five years old, never used. My wife explains to others: "I think if he'd have to cut a tree down, he'd cry.") Yet strangely enough, I find this junker of a roto-tiller somewhat engaging. I like the feel of its falling apart right out from under me—and there have been times when pieces have fallen off right in the midst of the row I was overturning. I *like* its unmuffled, banging/popping, grinding, bone rattling sound. Best of all I like the feeling of aloneness and the earth out there, under a warm, fading afternoon sun. Meditations of Man with Machine Upon the Earth. Yes, something like that. Zen mindlessness: the vibrations and noise of the machine centering me in stillness, the blending of the earth, the rows the tines make, the wheel ruts of the machine. My own footprints as I glance back to find them herringboned into the moist, freshly overturned earth, now ready for seed. *All* of this. Sweet smells too. And slight wind. The beguiling heaviness of late afternoon light. I take my time, yet race with the shadows the sun begins to cast on the west side of the garden. A perspiration upon my body I find vaguely sweet and comforting. I would like a cold drink of water, a cigar, but I will not stop for anything! Better a warm bath and a cold beer *after* I'm disengaged. I hold that before as something to deserve after the work is done. At the moment, there is not another place in the world I would rather be, no other life I would trade for. Old pants, torn shirt, funny green fishing hat with blue jay feather, and old, old army boots stomping in cowshit, earth, weeds, straw, egg shells, coffee

65

grounds. Find me anybody else so alive this moment, wading through earth, preparing to plant himself . . . harvests of his own.

May 4   At Day's End

Night sounds . . . spring . . . twilight . . . the first call of the whippoorwill . . . a chorus of spring peepers . . . short notes of robins settling themselves in the trees. And off in the distance, a sound I barely recall from years past, though I am almost certain it is the owl. All these sounds, distinct, mixed with other bird sounds and insects, create an air of jungle intensity at day's end. The world cries sleep, yet I linger to spend the hours listening till the last sound dies.

May 5   Reflections

Mud Lake: the interior, the pine soft floor of the bower where some of the outside world must be hid. The path seems fresh after winter. A silver colored bolt. A green bottle. The stone fence. The weeds here, rust-colored, have been flattened, knocked down, as if it were a winter resting place for deer among the cedar. The earth feels spongy in places. Still, I wind the dry place, the sun. Birds call. Hawks glide into the private sky. Stripped to the raw, consummation, the ultimate expression of all wonder. Wind upon the singing skin. A water hole nearby that holds the light. Eyes dazzled by spring's rush. The lovers' reflections of themselves upon the earth.

Joy in the work completed. Another expression in the termination of a winter's obsession with words and stories. To say, to speak to the new green life in fields, the tiniest of leaves upon the earth, the hawks wheeling, kettling overhead: in this ending of a story, in this way too am I new as the marsh marigold, as certain as its place and time, as real/unreal as its color on the water.

What looks like a possible nesting place for storks in the highest, barest branches of a maple tree out back, transforms itself (heavy, bristling, gnawing) into a porcupine glaring down, paws tucked into a massive chest, observing the curiosity of a man. I stand in wonder and confusion, aware of its destructiveness—one of its kind, some springs ago, eating away at the center post of my garage. A dumb beast, say the natives, harmless. (I have seen a native club such a creature to death with a baseball bat.) Such violence exists in me too, no doubt. Yet I cannot move against any living thing in that way. Even trees intimidate me as I approach them with a chain saw, then turn away again. It is all I can do to set and empty a mousetrap, let alone beat the life out of an innocent creature, potentially destructive to my habitat, yet nevertheless part miracle, part mystery, part of the very nature of this place I need, know, seek, to make part of my own spirit. So, instead, I stare. I smile. I love its just being there. And my being able to hold it against the sky in my eyes, keeping it there.

Manic season, manic moments. The day, at this time, taking on the mood of the man. (Do I make the day?) Sun/rain. Sky gray/blue. Warm/cold. A gray day, then, for the man today. A rejection of a book to coincide with the dark mood of the day itself. No clarity. No real joy. Hope remains somewhere out of range, far from this man's eyes to dream, to realize. This will not, ever, disappear, as the circumstances of one's life and art are not to be controlled. Man and mood are one. Gray sky, gray spirit. Nothing takes life today. No meaning even in the tight white bud of the trillium.

Dream messages again. I am taking notes, I am recording, I am aware that what I see, what I witness, what is being revealed to me is significant in my own life, and the lives of others. I know what I am putting down (what is being told to me, shown to me) is the stuff I must render into art. And I am confident (in a semi-conscious state) that I have it all down, that the task will be easy and true and right, and I will be satisfied in the meaning and pleasure it will bring others and myself. It is *so simple!* And soon after these experiences, a painting appears, colors, violet, with three figures, rather geometric, somewhat in the vein of Picasso. The background color, violet. The three forms: one a column, one L-shaped, and one a cube, have a grid of other colors within—oranges, yellow, blues, white. The most engaging is the cube, which seems to sit at the base of others with something like its own lips. It is titled: (something) . . . Ice Cubes. Is it a painting I have done? I'm supposed to do? I seem to immediately recognize and delight in its meaning. And of the title, I am certain. And satisfied. And comforted. But upon waking I *do not* have the messages of "art" or "composition" I seemed to be recording. And I have lost the title of the painting (but for "ice cubes") and all the significance I seemed so certain of.

An increasing feeling of alienation between me and this place. Part of it, perhaps, the season—something I must look into more carefully again. Does spring tend to keep one at bay, more cognizant of the magic of the surface—flowers, returning birds, buds, the glaze of rain—while winter, in its solitariness, draws one to the inner depths of snow and ice? And while I do not miss the winter season, I miss the inner journeying which somehow this season of green, blossoms, and sweet air, does not invite. Estranged. Outside the burning centers. The society of spring fanciers rather than the loneliness of the solitary seeker.

May 11   *Spring Again*

Trillium. Bluebirds. Rose-breasted grosbeaks. And those bright orange slices of Baltimore orioles against a blue sky. Moments of such a morning.

May 12   *But This*

Midmorning, wandering . . . trying to find "place"—something in the beauty of the day to hold me. Thoughts—scattered. Feelings—desperate, edging toward a calmness of not caring . . . which doesn't last. East of Ephraim, down Towline Road I turn left down the gravel road called Settlement. Almost instantly I am in tune with dirt roads, back roads, the true paths of the countryside once again. I stop, roll down the window of the car near a field and wild apple tree. There is nothing to the day but this: warmth, sun of the fields, and a red-winged blackbird in the slow budding wild apple tree. I watch the bird, its jerking motions from branch to branch. I listen to it chatter to itself. Entering the field. Closing my eyes. Being part of the stone fence. Briefly, I have found the way back in.

May 13   *Reconstruction of the Bird*

It was dusk. It came across the road from the shadowy edge of a field, entering my shadow, the sun behind the moving car. The flight was low, playful, the kind of skittering low flight one associates with birds at this time of year—jays, robins, meadowlarks, even swallows—something akin to love on the wing, yet near enough to earth to rest momentarily, make contact, and sweep up again in wing. This robin, I wonder later on, the pursuer? Or the pursued? Crossing the quick moving shadow, trapped beneath the engine and the fast moving wheels of my car. I hate the sound, the sight, the inevitability. There is nothing I can do. I am not in control. (I am reminded of fall and the seemingly mass suicide of Monarch butterflies fluttering against fast moving cars.) Looking back through the rearview mirror, I see the desperate one-winged flutter of a fistful of charcoal gray feathers . . . the setting sun . . . the traffic still moving. I pull to the side of the road, determined to end it quickly, but cannot move, cannot come to terms with the accidental killing of "bird," loved for the freedom it is. I want the wheels of the next moving vehicle to find the crippled remains and end it in the wheel's turn. In my own mind, the sun reflecting in the rearview mirror, I think Indian, pay homage, reconstruct the bird, and see it sweep the far field, the other side.

May 14   Loved and Unloved

Dreams of the journeys not taken, books not written, paintings not painted, women not loved . . . the journey taken, the books written, the paintings painted, the women loved . . . and the loss of it all. Again.

May 15   The Leaf

I try each day to see just how much a single leaf of a small maple tree outside my coop window opens. Yesterday? The day before? Last night? This morning? Now? Now the leaf, like the new wing of a Monarch butterfly that has just left the chrysalis, hangs there in the sun, wrinkled, unsure, drooping, shuddering in the slightest wind. It is not as it was yesterday. Yet it seems far different from the day before. I am in awe of the change that happens before my eyes. An understanding of a sort comes in the quiet acceptance of the final revelation. It is *being* a leaf. (And me?)

Three things: the white trilliums scattered upon the green earth outside my window—a memory of winter, the rush of green through the dead fields— the rust of last year's field changing before one's eyes; and on a warm afternoon in the coop, basted in silence and sunlight, I recall the winter scratching and skittering of the mouse overhead and wonder of his absence—which field or wood pile he now occupies—and his nocturnal wanderings under a spring moon.

Cultivating around the grapevines, late afternoon, late, gray afternoon. Wind rising. Vague intimations of the only man around, the last farmer on earth, the time of November: dismal, depressing, the center of aloneness. Reaching down to free the tines from the entanglement of roots, my fingers pierced by thorns and sharp rocks, I see the earth from below . . . the web of roots and rock and soil, beetles buried in their hard black shells, the tunnels of worms, the pathways of ants. All manner of insect habits and habitations. But mostly the secret life, the damp dark breath of plants *everywhere* extending themselves, intermingling, a private, frantic possessiveness for the black, nourishing places. My hands, sore, bleeding, tearing into this domain. First in anger, then silence. Finally in reverence that acknowledges my own defeat. My "undoing" will remain inconsequential. My violence to wrest a place for my preference of plant is but a momentary madness. The earth smirks, knowing what it is about.

A walk in an early morning, gray day rain. Robins ahead of me on the road, drinking from puddles, picking away at wet worms on the pavement. The sound of the dog's wet feet padding behind me. And the glorious sound of birds. I come back to this, imagining my life here without their calls and songs, their life in the air, on branches, fences, in fields. Their slightest movement instantly absorbs the walker, makes his presence and theirs something primeval, something sacred. The world this morning is only the sound of the red-winged blackbird balancing on a weed in the field, singing, calling in that sound part crackly, part song. In the mist, in the rain, in the morning, in black and red, its music stills the man on the road into transparency. Nothing remains. It is all in the field.

71

May 19   *Ribbon of Mist*

Waking at 4:30 a.m. . . . on the road to meet the mist, the sunrise at 5:15
a.m. a pearliness to the atmosphere . . . the morning the color of the inside
of a seashell. A ribbon of mist, not immediate to my touch or movement,
but in the near distance, wound around the middle and tops of trees, extending some height into the sky where mist, cloud, morning are one. Then
the ball of sun. Molten. The swallow on the wire, on fire. Then the day.

May 20   *Working, Sleeping, Dreaming, Leaving*

Summer-like warmth and sun: days of no time, evenings all light. Moments
spent gardening, tying the grapevines, turning over the earth along the
raspberry path, hunting morel mushrooms. There are never enough days
like this. Even the weariness at day's end seems somehow vibrant, alive in
the flush and tiredness of my own body. Opening the bedroom windows
wide to the night, hearing the whippoorwill, the sound of moths brushing
the screen, I turn off the bedside light, feel and hear the cover of wind
rippling across my bare body. Tomorrow, the journey to Chicago. Then the
flight to Santa Fe, New Mexico.

May 21   *Destination: Chicago*

The drive out of Door this morning, a morning so wrapped in spring . . .
the day will be warm, the highway hot and hotter as I leave the coolness of
northern Wisconsin woods and waters for the broiling highway that rushes
through and into cities. Destination: Chicago. Farmers plowing fields in
county after county, township after township. Marsh marigold blooming in
all the creeks and swamplands. Hawks on the prowl, hovering overhead,
perched on the tops of telephone posts. My mind split . . . part natural
longing, already feeling the press of urban man/imagination . . . the air not
as sweet as I near Milwaukee, the green of fields and trees, a different green
. . . traffic increasing . . . part of the mind still engaged in all the writing yet
to be done. I am in how many places this morning? Back home in Ellison
Bay, on the road, already in Chicago with friends, back in the neighborhood with family, already in New Mexico, in the Loop, walking the arroyo
outside Ross and Arlene's house in Cerrillos, drinking scotch at the bar at
Harvey's, Ralph Rausch, Howard Orr, sitting in the Plaza Bar in Santa Fe
with Jerry West, bullshitting with Charley Southard in his studio. Christ, I

am everywhere as I drive, driving as I do this morning through a patch of landscape almost surreal, dead cats and dogs flattened everywhere about me on the highway. Then, head-on, a runaway dog pacing the center of the highway, a long broken chain trailing behind him. He looks straight into my eyes with a sense of abandonment that settles inside me and shades much of the next three hours of the journey.

May 22   *The Gangway, The Prairie, The Backyard*

Sitting in my childhood bedroom near the screened window, remembering the vines that grew up the brick wall of the house next door. How the birds built nests in there. The sound of the rain on those leaves, the wind drifting through the gangway. Long before Door County, this was "nature" for me. The birds were sparrows and robins. The largest parcel of pure land was the corner prairie lot. Other than the wildness of that, one grew up with, experienced mostly the nature of his own backyard: lawn, lilac bushes, tulips, irises, and perhaps one apple tree. Occasionally a vegetable garden of mostly beans, carrots, and tomatoes. Living away from this for years now, one nevertheless still relishes the nature that was neighborhood.

May 23   The Language of Place

Absent is the space of fields, the depth of woods, the glimpse of horizon, the nearness of water . . . all the purity of water I live amidst and read in a way up North. The quiet alone so defines the quality of the natural world up North, whereas here, one wakes early (and all night, in jumbled sleep and dreams, cars rap down the streets, jets ply the skies, trains rumble, sirens scream through the walls and rooftops) and the sounds sink immediately into one's consciousness. The very air outside the window hums with the force of the city, the people, the neighborhood. I retreat to the silence of the backyard—sparrows, starlings, pigeons—and though the sound level of the city is still intense, the very presence of lawn and birds and roses stills me. I realize again that the quiet I once knew was precisely this: a quiet I may have ministered to myself above all the man-made urban energies. The true silence of the countryside was unknown. A language of wind and weather and space awaiting me in other countries (Greece), other places (Door County, Wisconsin) other landscapes . . . the desert Southwest, the mountains of New Mexico.

May 24   Takeoff and Landing

Slightly overcast sky: front lawns, trees lining the center strips of main boulevards. A robin. A cardinal. The small garden behind the house of a friend, Ralph Rausch, in Western Springs, Illinois. "Look," he says, "The lettuce is coming up." Then the drive down the expressways to O'Hare airport. The world is concrete and steel and smoke and speed. Inside the terminal, people in their anxiousness to be in other places on time. The aircraft scream or sit in a silvery silence outside the gates, sleek in their sullenness, awaiting man-made force of fire to be airborne. The thrust of takeoff—a force unknown to the wings of any bird. Nature returns in a still-life at the height of 30,000 feet—the wispiness of clouds, the sun lighting earth forms geometric, natural, serpentine. I remain at a most engaging level for what I see. Both earth and sky have never been closer. No division exists. What I see I know. We all fly; it is merely a measure of space, immeasurable. Touching down at Albuquerque, I am met again by mountains in their mountainness. The vista hovers as I walk the earth again. Sitting on the patio of the Loretto Inn in Santa Fe, partly in warm desert sun, partly in shade. Swallows scoop the sky, complement the mountain tops. I am held by a backyard peace once again of a very different neighborhood, a peace reaching far beyond, into an old, old silence of soul. And I read and speak this language now, with a drink in hand . . . the flight of birds, the poetry of baked earth, sun, and mountain gods, the stillness of Indian everywhere.

May 25 *Arroyo*

A walk down the arroyo this early afternoon. The shifting forms of earth rising, dipping, rolling, turning, at times, upon itself. The landscape marked by clumps of piñon trees, flowers (nameless) in waves of purple at times, highlighted by unexpected, small, fiery red touches of desert flowers. Most amazing, the shifting vision of the landscape. Most beguiling. I am of this dusty, sometimes flowered earth, of the spiraling sky within reach and the mountains, now here, now there, now a gray blue, now washed in yellow, and a slightly pink. My feet fall flat and hard (yet soft) upon the arroyo's powdery floor. Something new and old in this feeling too. A sandy beach? Possibly . . . but finer, much finer. My steps dissolve the earth in dust. Shifting light. Shifting landscape. Piñons dance along the arroyo's banks. Mountains undulate. I follow in this ancient dance, my footsteps leaving clouds.

May 26 *Puye*

In Puye this morning . . . the ancestral home of the Santa Clara Indians, following the trails, climbing the ladders to the ancient cave dwellings. As if space itself were breathing, a steady giving-way at my back. Vista. Sky. Mountain. The only surety—a rising of body-self to heights meant for gods and birds. The openings into the mountainside . . . shapes one wishes to fondle, their loving, flowing free forms. Cliff-swallow men lived here, so it seems to me, though *puye* means "Meeting Place of the Little Rabbits." Inside my own cave now, I view the heavens through an opening above me. While other openings before me—curved, circular, some vaguely reminiscent of the forms of standing me—lead to mesas, mountains, the wings of ravens passing by. Such sacredness of vision. Such purity of mind. Language is just this . . . and wind . . . and light.

May 27   *Wind Dance*

The view of the wind coming up this afternoon, its presence as it rushes across these flats, animal-like in leaps and turns and cries, comforting and mysterious. The dryness of it. A fickleness, like much of what I feel here—two natures: Eastern, Indian. It gathers suddenly and strikes with searing force, returning, sometimes in shadow, breathing remarkably cool. Standing in the midst of it, I let it gather round, as a dog or cat might brush its back around one's legs—a wind that begs to be coddled. Reaching for it, I feel it rustle through my fingers, rest upon my hand.

May 28   *Naked*

Naked in the sun, stretching out upon the dusty earth, bathing for the first time in a long time, in the sun. Silence . . . and the warmth spreading itself in waves upon the flesh, a flesh too long removed from the sun. Settling into the center, the solar plexus, the cock and balls, feeling the strength and peace, rooted so in place. Rising hours later, feeling sun, seeing mountains and earth etched in blinding white, I step nakedly upon the earth, moving in a time when men were light.

May 29   *Skylight*

Night moon, full, pouring thick cream over the flats of Cerrillos, covering piñon, cactus, desert floor. Moon set in a lapis lazuli sky, while in the far west, over the Jemez Mountains, the blue of the east and above, thinning into turquoise. A night of no darkness, met by a dawning of gray light suffused with yellow, then orange-red . . . then the same night scene now above with the clarity of crystal light, the softest of breezes. There are no clouds, not the faintest suggestion of white in solid blue, only a bleached skull of last night's moon. A transparency of day.

May 30   A Memory of Trees

The gathering of friends in the small, unfinished patio of Ross and Arlene's house. The planting of two trees, a cottonwood and an apricot, in memory of Ross' mother. The people—men, women and children—seem one in spirit, people touched by the special qualities of this landscape, touched in turn by the warm energy of each other, and all of them touched, in turn, by the special caring powers of Ross. The death of his mother is a loss to be shared by all friends because we all, through him, have been touched by this death. And the planting of a tree in this arid landscape so barren of trees reflects a perfect act in memory of her. The tree, so precious here, so dependent upon forces outside man's control. Yet here, close to a stunning adobe home some of the men present have helped build for Ross, the tree will have water and attention. Here it will grow, glow green and gold, bear fruit, and provide the solace of shade in a place that speaks mostly in sun. And so the ceremony of the tree is performed, each of us handling a shovelful of sandy, New Mexican earth, while one, a woman of powerful potions, pours a special mixture of essences to sanctify growth. In such rituals do we all live imaginatively, honorably, in and beyond time.

May 31   To Be Here, To Be There

Walking Canyon Road in the late afternoon . . . the sunny, incredible brightness of a quiet Mexican town. A memory? 20 years ago? The clay pots of red geraniums on tile patios, in windows . . . bougainvillea, purple, color, fragrance, sun and shadow everywhere. The green of trees and bushes showering over earthen walls. The single song of an unseen bird. I glide in and out the shadows in an invocation of nature unknown in the north country I call home. The secret of this place? A special stillness in the earth, a gathering of spirit in the serenity of sun that holds all things darkly, religiously in spatial, silent, mountain light. To be here is to be there— where you've been or might be. The transference is mystical, rare, understandable only in a knowing beyond telling.

The Plaza in Santa Fe, late afternoon. I become what I am, what I've been, what I know of myself, half-urban, half-nature. The Plaza, the coming-together of natures, ways most human. The gathering of people: children, men, women, Indians, Chicanos, Anglos, drunks, drifters, lovers, gays, lesbians, musicians, madmen, mothers with babies, policemen, old men asleep, grandmothers knitting, travelers resting from their various journeys. The humanity in all this. The force, energy, most magnetic. The trees so green, the grass, the bushes, the birds, the vendors, a quietness of sorts, while on all four sides, the busyness of Santa Fe continuing at its own pace. The Indians hawking their jewelry under the portal of the Governor's Palace, the comings and goings of the Plaza Bar and Café, the Ore House above, the posh jewelry and fashion stores, Zooks, the art galleries, Woolworth's, and the famous La Fonda Hotel, with its own traditional centering of forces most human. In the Plaza, in sun and warmth and shade, I sit on an ornate white iron bench watching the scene, being nothing. A pleasure close to prayer. A peace going back to neighborhood parks, city parks in downtown Chicago, parks in London, Paris, and Eastern Europe. Not unlike the Old Man's Café, which I haunted sunny afternoons in the village of Lindos, on the island of Rhodes, Greece. Not unlike the alameda in Saltillo, Mexico, smelling sweetly in the morning as old men washed the pavement with a hose. Somewhat of the same peaceful landscape I possess almost boundlessly in Door County, though it lacks this reverie of humanity.

June 2   *Indian Vision*

I want to be still, color bright like the Indian under the tree sitting in the morning sun, the mountains, the moon, the horse, the earth circling around him, seeing through closed eyes.

June 3   *Benediction*

Nothing but sun since my arrival: a monotony of weather some might call it, yet the effect on me (on native New Mexicans?) is most beguiling. Certainly perfect (what men inevitably seek in a lifelong desire for peace in place) is a condition of light. And in this "permanency" of daily sun, one moves (internally and externally) in waves of freedom, hope, desire. Walking like gods, absorbing light, reflecting the source. Then the clarity of night's sky . . . stars and moon . . . yet another benediction. *This* is the universe I am.

June 4   *Charley's House*

Following the bone-jarring, rutted, washboard dirt road to Charley Southard's hand-made new house some distance beyond Ross' and Jerry West's place. The wooden gate to keep his horse corralled. Then a slight turn in the road's approach, and there, the house tucked into the side of a hill. A Truchas house, he calls it, every inch of it somehow both realistically and magically conceived and expressed in the free human spirit that is Charley. The color: Chamisa green. A tin roof (Truchas style). A portal overlooking the mountains. A greenhouse. All the wood trim around windows and doors, beautifully carved. Above a small window in the greenhouse area, a carving, Indian-like (almost a petroglyph in feeling) of a frog, splayed out—arms, legs, torso. An omen, Charley calls it. "To keep the insects off the plants," he smiles. "Old Indian trick." An aura to this whole setting I've rarely known before. An immediate effect: the man who lives here, who has made this house, who has utilized the sun for heat, the windows for knowing/watching space and mountains, a portal and railing with a specific height to enhance his seated view from a rocker . . . this man lives spirit, speaks silence, extends himself through love, through landscape, outside time.

June 5   *Flight*

Driving south of Santa Fe to Las Vegas, New Mexico, the land opening up
to an incredible flow of hills, mountains, and horizons. Driving, one feels
himself flying at low altitude, moving across desert plains, arroyos, up
mountainsides in graceful sweeps, now a canyon, now a forest of pine, all in
sun and sweet, swift breezes. I am the shadow of the hawk. . . .

June 6   *Santa Fe Sunset*

Both this evening and the evening before, the sun stealing over the adobe
buildings of downtown Santa Fe, a wash of earth tones . . . golden orange,
deep rose, fiery sienna. The Spanish people themselves, the Indians, moving
in their own earthy shadows, eyes inevitably drifting toward the burnished
clouds and deepening violet sky within reach, merging, melting over the
adobes, streets running in gold.

June 7   *He Rides in Darkness*

Wind and the night sky . . . moon, masked, unmasked . . . ghostly scarves
of clouds bannering the stars. A southwest wind scattering whirls of dust
behind the pickup truck as I move up the hill from the house, down the
road. The empty highway whistles in the blowing darkness. Tumbleweed
(chamisa) scurries across my path like skeletal shadows of lost animals. I
know the mountains lurk somewhere alongside of me. And the moon,
playing games with light. Inside the dark cab of the pickup I feel the weight
of my own bones clutching a steering wheel into a familiar oblivion.

June 8   *In Absentia*

A day slightly overcast. Last night's wind still lingering. So accustomed to
the daily sun, one suddenly feels fear, entertains a certain disorientation in a
day not quite the same as yesterday, and the day before. In the absence of
such variety of weather experiences on Wisconsin's Door peninsula, one's
whole body/spirit seems less adaptable to sudden change here. Having
swallowed a daily dose of sun, a level of satisfaction: serenity seems ever

constant, my nature and the nature of this place are one and the same. But then the unexpected . . . a sunless day. A cold streak of angst enters the psyche, and for reasons unexplainable, the man (this man) seems doomed, begs the light that saves. (A clipping from the Door County *Advocate* reaches me today: "What Ever Happened to Norb Blei?" it says.)

June 9   *Taos Mountain*

The Rio Grande Gorge, and the river sunning swiftly: white water breaking, eddying, sound of the river song, vista, haze over Taos Mountain. The sacredness in setting. Soul of everything alive circling the mountain top. Wanting the closeness of its magic. Knowing religion, faith, meaning, myth become us in mountain presence.

June 10   *Blue Doors*

Patio garden, adobe home, doors from unknown rooms (bright blue doors), opening into the outside . . . in. Light contained in a garden hollow of a house . . . sky, and one's own piece of it. Garden earth, black against the adobe wall . . . bright floor tiles. Then the green of jungle plant, rose, flowering pink hibiscus, red geranium, and tree growing under, through, beyond the very center of the house, coaxing sun, sky. The warm, green smell of plant life. The familiarity and certainty of inviting the outside in. Living it.

June 11   *Departure*

The plane climbing above Albuquerque, above the Sandia Mountains . . . that, all of that, all of New Mexico falling away from me, thinning to a vapor, losing it all through my fingers, as if my arms were extended as wings, becoming wings as in the Jerry West print of men hovering above the city like airplanes. Feeling this in the sharp ascent, knowing it throughout the afternoon in cloud breaks, the Georgia O'Keefe sky, glinting sun, the leveling off at great heights. Then, hours later, the descent. The grandiose turning of the huge body, the rising of one wing tip, the dipping of the other. The shifting patterns of the earthscape, so primitive in the Southwest with meandering canyons, mountain roads, dirt roads deadening, turning upon themselves like Indian designs in old rock carvings. Now, outside Chicago, suburban green again. The geometrics of rectangular backyards, circular swimming pools, concrete/asphalt roads linear, curving, of precise destination. Lagoons, rivers, small bodies of water accentuating the landscape, reflecting light, opening the earth upon itself. Wings in descent . . . the earth rushing into the body . . . Lake Michigan in a silver-blue distance, returning. In my absence of this familiar terrain, I am wondering if I ever missed it.

June 12   *Re-entry, Wisconsin*

Earthbound, driving into Wisconsin, but still not of this earth. A difficulty in grounding body/mind. The landscape—unbelievably green, so cluttered with cars, people, urban sprawl. Neither happy nor sad. Mindless. But aware this home setting is very strange compared to the one I just left and still living in me—mountain, mesa, desert, an emptiness full of being.What I see before me seems less than real: white frame houses, red barns, fields rich in black soil, fields coming alive with the tiniest green leaves of corn. And moving through it all so smoothly (not the bounce of Ross' pickup truck over dirt-rock roads) I see a Midwest vaguely transformed into adobes, clumps of juniper, occasional cottonwoods, jack rabbits, coyote fences, turquoise-blue window frames . . . this flat green/black land suddenly rolling off into desert earth, pink and gold.

First it was the smell of the land working on me. There was an air of sweet clover to the fields. Sweet, white clover. Then hay. The sight of hay cut and baled. The smell of fresh hay in the air. Barnyard smells drifting by. The unexplainable sweetness to the Midwest countryside in June. Something to do, here, with wetness, water. Even a sense of moisture, so alien to this nose, this skin, these eyes so dry, so long in the Southwest. A dampness pervades. Something life-like and bodiful about it, as if a whole dimension of water once again occupies this body, floats it, flows somewhere beneath the skin in a thin blue film as interconnecting and complete as flesh itself.

June 14   *Shedding*

I am aware of these continuing body changes, but I am not yet back, not yet "here." The coldness of the North Woods landscape returns this morning with a dense and beautiful Oriental-like fog. I walk amidst it, feel again the moisture, despise at this time of tradition the cold. I have lost the sun. My skin is bronze, and I am peeling back layers of Wisconsin white white birch.

June 15   *Learning to Walk Again*

Still away, though the green is thick and blinding, though I reacquaint myself with the garden's growth, the yellow and orange hawkweed growing along the roadside, the white daisies. It is cold. My mottled brown skin seems warm. The adobe, the mountains, the mesa fade from my inner landscape. I am somewhere learning to walk again this very different terrain. But I am not yet here. I am no longer there. It will take time to find this place again.

June 16   The Clearing

Entering the Clearing yesterday evening for my week's teaching stint, I am instantly aware of Jens Jensen's subtle communion with the landscape in these parts. And now this morning . . . stone stairway, stone path, stone lodge, the root cellar built in his 90th decade, the Oriental orange poppies glowing in front of the cook's cabin, the greenness of all things, fuzzy moss on the cedar roofs, the dappled light raining through the trees, the water in sound, in sight . . . all speaks a man whose vision is one, is mine, is anyone's who enters his clearing and breathes the stillness of the territory within.

June 17   Empty

"The way to do is to be." Lao Tzu. To begin with a class of writers (ever so doubtful, always so insecure) with a variation of Lao Tzu: The way to write is to write, I tell them. Emptiness and the landscape of the Clearing. Does the space not shout out in stillness? Emptiness as awareness. The revelation of things through the very emptiness within them. "Cease striving and there will be transformation."

June 18   A Door Half-Opened

A haiku morning . . . the perfect expression of nature, in a Zen-like way. Stillness. Insight. Gensha, the Zen Master: "Do you hear that stream?" "Why yes." "There is the way to enter."

> The white peony;
> At the moon, one evening,
> It crumbled and fell.

"A haiku is not a poem, it is not literature; it is a hand beckoning, a door half-opened, a mirror wiped clean. It is a way of returning to nature, our moon nature, our cherry blossom nature, our falling leaf nature, in short to our Buddha nature. It is a way in which the cold winter rain, the swallows of evening, even the very day in its hotness, and the length of the night become truly alive, share in our humanity, speak their own silent and expressive language."—Blyth.

The concrete image, I tell my students. Just so much and leave it be. Stevens' "the thing itself."

Alan Watts on haiku: "To my mind this is beyond all doubt at once the simplest and the most sophisticated form of literature in the world, for the invariable mark of great artistry is its artlessness. It looks easy. It looks almost as if it were a work not of art but of nature . . . It seems to be a poem just begun but left unfinished. But with a little more familiarity you realize that haiku poetry excels in one of the rarest of the artistic virtues, the virtue of knowing when to stop; of knowing when enough has been said. And there are other respects in which this is the secret not only of art but of life itself. Haiku represents the ultimate refinement of a long tradition in Far Eastern literature which derived its inspiration from Zen Buddhism . . . The unique quality of Zen Buddhisim, and of all the arts which it has inspired, is a profoundly startling simplicity. There is a complete lack of the unessential and a marvelously refreshing directness."

June 19   *The Clearing*

Rising early each morning this week, practicing yoga at 6 a.m. in Jensen's schoolhouse under the tutelage of one of my students, M.B., skilled in the yoga way. Some ten of us each morning assemble quietly, carrying our blankets, establishing our place on the floor before him, before Jensen's grand window facing the waters of Ellison Bay, the cathedral-type window of which he was so fond. His feeling was that such a window should put a man immediately in touch with earth and sky, as this one does.

The Yoga Man, his back to the window, moves in the blueness of morning shadows. Sunrise time. Eastern music (Zen meditation music and the flute music of Paul Horn) fills the air, settles one comfortably inside oneself. We lie still, empty. I concentrate on silence, listening. *Prana*-breath-force. Stilling the mind—but not too consciously. Letting whatever positions itself there, flow through. Not to reject thoughts, to let them be . . . to dispense themselves. We begin then with the sun salutation, standing, in a position of prayer, palms clasped together, fingers extended upwards. I see and hold, ever so briefly, Jensen's own vision through the cathedral window of his schoolhouse. This morning will return to me forever. "Faith is built on knowing we have listened to the voice of the living world."—Jens Jensen.

June 20   *Zen Images*

Sabi . . . the pond outside Jensen's schoolhouse. The empty rock path, wet with rain water. The essential loneliness of things. Myself, the pond, the stone, the fish. . . .

Wabi . . . knowing a moment's desperation, depression, blackness of mood . . . and then, the orange poppy. The surprise of "in-ness." In that revelation, *wabi*.

Yugen . . . mystery . . . the unknowingness of all existence . . . Jensen's own cliff house of meditation. *Yugen* in the horizon he faced . . . water/sky . . . a gull hanging in the universe outside the window. No attachment.

June 21   *Change*

This week has passed in green, gold, and blue water. In the emptiness of teaching I am full. In the fullness of students I am empty. The white birch tree neither points nor roots, but bends. Change. "Life is lost in all forms that last." The final lesson: "If you meet the Buddha on the road—kill him!"

In transit once again. Still the feeling of never having quite landed from New Mexico. Images of people, streets, moods, persist. Merging into that, the past week spent teaching at the Clearing. *That* landscape—North Woods, Eastern—contrasted with the desert Southwest. The East in both places. All of this placing me, holding me, in some state of suspension as I drive with wife and children to attend a wedding in the west suburban area of Chicago at 3 p.m. The feel of Milwaukee/Chicago urban humidity begins seeping into the car. Stickiness. Dirty air. Crowded highways. Exhaust fumes. Through much of the journey I doze, I sleep, I see again Santa Fe, the Clearing, the faces of people I love. Nothing stays in place.

Nature is miniaturized again. The backyard of my inlaws in Berwyn, Illinois. The patch of perfect green grass. The blazing red, climbing rose bush. The Russian olive tree. The borders of flowers, dazzling to the eye. A robin, a rabbit, a rose bush. The tiny section of black, rich earth alongside the garage. My father-in-law's garden . . . the one place above all else where he makes himself known—a quiet, kind, old man . . . a life of such little ambitions: to grow a bright rose, to raise a juicy tomato from seed. In such everydayness is a simple life led. Of such communion, fingers to soil, is a meaning unexpressed—probably called faith. In such quiet acts (summer after summer) does the man confirm his peace, and pass it on, unconsciously, to his own daughter (my wife) whose love of earth is partly the love of her own father. I see them together, hunched close to the earth, their hands wrist-deep in rich soil, saying nothing, knowing the love-language of plants. In the dark night, alone, I pass through the fragrant backyard garden on a solitary midnight walk through the neighborhood. A rabbit jumps in the shadows. The long lost fireflies of my youth—the lightning bugs of all my summer boyhood days—surround me in a hymn of such special light, that for a moment I feel the night air before me is raining stars, and I put out my hands to grasp them, hold them, retrieve the light.

A muggy midwestern day. Driving back to Door. The humid heaviness of the city air. A haze always just in front of us. We head north, knowing that somewhere beyond Milwaukee (we have a faith in this) the air will slowly, sometimes dramatically, change. The coolness of the North Woods will prevail, the natural air conditioning that Chicago and Milwaukee people labor so hard for all year long in order to know it, to have it, to feel it in the heat of summer. It hits, for certain, along the lakefront in Two Rivers, Wisconsin. We drift along with it through Kewaunee, along the lakefront. "Ah, finally . . . fresh air . . . farm smells," my wife says. We open all the windows and breathe deeply.

June 25   Sun & Water

A heat wave of sorts, the first this year to even touch this place. Though the coop remains comfortably cool as I adjust myself to the act of writing, of being in one place again, I know and feel the air outside to be unnaturally hot for this county, this time of year. The trees in full green leaves, the whole landscape seems uncomfortable with such temperature, twitching in place, curling, beckoning the relief of rain. Late afternoon, I move instinctively down to the water, place my blanket upon the hot sand, strip down to essentials, and move mindlessly into cold, blue water. Buoyant, eyes closed, touched by the hot sky, I float in a freedom unborn. Fire and water: Perfect balance.

June 26   Body Peace

Last night in bed, stripping to the raw, opening all the windows in the warm upstairs, waiting then through much of the night for the summer wind to finally stir the trees, rustle the branches, fan the leaves, and enter the bedroom window with a coolness rippling along the flesh like water. Even in winter I wait for these special moments of a night summer wind, the communion of cool air after a day of finely honed hot temperatures. Wind, at night, upon such a night, turns water to me. I fight a deep sleep, desiring either wakefulness through it all, or at least a consciousness of knowing/feeling the prayerfulness of cool wind on a hot summer night of the body.

June 27   Wind Change

Retreating to the beach again, a hot afternoon, lying on the sand, feeling so suddenly the shift in wind. A blue sky, quickly sailing clouds out of the northwest. And then: the wind, the instant drop in temperatures. Within the span of a half hour, the day's temperature (high 80's) drops 10, 15 degrees. The beach people pack up, disperse. I comfort myself in a long sleeved shirt, buttoning the sleeves, turning up the collar, watching, waiting, marveling in the dramatics of such a summer day.

June 28   *Floating World*

Early evening. The sun dropping in splashes of yellow-gold upon the green fields, the green woods. Yellow-gold, then orange. Making my way north down the back roads, north toward the tip of the peninsula, I witness once again the magic of weather at this time of year. The land, warm . . . hot. And now, once again, the visitation of cool air from the lake moving inward, transforming the entire landscape into an Eastern painting of mist. Treetops float in the horizon. The sun, muted tones of orange, glows in a gauze so ethereal. I transfer concentration from the mechanics of a moving vehicle to the transformation of land, water, air . . . this sense of self lost in wonder.

June 29   *Spring Showers*

Their unpredictability. I love that even more than the rain itself, the intensity of color it lends the plants, trees, earth. Their coming and going. The momentary clearing of blue sky. The unfathomable return of gray clouds. Even an absence of thunder. The not knowing of it all. I care not what the weatherman predicts. My faith is the faith of a spring and summer shower. I welcome surprise.

I have no time, it seems, even for the flowers along the road. The goatsbeard, already in downy fullness to match the moon last night. The orange and yellow hawkweed dotting the roads and fields in perfect free-style flows of color. And the white daisies, singularly, the most beautiful petaled flower. These my daughter secretly gathers for me in a small bouquet for my desk. Through the white daisy we both speak summer, though the act is one of silence. I will enter the coop, usually in the early shadows of morning, flick on the desk light, and there, in a white vase near the typewriter, a small bouquet of daisies. And that will set the day—a child's gesture of unexamined love.

July 1   *Freddie & Friends*

Backroads, cornfields, abandoned farms, country graveyards beside white churches . . . settling into the rural today with poet/friend Dave Etter. "I like this," he says. "The smell of the country." A time for me, too, to readjust body/mind to this texture of my habitat. We sometimes see things truest when finding them for others. So I show him "my" land . . . "my" orchards, trees, barns, fields, silos . . . and finally, people. People like Freddie Kodanko, who are defined by the very land itself. Freddie and the six orange kittens piled on top of each other by his doorstep. The open door, the empty boxes, the tractor parked nearby. The polka music pouring out of his living room. "Freddie!" Perhaps too long a time at the A.C. Tap last night. Freddie maybe still sleeping it off this late morning. But the polkas go on. The flies buzz around the windows inside. And now here comes Freddie, rubbing his bloodshot, tired eyes. He smiles. A grin of recognition? One never knows with Freddie. He just starts talking and laughing about tying one on last night. I've come to buy one of his handmade wooden boxes, I tell him. I've come to introduce my friend, Dave Etter, to him, a poet of the people. Freddie. Freddie the farmer, box-maker, hired hand, polka music lover, dancer, drinker, lost soul, fool perhaps. Freddie the best damn truck farmer around, showing us his cukes, how he goes up and down the rows with his fertilizer, how he weeds. He's got beans! he says. He's got onions, tall ones going to seed, "Cause that's what I want 'em to do." And he's got boxes, handmade wooden boxes: "These are pine, these here are cedar. These are $4.50 now. If you come to Baileys Harbor for the 4th of July," he says, "I'll play some marching music. George M. Cohan . . . 'The Stars and Stripes Forever' . . . and some polkas. This box here I made, this is a new one, is for shopping. Instead of a shopping cart you put this over your arm see and you go down the rows and fill her up, then you set it down on the counter and you take it out and then you fill it up again see." He's got some good stuff inside to wet our whistle, he promises. Walking around his Ford tractor, he shows us where he carries his console stereo on the back wagon, going from town to town for summer celebrations and parades. He brings his polka records along. And does his dance. We follow him into the house where he gets out his collection of polka records, small town, small label, little and big name polka players he loves. "Listen to this . . . that's quite a band! A dulcimer, a piano, a banjo. And, ah, here's one I like, The Peacock Waltz." Waltzes, polkas . . . nothing but music in this man. Small, disheveled living room . . . a cold plate of half-eaten beans on the table, the faucet dripping, the lumpy stuffed chairs. An old pair of very worn shoes on the floor. Freddie now dancing, smiling, turning around himself. "That there box of records is full. That there one too." Friend, Dave Etter, just smiles and shakes his head. This is his Midwest. These are the people indeed. Freddie makes no sense anywhere else. He's just right here, dancing between us, where we leave him, where he's supposed to be. He doesn't even say goodbye.

July 2   *Ferry Boat*

There's something about a ferry boat, early morning, tied up at Gills Rock
in the sun, in the sparkling summer water, the day made for those of us
partly made up of islands. The need to cross the water and feel the isolation
of the land. The need to come back. To be always comforted, though, with
the presence of islands in one's midst.

July 3   *Ballfield*

An abandoned school and playground. The chicken-wire backstop rusting,
torn apart. The ballfield gone to weed, gone to daisies. "I can just hear the
kids," says friend, Dave Etter. "Come on, let's play!" Wind ruffling the
knee-deep daisies. "Imagine that."

July 4   *Morning Rhythms*

Muggy morning. Insects follow me down the road, buzzing above my head,
in my ears. Hot summer morning of no breeze. The heat is already in the
branches and leaves of every tree. The tomato plants drink up the hot light.
Corn stretches. My eye-lids seem weighted down with sun. No birds sing.
Remnants of a dream wisp through. But it is not a dream to hold. Heavy in
hangover of good jazz last night at the Common House. Jazz and
margaritas and friends, Ralph Rausch and Dave Etter. Some of that music
remains: the brass, the bass guitar, the rhythm, the improvisation of
musicians. The writer meets the morning, feels the quiet, the beat of heat
. . . and improvises another day.

July 5   *Whippoorwill*

Whippoorwill sounds at dusk. Whippoorwills moving in, staking out the
wooded territory along the edge of fields. Moving in closer at night. Cool
breezes. Sleep and the dream of the Indian woman. She has found the gift I
have hidden for her in the house. She sits between us as my father drives us
toward the city, toward his house, the house where I grew up as a boy. The
Indian woman is smiling, holding my arm with both hands. My father is

comfortable and happy. My hand roams and strokes the Indian woman's thigh. She has thrown both her legs over my knee. My father is taking the long way home. He too may be in love, or attracted to the Indian woman. The whippoorwill calls from the dream trees outside my bedroom window: whippoorwill, whippoorwill. . . .

July 6   The Eye of the Deer

A sunny, cool morning down Daubner Rd. A deer stealthily stepping upon the edge of it. Stopping. The stillness of its form . . . part shadow, part sun, an air of the dark woods, the green fields in its presence. I hold the deer in my eye; the deer holds me, neither of us moving. The distance is safe between us. The deer turns its head in the direction from which it came, pauses, then proceeds across the road, a small fawn following it. Touching down upon the field, the deep leaps and runs, the fawn taking after her. Only the head and hind of the deer in an undulation of tall grasses. The fawn, unseen, bends the same tall grasses in the wake of its mother's path. The eye of the deer, the eye of the fawn, the eye of the field, the eye of the man in a summer morning sun seeing, once again, the eye of the November hunter and the blood upon the snow.

July 7   Water on Glass

Dreamscape . . . though there are qualities of the setting that reflect the sand dunes of Whitefish Bay. White is the color that suffuses this dream. An ambiance of white yet not white. First a milkiness, then a transparency the color of frosted glass. I watch hills and mountains of this clarity (it is not hard nor glass, but soft) from some distance—possibly another mountain/hill/dune. And while watching, the scene transforms itself to no form, only a blur like the sight of water on glass. It then reassembles itself in white, in the clarity of glass; then, by its own force, distort it in an exquisite blurriness touched with light. I stand amazed and loving before this image, so like rain, yet so far beyond any phenomena of water/clarity/transformation I have ever witnessed. The beauty of distortion moves closer, it seems, each time. I am not afraid, though what I see borders on the miraculous. And I do not want it to end.

Dusk. On the road just beyond the house. The quality of air is vaguely hazy. Green, the bright green of birch and maple lends a light to the road itself. The scene, but for the asphalt, touched with the primeval. I appear unannounced, my own steps as quiet as leaves. Three fat black ravens hold the ground before me in various poses of stealth, suspicion, bewitchery. A foreboding fills me at first: the shininess of their black feathers, their movements—a trance. They unfurl huge wings in my approach, gliding first above the weeds, then to higher branches where they set, holding me in their eyes. There's beauty to the black death they evoke in summer green, at day's end.

For almost two weeks now, the fevered pace of keeping up with summer, with the work of summer around house and garden, summer schedules of the kids, summer visitors. The heat and time of day and night itself consumed by a mental energy, a physical running-in-place, both fatiguing and exhilerating. I run (I feel) on the exhileration, taking little time to pause (as I do in other seasons) to wonder what I'm about, where I'm headed. I push on with all the other crazy summer growth—a grapevine, the thick snaking squash—in whatever direction the sun, the moisture, the earth call. Growing, even in the night, as corn and the scent of tomatoes permeating the air. Gathering all the light within reach, absorbing all the warmth. The only evidence of time, the day and the night. And a numb remembrance (unacknowledged) of the same landscape, stark, and the loneliness of winter.

One of the hottest summer days I have known here. On Europe Bay beach by midafternoon, enjoying, celebrating the cold clear water of Lake Michigan, reveling in the relative absence of tourists, of others. In the distance, clouds of gulls hovering over Gull Island. In the north, a gathering of clouds. A possible storm? Rough, they look less than threatening at this hour. Yet—knowing the dryness of the land, our garden parched, and knowing the beauty of sudden summer rain—something inside me cries out for thunder, for storm. By 5 o'clock, the north cloud cover has spread, though it seems to be headed in a grand sweep, southeast, missing us at the top of the thumb. I would like, if I could, to coax it inland. Touch us, touch the earth, I plead, loving the cool lake water again, floating, sinking, diving, jumping, entering it, letting it enter me so that I am water. Moving along, further down the beach, I discard the denim cut-offs I wear, and truly meet the water, feel it thrill the naked body as it should. Some hours later on the road, in a movie house in Baileys Harbor, the sound of thunder, the distant rumble. Then the wind. Then the rain. The night sky disgorging itself of water. The night sky, electric in soft yellow light. In the car, driving home through downpour, I think of the beach again. I think of the fields drinking at night. I wish to be there, under the rain, knowing the water, the sky, the summer night in the heat of July. I roll the window down and feel the drumming drops upon my arm. In the morning, the earth wet and black, the garden fresh green.

July 11   Orchards

I watch the orchards now as I drive the back roads of the north end of the peninsula. How the white cherry blossoms of May fill the trees with popcorn, changing with the constancy of summer sun. All green. Then, in mid to late June, the evidence of the cherry itself, a hard white sphere, testing its form, feeling its weight upon the bough. Clusters of them follow, white pearl turning to yellow moonlight. And now, though the eye never quite sees the moment, a cast of the lightest shade of pink. The intensity of the tree, the blue sky, the sun, the powers of earth and rain conjuring the final transformation to a red/orange that ripples through the moving countryside like a wash of watercolor. In the redness of the vision lies a staccato of pure form that lifts the trees and gives us special summer light.

July 12   *Peas*

The sweetness of green peas, fresh from the garden, early summer evening, the sun in a low angled slide through the trees, scattering a patchwork of light upon the plants. "Puk, Puk, Puk" . . . pulling the fat pods off the pea plants, running a fingernail down the seam, opening the halves in bright green wonder, tearing them, teasing them gently off the stems between my lips, tasting a summer sweetness, natural green. I walk the rows, munching peas, pulling weeds, inspecting potato blossoms, feeling the day close in a fragrance of growing things all around me.

July 13   *9 p.m. Sky*

A 9 o'clock sky, driving home from Algoma down County trunk S after seeing the movie *Black Stallion* at the local show. A 9 o'clock-in-the-evening sky of pearl and gray infused with the lingering apricot light of a hot sun that set some time ago. Windows of the car wide open, breezes from the lake beside me. The sky forms its dying light in saber curves reminiscent of the North African landscape I just viewed, where water and sand turn upon themselves, graced by desert light. Rows of corn here, though, and barns open to the coming night. An owl swings across the road. I curve amongst all of this in mind, in love with the whorls of such summer night.

July 14   *Sunflower Reveries*

A wetness to the earth today. A wet time. The skies bursting with thunder and rain, early morning on. The sunlight, when it does appear, is hazy and quite momentary. The work of rain is the business of today. Wetness to stifle, again, the strange constancy (for here) of heat and sun. All day long a grayness pervades. Standing in the garden later in the evening, walking the rows so green and bursting with green—snow peas, sweet peas, lettuce, spinach—the grayness wrapping itself around my shoulder, entering me, filling me finally with a winter-mind of snow and an all-encompassing reminder of this garden in another time. I stand before a growing sunflower, only waist-high in mid-July, anticipate its reach far beyond me in another month, topped by its great head exploding in homage to the sun. I feel the grayness again. And see the same stalk, bent, seed spent, faced with a death of drifting snow.

The mugginess of morning, 5 a.m. All the windows of the house covered with a heavy moisture, so unlike this place of summer mornings, ever clear, ever light, ever cool. I step outside into the soggy air. Inside the coop, well-insulated and tucked into the thickness of trees, a woodsy coolness prevails. Placing a blanket on the floor between writing desk and painting table, I face the east window and meet the morning in a yoga way. I feel the sun stretch.

July 16   *Kite*

Finding myself in the dreamscape of July 7th now, witnessing the dream itself, parts of it, become real. Watching myself, the scene, this moment on a dune in Whitefish Bay. The light . . . the waters, the horizon, the sand itself a bright steeliness to it all. Not quite the beauty of blending, the wateriness of blur. But enough, enough to say inside myself: I have been to this place before. And then the recollection of the dream, my own. And to it, add the dream told of another, the snake dream, the garden-of-Eden dream. The woman, now. The gift of kite, unfurled. The colors . . . hers. And possibly a moon? No, a snake. A snake-kite, drawn primitively, heart-shaped. These spaces of image—feeling, love, living beyond time—touching those now within ourselves.

KODAUKO'S TUG
=/9/76

July 17   *Fresh Fish*

Scent upon this landscape, unknown in winter. But in summer, driving the
shorelines, nearing the docks where some of the natives of this peninsula
still work the waters, smelling, remembering, and in ways most unexplainable, thanking the clear sharp smell of fresh fish, boatloads and boxes of
the flashing, living, silver life. Even inland, miles away from it at times, the
fish scent trails, and I know I am here, always near the water.

July 18   *Flower Watch*

To see Queen Ann's Lace floating cloud-like in the fields already, fills me
with a sadness that speaks autumn.

July 19   *Web Light*

A morning of magic, of fantasy, of fairytale, a sunny summer morning of
heavy dew, a morning I witness perhaps once a year, though years may pass
when I fail to find such a fine magic to the day at all. A thin morning, a
morning of webs. The dew must be present . . . and the sun, at such an
angle, and the time of day so precise (after 6 a.m.?) that the delicacy of the
moment (light and dew) can easily dissipate before one's eyes. But they are
there now . . . here in the field . . . thousands of them surround me, my
shoes and pantlegs wet with dew. The magic, the mystery, the secrecy of
spider webs set so surely in the private places of the weeds and flowered
fields. Their inspiration, their artistry caught now, revealed for the moment
by heavy dew and morning sunlight . . . glittering, the intricate spaces
aglow all around me. A sense of catching nature unaware, seeing something
I was not supposed to, like the nakedness of a woman alone bathing in the
sun. The webs spin in their own light like ghosts of flowers.

July 20   *Leaf Watch*

The foliage, though thick and vast as a bright green umbrella, sheltering me
in these woods where I now sit, shows intimations of other times, spreading
through their green machinery. Isolating a maple on the road, this gray-sky

morning, staring into its very center, individualizing the pattern and color of the leaves, I see for certain the days of deep green are over. Already, almost a transparency, a thinness of color to the leaf. And along the edges of three leaves—yellow, an insinuation of red—the seasons intermingling, the way of life, a blend.

July 21   *Deer Darkness*

Wet country backroads, a night after the rain. The smell of rain and the fields and the farms. The road ahead a soft shiny black in my headlights. I light up the ditches too: cat's eyes, electric; Queen Ann's Lace; the deer. A wet summer night of the deer standing in tall grass, waiting in ditches, cautious of the headlights. They stand statuesque, still. Heads turned toward the field and woods they came from. Deer everywhere along the road this wet green night. Traveling in such silence. Standing, sometimes bounding at my approach. I love their eyes, pools of this wet summer night. We exchange the light. We handle the darkness of each other, in passing.

July 22   *Tree Talk*

Talking trees, talking leaves . . . wind . . . light . . . a branch of leaves, a child waving goodbye . . . a rattle of leaves, a clutter of leaves, a rush of them, waves of them, shimmering, shimmering in the morning light. Now serpentine, now doddering. Flashing. Twirling. Rippling. A rippling mountain stream of leaves over pebble-like forms of light on other leaves. A noisy summer morning, good leaf-talk among the trees, bathing now in their green splashy ground.

July 23   *Dream Horse and Michigan Farm*

Hollyhocks, tiger lilies, sweetpea, Queen Ann's lace, purple thistle, black-eyed susans, chicory, daisy, mullein, all wrapped in sweet-smelling white clover in a rural bouquet of a summer field in the Midwest. The summers of my youth spent on Grandma's Michigan farm: all of it is here, here in this sweet clovery smelling, flower dancing field. Grandma amidst the grapevines, the orange tiger lilies lapping at her legs, Grandpa on the bench under the apple tree, the horse nodding in the thick summer light.

July 24   *Silver Waters*

A rendezvous of the rivers. The coming together of swift forces. Then the quietness of the lake: woman and water and the sun's reflection of all this, the lake nibbling the shore in its song of silver, silver goblets of wine the color of her hair, the Queen of Cups, Tarot. Surely there is beauty, imagination, love, in such a time and place as she, the fortune in the moment taken as morning sun moves in gentle passion to noon and the dying of the day. The cups are cold. Our fingers engraved in silver, in ice, in passion. We drink the light of each other while summer spreads the tree around us in shade, and sets the lake on fire.

July 25   *Red Raspberries*

A raspberry morning, the soft ruby caps plucked from the plant, gathered O so red, between fingers, in the cups of hands, slipped between the lips onto the tongue in the way of communion wafers in the Sunday mornings of my youth, though I tongue their velvetness, press and search for the thinness of seeds to crack and crunch pleasurably between the teeth. This nurturing again, on mornings in July, mostly raspberry, red, red, red, raspberries in a blue sky and the cold pitcher of cream set on the table inside.

6 a.m. . . . the rising sun burning off a cloud-like cover of low mist in Charley's and Carlson's fields. I watch for the precise moment when the warmth of light seems to lift the mist, dissipating it all in an instant. Midday . . . clouds of purple thistle and blue chicory float on the fields, shimmer, mix, turn the earth into living watercolor. 11 p.m. . . . the same scene as morning, only now the white light of the moon casts a cool and calm effect upon a low settling ground fog that wraps this summer earth thicker and thicker into night. I move, under moonlight, toward, into, such final and perfect dissolution.

July 27 *Peas*

The morning, of such wonder and promise, cannot rid me of myself today. I live the day disguised, looking for salvage along a hard row of peas too old to pick, too tough.

July 28 *Roses and Crippled Bird*

Backyard roses . . . Chicago, the Cicero neighborhood . . . home again. Pink and red roses, a thickness of them, and my father feeding the birds promptly at 3 in the afternoon. "George," my mother says. "Your friends are here." Sparrows and starlings and mourning doves line up on the edge of the garage roof, the fence, the telephone wires, waiting for my father's scheduled feeding. "I don't feed the birds in summer," I tell them. "In the woods, in the fields at my place, there's enough for them to eat. In summer, they're on their own." A small starling flutters beneath the rose bushes. "Oh, George," screams my mother. "He's back again. He's hurt! Keep the dog away from him. Do something." "The bird is crippled," I say. "A cat, something got him." "Oh, he'll be all right," says my mother. "No," I answer. "No, he won't be all right. He'll never fly again. He's a victim, a target now." "Put him under the rose bushes, George," she says. "Put him in the next yard. Do something." In the starling's eye, reflections of newly mowed blades of green grass, and fallen pink petals of the rose.

July 29 *Baseball Moon*

The moon rising over Sox Park and the night ballgame. The stands full. The outfield so green under the lights. The players in motion around the bases.

And then the moon, solid, full, a rich creamy yellow, hovering over the right field bleachers. A tiny white ball sent aloft in the face of the old moon itself. My eyes follow the ball, but stay with the moon. I place it, myself, over a summer field in Wisconsin, over the waters of Lake Michigan. The city recedes. The ballpark has become prairie again.

July 30   *Stone Fence*

A sunset walk across Timberline, into the field toward Gus's beehives. I stop to take in the stone fence running beside the stone fence, the purple thistle, the Queen Ann's lace . . . the field of it. And all of it, touched in the falling orange light, moving, as only stone fences move, cradling purple thistle and white lace to the round forms, the openings of laughter and sighs.

July 31   *Bleeding Hearts*

Comfort me in hollyhocks and hummingbirds, bleeding hearts in black hair, and the violets you shed from your skin, the white light, the white light. . . .

Behind the large garden, the back garden (the "other" garden of my own tending), where I once planted grapes and sometimes tend the vines and sometimes harvest them before the birds or frost. Where, this year, I planted two rows of extra onions between the two long trellises of grapes. Harder earth back here. Rocky soil. Unfertilized. Unkempt. Weeded, trimmed occasionally in spring around the grapevines, but it all gets away by July. The wonder of weeds, small trees, wildflowers. I give it its head, its nature, and tread in mostly unaware, like a stranger. The leaning fence posts and sagging wires the grapevines grasp and wind and hang themselves upon, retain some permanence within the orgy of leaves and roots, and the wave of young poplars steadily moving in. The grapes, I tell myself, will always be there. Further in the back, beneath a healthy white birch tree, the yellow bench, once part of a swing, rests, decayed, on the stones I once set it upon, years ago. It was (is?) a quiet place to visit, to sit and tend the grapevines in late afternoon sun. Charley's old stone fence. The small grave of my son's first hampster, and the small wooden gravemarker (with a red heart and a black cross) proclaiming, in his words, age 12: "Harvey . . . He was wondrous and ambitious Sept. 1975 to March 1976 R.I.P." The three old, wooden birdhouses leaning in every direction, their tops held on by large field stones. Beneath the third, the furthest house from the road, a tiny patch of herbs, lemon thyme, passed through the hands and gardens of friends, but beginning in the hands of the consummate gardener of the mind here, the late Bill Beckstrom. I remain still amidst the growth and decay of this private piece of earth, relating the abundance, complexity, madness of green growth to something almost South American, realizing the death is here too, as strong in all these things. Sitting on the rotting yellow bench, the birdhouses of swallows and bluebirds now abandoned, I garden the spirit of this place, the spectres of flowers, fruits, all animal life, stones and friends.

August 2   *Garden Spirit: Lightning Birds*

On close inspection, discovering the third birdhouse in the back garden (spirit garden), along the stone fence. The back wall, with rusted nails protruding, still attached to the top of the post, but the top and other three sides, gone, pulled apart, perhaps by some anxious animal. A racoon? A stray dog? Cat? And what did the nest contain? Young bluebirds? Swallows? Some distance away I find the other three sides of the birdhouse, still intact. And along the stone fence, the top. Fitting the three sides into the nails protruding from the back wall, I set the house reasonably in place, back together again, still wondering about the force of an animal to pull apart so tight-fitting a box. I return the top, placing a large flat stone on top of it to secure it in the wind. Only then do I notice the burn marks on the cedar birdhouse. Only then do I visualize a strike of lightning in a summer storm seeking out so precisely the small nailhead, and wrenching the house off the post in a somersault of blue-white light . . . feathers and fire . . . lightning birds.

August 3   *Summer Itch*

In the garden, I weed the rows between the corn, early morning, late evening, and do not see them setting upon the backs of my arm, neck, cheek, forehead. Nor do I feel them, at first. Later it begins, usually when I leave the garden and my skin responds in a patchwork of fire. I hear them on the road too, following me. Hear their buzzing above my head, feel them pick up my scent, now, set down in the quiet pools of perspiration upon my body, and leave their handiwork. This morning, as I walk toward the coop, I feel them hanging in the muggy air. Unknown to me, I must carry them into the coop on my pants and shirt, or harbor them somewhere in my hair. When I sit at the desk in the absolute stillness of this place, then their presence is most manifest. In the furthermost corner I hear the maddening buzz of the tiny single insect. I trace its sound, picking up the warm, human blood trail, as it flies, often unseen, above and around me, while I grasp at the thin air, hoping to capture and extinguish the sound and life. It's that moment, when I've missed, that I am most suspect. Where, upon me, has it lit? Is it still here? And then the slightest sensation is felt just beneath my elbow. Then the scratching which continues till the familiar pink and white welt appears upon the skin, and I numb myself with persistent scratching till I eventually draw blood, the satisfaction, bordering on meditation. Moments later, near my ear, I hear its slow, droning, sluggish flight. Moving toward the sound in a frantic hand slap, I slowly lift my hands off each other and with unexplainable satisfaction, delight in the bright red blood print in the palms of my hand and the death of my most baneful reminder of summer. In peace and satisfaction (and desultory scratching . . . for in truth, one dead mosquito recalls a thousand other bites—the neck now, the leg, the ankle, the shoulder—itch, itch, itch, scratch, scratch, scratch . . . ah . . .) I resume my quiet way with words. In the distant corner, another drone begins. Concentration destroyed, I will do no work now (for minutes bordering on hours) till I have secured this place, regained the peace to write again.

August 4   Rain Storm

A day, comfortable enough, deep, wooly, buoyantly gray. Huge dark clouds rolling over the waters of the bay, the lake, and onto the countryside. Wrapped in their dark thickness, wanting all the heavens to break loose and empty the skies of rain, coaxing the thunder, speaking it in one's very bones, guiding the lightning in one's eyes, bringing it in, closer over the woods, above one's own head . . . now, now! Split the solid rock of summer, open us all to the wash of rain, play the music on the leaves, preening so in the wind. Let loose the late sun, then. Fill the road with worms. Make the green grass thick and alive with frogs and toads. Bridge the late wetness of the day now with a rainbow in the far fields. The air is a mist of gold.

August 5   Fishtug

The time: before sunrise, somewhere after the hour of 6. I walk the quiet road again and hear only the sound of birds—swallows and bluebirds already on the wires—and then, across the fields, slowly taking on more and more light, I see the fishtugs (though I hear them only) gently rippling the quiet surface of the water at Gills Rock, smoke coming from the stack, gulls etching the skies directly overhead . . . the tug now turning into Death's Door . . . the pilot fisherman (Tim Weborg, perhaps?) slipping between the buoys, chugging, chugging, chugging a waterway toward Lake Michigan. There is more movement to the water now . . . the tug itself begins to rock and sway and dip as it meets the force of lake waters. The fisherman tightens his stance, the muscles in his legs rippling. The gulls sweep higher and wider. The sun rises. The fishtug, the water, the horizon, the gulls, the sun, the fisherman, the man on the road overlooking the field this morning. And the dark silent nets and their mystery of light under water.

August 6   *Night Flyer*

Cool, warm. The variation of degrees in a single day. This the whole body basks in—not the waves of water this time, but the waves of air, of light. In the loving field, insects hum, black-eyed susans drink the sun, red mushroom glow, Queen Ann's Lace sways. The earth is hard and soft. The pines call. The sky wraps and unwraps itself, now blue, now gray, now blue again. The skin perspires upon touch, breathes cool as the gentleness of air wafts over it. Warm wetness intermingled, disengaged, while the world sighs in a brisk breath of pine. Evening, I ride the countryside, cool, windows open, coffee, wine, tobacco smoke, cherry orchard wind, purple thistle wind, pink and gold and violet bay water wind. Lights go on in the windows of old farmhouses. Stars rain down my neck. I shower in tall corn. These wheels leave the pavement as I glide high into the cold water sky, nodding my head to the hot sounds of radio rock.

August 7   *Stone Sculpture*

The play of light on my "spirit rock sculpture" outside my window at this time of day—2:33 p.m. The big one, the Buddha, is sensational. Also the new one (actually an old one) which I've transformed into another spirit-person-type. I feel he's the Shaman—dark stone head, white torso. An Indian type shaman . . . wrapped in a blanket maybe. And the stone woman still stands alone out there in the southernmost distance. Not as imposing or dramatic, but a presence. In this light, they're all dancing. . . .

August 8   *Summering, Solitarily*

I revel in the aloneness of this savory summer day: the walk to the coop in the cool light of morning air, the work, revealing itself so well, so true, the solitariness of going for my mail, basking in the love of friends—where are they now? What do we share? And answering their words with mine, all the way home. I delight in the aloneness of lunch, picking greens from the garden for a salad; munching, while there, on snap peas, biting deep tracks into wet ripe green/white kohlrabi; dining alone in the kitchen booth, a lemonade lunchtime, with music by Paul Horn, Cat Stevens, Buffy St. Marie, Jimmy Buffet; chewing and eating and drinking and listening and reading *Time,* the New York *Times,* the *Trib,* the Door County *Advocate.* Peeling off the short sleeve shirt for an afternoon writing session in a good old neighborhood type white tank top undershirt because I like the freedom of movement in such Old World-type garb; thinking of the oldtimers in the neighborhood, watering their lawns on hot summer nights in these under-shirts. And for awhile, I am *that* here, this summer day I can smell, feel, taste, touch. Late afternoon, I stretch under a tree, resting on my elbows, pulling thin green weeds to stick between my teeth. The wind blows blue under my arms. I am buoyant upon this earth, feeling weeds wash over me like waves.

August 9   *Garden Count*

Potatoes are dying . . . carrots, thriving solidly thick within their row . . . one egg plant shining like a bruise . . . second crop of snowpeas (snap peas) now in blossom and still climbing the chicken wire trellis . . . tomatoes thriving, but mostly still green . . . corn as high as an elephant's eye . . . pumpkins, green and burgeoning . . . yellow, crook neck squash making themselves distinct . . . celery almost ready for chewing . . . lettuce, salad green and growing with profusion . . . cauliflower showing its rough white hide, ready now for tying, kohlrabi begging to be pulled, peeled, chomped, cabbages developing a ball . . . pickles and cucumbers running wildly across the ground, popping off, it seems, extending themselves right before one's eyes . . . onions, fist-size, popping out of the soil, their thick hollow stems, bent, broken, yet musical to the touch . . . garlic both in seed and ready to be pulled, dried, chopped, into salads, melted in butter for garlic bread, slipped into tomato sauce for a winter's meal of spaghetti . . . green beans trail the earth, still in blossom . . . dill clouds the garden air in blossom and smell . . . while four sunflowers, still green, continue on their upward journey, still keeping their color to themselves.

August 10   Clouds

The clouds just before the sunrise . . . streaks, ripples, puffs of them, all steely to light gray, and overhead, white. There the carrousel, here the woman, supine, there the lion's head. And all changing, the whole line of sky above the trees, as I look upon them, trying to see, to know, to realize the slow progression of the rising, spreading light. For those who feel there is a measure to time, let them document a sunrise. A time beyond time. No time at all. No thought. Only the image. The northernmost band of clouds, now suffused with a white, golden light, while to the south, the same band rippling, spreading, with a light like the skin of an apricot. The sky above and behind me gradually open as the stone doors of an ancient temple. No longer walking forward, I step backward, my eyes still on the rising sun, the cloud line, pearlish pink, casting sprays of the same pink toward the clouds overhead and behind me. Each, receiving the light, transforms it into a fiery nimbus. The stillness of it all in the time it takes a tree to grow its bark. The cacophony of it all, the rumble of thunder, the miracle of lightning. Nearing my drive again, still walking backwards, I catch the tops of the trees so green with fire. The light opens the woods, spreading the trunks and branches in an invocation of the day. A jay cries. Clouds return, white with day, forever reshaping themselves in wonder. Clouds disintegrate in light. The sun rolls into the sky. Nothing is the same. In Tibetan Buddhism the white clouds signify the creative power of the mind, assuming any imaginative form. I make the day.

August 11   Cloud Passage

Clouds again this morning, layers of them—silks, satins, gauze—some low enough to touch, others infinite as a clear night. Movement was their beauty in this moment. Unfurling, streaming out of the northern sky, shot out of it in the manner of fireworks fired laterally, then spreading overhead in color. The light of the morning sun somehow above them all, raining down in muted tones of pink and peach and white. Planted firm upon the ground, with animal, stone, weed, tree, I seek the transformation of transparency, the diffusion of flight.

August 12   *Dunes*

Sand dunes and sun on the Lake Michigan shoreline . . . finding the quiet
hollow that is hill, that is sand, that is dune grass, wildflower, white birch
and the biting of flies, the droning of insects. The grittiness of hot sand
soothing the skin, warming the flesh, turning the mind over with hot licks
till evaporation is imminent and nothing remains but the silent blue water,
flashing, on fire.

August 13   *Birds on the Wire*

Birds on the wire: I don't even care to know their names. I just like them
there, from a distance. Gray skies and black birds strung out in pairs, in
large groups, or all alone. I like to watch them set, so carefully, so
accurately, so still. I like to see them suddenly sear the air in flight. Mostly,
though, just seeing birds on the wire, knowing they are there, fixed and
unfixed upon the landscape. A peace, for these eyes, in the transitoriness of
dark wings.

August 14   *Bouquet for Charley*

One Queen Ann's Lace flower, white with its tiny violet center; two sprigs
of sweet pea, a fleshy pink-violet; one small spire of goldenrod; one sprig of
the soft purple milkweed flower; one buttercup, yellow enough to light this
room. All of these from Charley's old flower garden, all gone to weed, but
for these kaleidoscopic colors lighting and lifting the tangle of growth of
green. A child's gift for me this morning, turning the desk, the window, the
whole room in the spiritual sustenance of live color that honors the old man
who loved them, and the child in love with giving flowers.

August 15   *Emptiness of Birds*

Their absence grows larger as summer wears on. Chicadees. Where are they
now? Their black caps, slate colored wings, white breast. I miss them at the
feeder by the breakfast nook window. I miss their delicate but sure picking

and pecking of sunflower seeds. How they look at you through the glass. How they light on branches and seem to twirl. Their gaiety, their joy. Bird people explain their summer disappearance (July, August) as natural to their kind, a time for nesting, deep in the woods. And with such a surfeit of summer everywhere, it seems unlikely they are missed. Sometimes, deep in the woods myself this time of year, I remember them and look, but find only such an emptiness of birds in the thickest of trees. Solace comes, knowing that even in their mysterious absence, I feel they are here, watching me. And solace comes, laced with joy, in knowing for certain the friendliness of their presence, their magic, will be evident again in the feeding window, all about the trees and house, in a matter of days or weeks ahead. And once again, this bird above all will ease the depths and isolation of my winter.

August 16 · Deer Kill

Moving steel, glass, a late morning sun upon the highway. Car-loads of tourists on a rush to everywhere. The county still singing fresh and green at this time. The birches glowing in their white bark. The Ellison Bay swamp at the bottom of the hill, inviting no one, yet harboring bird and animal life, thick in the solitude of the privacy of trees, green growth, and water. Skunks and porcupines dutifully venturing across the highway to retrieve the swamp silence of the other side, falling victim to their own instinct, blindly meeting the fate of speeding cars, the thumping flesh of animals ripped open, flattened in fur, blood, and guts. This late morning, a kill even

110

more poignant: a deer—a large furry buck—feeling the onslaught of fast moving steel rip into the furry softness of its flesh. The cars pulling over. The continuous stream of tourists, gaping. The officer of the law, a leg on a bumper, writing the accident report. The concerned citizen directing traffic. The deer, stretched on the side of the highway, its head gracefully bent back, its black nose sniffing the grandeur of the forest lost, the swamp that was the completeness of its being. Its antlers, scratching patterns of no meaning in the gravel of the road's edge. Its eye, a large black pool in which I swim.

August 17   Green Wind

It's the gustiness of the wind today, the green leaves outside my window turning, twirling on stems, the very flat green of their undersides more evident than the shininess . . . the way the branches bend, sway, the very trees themselves seem to shudder in the turmoil of such a cold, gray day. A gray windiness moaning through the mind, blowing the windows of eyes open, the doors of ears shut . . . then closing the eyes, opening the door, a winter's cry of ice entering the bloodstream. Viewing it all from the inside, I sit behind this window nursing the first pangs of the solitariness of winter to come. Stepping outside, entering it all, my eyes rest upon the frenzied green, remembering it's still summer after all, and there are days and days of sun yet to come. This is but the other side for now. And in the splendor of each season are intimations of what was, and is to come.

August 18   A Thousand Robins

The wind of yesterday giving way to the rain of last night, leaves the road this morning wet with worms and what appears to be a thousand robins, many of them in speckled breasts, feasting on what the earth let loose in last night's rain and yesterday's wind. Charcoal gray on blue-black asphalt glistening in pools, reflecting the pink, fiery sky opening to day.

August 19   Garden Feast

A second crop of snap peas ready to be plucked off the vines, still trailing, still blossoming white on the chicken wire trellis. Both pickles and cucumbers in abundance spread across the earth, plants entangling in plants. The cukes and pickles growing, inches and inches, before one's eyes. The green ready. Pulling them from the leafy underside of the plant. The cardboard "gardening basket" filling with a mixture of sweet snap peas, green beans, cucumbers, pickles. There a yellow crook neck squash, there yet another, another, snapping them off the vine, tossing them in . . . tomatoes, ripening, 1, 2 3 4 5 6 ready for picking. Pull a kohlrabi . . . pull two. Add some fresh bulbs of garlic, an onion or two, and red potatoes, accidentally dug up. Wiping the mud from the skin. Slicing off a head or two of broccoli, a clump of cauliflower. Some sprigs of dill. Peeling back a bit of the husk on the corn . . . not quite ready, but coming along real fine. Bringing this morning's summer harvest to the kitchen now. B readying the large blue pot on the stove, the mason jars . . . washing and slicing the pickles. Ah, the aroma . . . it's dill pickle time. Lunch time too, garden fresh lunch, the knife slicing through bright red juicy tomatoes, cucumbers prepared in sour cream, yellow, crook neck squash sliced, placed into boiling water, small red potatoes boiled in their jackets, the broccoli boiled, the cauliflower eaten raw with a dip. Biting into the sweet snow peas, while dishing out the yellow squash and broccoli, buttering it, salting it slightly, consuming it all. The taste of sweet earth, the body sanctified. A certain holiness consumes one.

August 20   *Blackberries*

The west field beyond the house is filled with them now, sweet, plump, wild blackberries. The dog wanders through the entanglement of thorns, licking the black caps into its pink mouth. I wade deep into the nettles myself, gently pulling caps from plants, feeding them into my mouth, bear-like . . . delicious . . . two creatures on a summer's romp, lost in a blackberry patch.

August 21   *Moths*

Though their beating on the black windowpane of night lends an eeriness to the livingroom of the man on the rocker watching the candle send shadows and light dancing on the objects in his vision, the rhythm of the mist-like moth wings and the candle's light play in unison, and the tiny jewels of light in the eyes of the moths burn in a self-consuming flame, and he would be this night, the ancient patterns on their wings, the night's thickness of branches and stars, their language of light in the hollow darkness of his rocking bones.

August 22   Theater

As the players assemble backstage of the Theater in the Park in Fish Creek, the playgoers filter under the night-reaching tall trees, homing, as it were, for the water's edge. The white pebbles. The water, horizon, sky, colored like a peach. Down the darkening path between pines, the quiet waters rehearse the sleeping fish for stars. An almost full white moon opens a way into the sky. While men and women rehearse their roles behind the drawn curtain, there are no masks.

August 23   Birth Daying

On such a day of birth, such a 5 a.m. morning on the road, mist hangs above the field in thin wisps of dream, the woman turns unclothed in sheets redolent of night's lovemaking and the silhouettes of distant trees stay spectred a while in early dew, the day opening like a peach, my birthing the morning star.

August 24   Creatures

The noises overhead, either above the ceiling or upon the roof, speak of life (rodent? bird?) trying to establish itself in this gray afternoon. Claws and busy teeth, wings and wiry feet, seeds being stored, small branches set upon. In the ignorance of what is, the noise itself shapes the room, takes hold of the darkest language within this man who, listening to the wonders of his own blood, wants the sharp instinct to detect the scent, seek out the movement and the noise, repossess the territory by cunning, guile or force. Kill, if need be. Returning to a state of grace.

August 25   3

The wet pavement of the worn asphalt road this morning, and the three blackbirds gathered around the pool of standing water, pecking at the stillness of the gray sky. A luminosity to the feather, the stones in the pavement, the rainwater, like molten silver.
In the field lay only a single side of an old shed. Through what was once a

window grows a bouquet of purple thistle, while through the doorway emerges a woman in white, dressed in Queen Ann's lace.

The full moon this night upon the farms in the center of the county, lifting cornfields, barns, cows, and silos in a heavy gentle mist of light glowing from within.

August 26   *Still Life*

The noises overhead this rainy day morning, blown twigs and branches on the roof, pecked at, stirred about certainly by birds. I smile, sit still, welcome the foray. The drumming of the rain and those sporadic scrapings of twigs and branches enters me with a need for nature noise this day, a familiarity beyond defining. A branch rolls down the back of the roof, wings flutter, the tree outside my window shakes suddenly in a frenzy of one, two, three, four young, speckled robins lighting upon the wet branches. All their eyes, I feel, gaze at me seated beyond the window in the desk's light. I turn the lamp's switch and we dissolve in the wet, slate gray of their feathers. A single robin drifts down to perch upon the head of the stone Buddha, giving the moment the weight of flight, the song beyond enclosure.

August 27   *Tree Kill*

Attacking a fallen tree in the woods with a chainsaw, committing a heinous
crime one reads about in cheap pulp scandal sheets, I am the man with the
axe, the blade, the hammer. In the maddening whine of the motor, the
sharp turning teeth, severing limbs and trunks, I view the murderous act like
a grainy photograph filled with bloody images of dismemberment. The act
completed, I drop the bright yellow machine and seek the solace of silence
again. Pray all trees to stand and fall in my absence, and the earth consume
us in quiet moisture.

August 28   *Ryder Moon*

Another Albert Pinkham Ryder moon this night, with the clouds both light
and dark, gray, blue, black, white, rolling in the near distant sky—a sky so
transparently blue-green, yet knowingly black—and the moon, the moon
blown away with it all, yet constant behind the wispy, wind-tossed shapes.
Oh, love, how we move through the turbulent nights skies, how our own
dark shadows turn circles in ourselves, the light centered in a distance we
can only hope to embrace.

August 29   *Smoke and Candlelight*

The scent of piñon smoke still hangs in the air of the coop this morning,
where last night the orange candle glowed, flickering light on all the
paintings, while the window glass turned black and both my words and
watercolors rested in the memory of sage, mountains, and the shadows of
love that hover inside the room.

August 30   *Fog*

The heavy, wet fog of last night, slipping into dream as I walk the road with
only the occasional light from the trunks of white birch trees to mark the
way . . . losing feet, legs, hands, arms . . . only the eyes which seem to
reflect themselves. Making a wide arc—part road, part field—in a return
toward home, a diffusion of light in the distance, a spilling, a glowing,

pouring through trees, onto the roadway. The house rests without foundation. Only light flowing and spreading through windows where even the furniture inside, the paintings, the books, the lamps, the clock and rocker turn in the night's mist, float upon pools of light.

August 31   Rainbow Man

In yet another morning, the heaviness of moisture in air slowing all the life processes—the trees themselves, their branches, all plants, bowed, drooping with the burden of air. My own body, fighting allergies of all sorts which seem intensified in the mugginess of such a day, sluggishly makes its way at 5:30 a.m. toward the coop. A night of little sleep. A routine of yoga in the dampness of the coop reawakens body/mind slightly. I breakfast. I return to the coop to write, but after an hour the typewriter keys seem to run upon the page, my head bobs, then falls. I clear a space on the cot in the corner, under the Jerry West painting of New Mexico, under the Hoppe paper sculpture, Antea (sender of nocturnal visions) and try to clear my head again with sleep. Staring across the room at a crystal pendant hanging in the east window, I see the sun, smothered in layers of wet air, suddenly sends a single ray that pierces through the crystal pendant loosening a spectrum of rainbows in the room, rainbows the shape of tears, the largest ring of them circling the room near the foot of the cot, each tear-shaped rainbow spreading, slowly from brightness to oblivion. By moving my head slightly, in these seconds that seem suffused with miracle and light, I hold one color of the spectrum—yellow—in my eye and watch it spread (through my own tearms?) in a cross like pattern, then star, a solid, center core of light, radiating in a color and spirit one could only call sacred, holy, cosmic. I discover, also, that I am in control here briefly: I can choose any color of the rainbow I desire, by a mere movement of the eye. I choose red then . . . fantastic . . . green . . . perhaps once the color of paradise . . . a blue I have seen only in the waters off Greek islands, or the color of Indian turquoise . . . violet, the petals of that same flower . . . I continue running these colors together, pausing at one to drink it dry occasionally, then redeeming the light, the day, the rainbow, in yet another . . . blue . . . I am this blue . . . or I am this yellow, turning gold, turning, lifting this room, this body, this moment into dream, into light.

September 1   Coop Aglow

The house behind me, walking west toward the coop, 7 in the evening, I see the cedar shingles of the coop walls, singularly silver through the ages, a

116

penetrating, polished black in rain, now begin to glow in the most radiant tones of rose. I turn to look backwards and then upwards toward the sky, where clouds, both stratas and clusters, spread the day's final light in explosions of pink, violet, and silver gray. The coop, in its repose, stands holy. I do not enter it for a long while.

September 2   The Land Returns

In the emptiness of the roads, the towns, the stores, the landscape, a feeling in this clarity of day, so cool and bright, that the earth, water, sky, sigh in the departure of summer people, and nature returns to what nature is.

September 3   Crescent Moon Lovers

Morning night sky, 5 a.m., the perfect crescent of a moon, lemon sliced, against a Prussian blue sky. One bright star, just beneath the lower curve, still holds the night, pulling fast the tiniest gray threads of day which will diminish it within the hour as the moon itself pales and one forgets how it was the moon makes lovers of us all.

September 4   *Day Perfect*

Perfect sun, perfect leaf, perfect sky, perfect water, perfect air, perfect wind. A day, sometimes one, two, three or more in that time, not yet the end of summer, not yet fall, where a man enters and, without a desire to, escapes. Only the closing of a door places him home again, uncertain where he has been.

September 5   *Hollyhock Seeds*

Rose red, pink, rose pink, fuschia, deep red, dark red, purple red . . . hollyhock seeds, the gathering of them, wild, from roadside field, homes of friends. Sifting the soft nuggets through the fingers. Containing them in sun, darkness, drying to be passed on in hollyhock love, to be seeded in other places now, in the still warm earth of these days, part summer, part autumn, till the summer of their tall bright blooming comes again and we shall know in our eyes they are ours in the field.

September 6   *Ascending into Day*

That kind of day again returns, as the day before yesterday, when, whatever the burdens of being human, we are lifted into the day's very special September light and we rise, miraculously, through trees, over fields, water, spangling countryside to meet and be the air, dissipating in love of all this.

September 7   *Black Morning*

A 5 a.m. study in black and soft silver haze . . . black the road, the sky directly above me . . . and the trees, black filagree against the silver haze and the eastern sky showing the slightest early morning graying. But it's the rich blackness of trees, of wires, of birds—one weak call of the whippoorwill—that holds the death in me, alive.

September 8   *Thunder*

A welcoming sound though the season grows late. It wakes me from my sleep—thunderstorms in the distant west, rolling in at 2 a.m. The first rumbles, barely audible, though the trees outside the bedroom window begin to rustle, drafts of wind begin a steady wave-action through the screen, over the bed in which I lie. I picture the storm clouds kettling somewhere high over the Green Bay waters, their blackness suddenly an illuminating dark blue, silver white, soft pink. All of this, moving steadily toward me. I track it, partly awake, partly asleep. In a way, I guide it, the strongest clap of thunder, the sharpest stab of lightning, the churning of the clouds on a path just above me. Then, when the thunder unleashes its fury directly above, and the house shudders, and the room turns blue, I wait, close to tears, for the meditation of the falling rain, stilling me again close to sleep, grieving the changing seasons, the loss of summer thunderstorms.

September 9   *Chill*

Clear puddles of rain on the gravel driveway, in shallow recesses of the asphalt road, the water holding the brightening sky. In the woods, the green leaves of maple trees shimmer in the falling sun. In the meadow of mud and weeds, yellow butterflies abound, while goldenrod lights the way through the fields. "Have you listened to a tree?" a voice says. "Place your ear to the smooth bark and you can hear all wondrous things, the life moving within it." To evolve to a higher form of life, we must shed. By nightfall, in the confines of my own living room, this body begins to chill, begins to register the first sign of the coming cold. And though I reflect upon the comfort of an old flannel shirt, I am unwilling to call an end to summer sun. I want July and August born again.

All summer long it has been evident, but the last two weeks especially, skunks, it seems are everywhere. Reports, too, of the county overrun with rabid skunks. Roaming dogs are in danger. Gardens are being attacked. On the road to town today, within the distance of a little more than a mile, three highway slaughters of skunks evident—flesh and furry bodies splattered—the lingering stench. I think again of nature in cycles, creature cycles, that summer when all was frogs it seemed, the backroads filled with them one night. You could not drive without rolling over frogs. Some spring mornings, too, of worms. Or snails. Two years ago when the front lawn was littered with robins, hundreds of them. That fall, and that cloud of Monarch butterflies. Or that time when grouse seemed to thunder out of every tree I passed. The summer nights of last year when whippoorwills were thicker than leaves just outside the bedroom window. Some summers it's bats. Cedar bugs. Tomato worms. Cabbage butterflies. And a summer (or any season) where there is excess of one creature, the next year, and often years to follow, there is little or no evidence of such life. Excess and nothingness.

The first chickadee spotted returning to the feeder by the kitchen window this morning.
One sign of fall.
They are returning from their summer's nesting in the woods. A second spotted in the pines at the Sister Bay beach.
And a kingfisher firing his body into the water on a direct hit. Woman in an autumn mood, reflecting on the day. A mood, later that afternoon, taking on the burn rather than the fire, while I stand in a woods of my own helplessly holding the smoking match.

Frog fetish, water symbol; the woman of love and fire who bore me goes under the knife this day, the time of her living and dying to be determined by what the secrets of the body reveal, once opened up. The rain, I knew, was a bad sign. My early morning prayers, the turquoise frog, the practiced silence. Nothing could quite control the revelation of the spread of death.

"They opened her up and closed her again," or so it went. Shit, shit, shit, I replied. I stood a long while in the rain, not cursing the gods, failed powers, or anything. There was still time. Purification came in many ways. She would wake, I knew, in anger. And that would be her cure. How powerfully she could reprimand the world—even a son. If the anger remained, there would be life no matter what. And that, I could feel, she would eventually bequeath to me in full measure. "Get me out of this fucking place," her first words after recovery. She gave me life again in all the rain of this moment, steel gray sky, turquoise frog throbbing in my hand, in my pocket. I move a large round rock to my garden, in my window view.

September 13   *Geese*

The first flight of honking geese sighted, 11 a.m. in Sister Bay. They lift the head, hold the eye skyward, breaking and remaking their V flight pattern in a soulful guidance system beyond one man's tracking.

September 14   *Corn*

Picking corn in the dreariness of the gray afternoon. Two bushel baskets, the muddy/gray color of the day, filled now with green ears of corn. Shucking them then. Picking and cutting and breaking away parts of the cob affected by worms. The hands sticky with creamy corn juice and silky tassel. Ah, the sweet smell of fresh corn.

September 15   *Deer Light*

Traveling to Chicago in the darkness an hour or more before sunrise. A silver blue glow to the rural world at this time. The stars bright but fading. No trace of the moon. A deer stands in the middle of the highway, transfixed by my headlights. I stop within feet of it. The head turns slowly, and the body bounds into the day, into the field lifting into morning light.

September 16   *Red Roses, Green Peppers, Purple Grapes*

Two drooping red roses from the back garden in my mother's hospital room. A small green pepper, a pink bow tied to the stem, my father picked for her from the plant along the backyard fence. "Bring some fresh roses tomorrow," she said. "You ought to see all the nice green peppers," he tells her. "And the grapes on the neighbor's fence," I add. "They're beautiful, a dark purple, ripe and so sweet." "Oh, I'd like to taste those," she said. Tomorrow, before visiting, I will take from the neighbor's grapevine.

September 17   Lakeshore Drive

Lake Michigan sparkling in the sun from the vantage point of Chicago's Lakeshore Drive, the same Lake Michigan only a few blocks from my doorstep in rural Door County. And though the lakeside, Chicago, is outlined in beach, concrete, park, Lakeshore Drive itself, towering apartments and condominiums, the mystery, the solace, the power of water attracts the mind's eye, restores a sense of nature amidst sirens and smoke, bikers, joggers and roller skaters, men from a rifle club shooting clay pigeons over the water in the morning sun.

September 18   Nighthawks In A Neon Landscape

A booth by the window, traffic lights, neon, police sirens, the clatter of dishes and utensils, the night people reading the morning papers and the track sheets. The waitress taking and delivering orders. The Seneca Restaurant, 1 a.m. The young man:
"Women, they're all fucking stupid. That's why I'll never probably get married. They're fucking worthless, stupid bitches and I don't want any one of 'em. They're married, even if they're married, they move on their man. You know? They all fucking move on their men."
Old man: *"Not all of 'em."*
"All of 'em. That's why I'm never probably ever gonna get married. Who needs that shit? They're stupid. Pussy is stupid. I mean, not your wife. Not your wife or my mom. That's a different thing. Different thing. That's a different kind of woman. An old kind of woman. In their days, there was nothing like these days. They didn't move on their men, right?"
"Yeah."
"But the broads today . . . all fucking stupid."
"Listen . . . a rod is a rod. Pussy is pussy."
"No, no it ain't. Pussy ain't pussy. Some pussy's like this, some like this, some long, some this way. . . ."
"Yeah, but I mean, it's all really pussy. Ya know? Pussy is pussy."

"No. It's different. Some of 'em are this way, some of 'em that, or they want this. You know, different. They're not the same." "Aw you mean, if you mean that some broads like to talk to you . . . you know, talk sexy, get you up. Some like that, yeah. That's something different. That ain't what we're talking about. Or they do it a different way. But all together, really it's the same. Ya get what I mean? Pussy is pussy."

"Ya mean if you had the chance, you wouldn't go after some strange pussy? Huh, you mean that? Some strange stuff."

"Ah, go on."

"Some strange pussy come up to you, you wouldn't look? Huh? Huh? Bullshit."

"Ya know, you're married 20, 30, 40 years. The same old thing. Yeah, it's boring. Some strange stuff, yeah. Ok. Some of that stuff. But it's over, it's pussy. But yeah, oh yeah, I know what you mean. Sure."

"That's why I'll probably never get married."

"Your brother's gettin' married."

"Yeah, dumb fuck. She's 18 years old, and he's 36."

"Well, you know what that is."

"She's a virgin. She ain't never fucked no one but him before. He's crazy. I could cry. Dumb fuck. He's 50, ya know how old she'll be?"

"Yeah."

"He's 60 . . , she'll be movin on him. Like all the fuckin' women. Not like your wife. I dont't know your wife like I know you. But still, not like your wife. Your wife or my mom. That's different. That's not like nowadays. You know that Bobby G.? I hate him. Can't stand him. If there's anyone I really hate it's him. I was at this wedding, you know, and he was there. And he comes up to Larry's mom. You know Larry's mom. A real nice person. And this Bobby motherfucker's drunk and he comes up to Larry's mom and she's wearing this kind a low cut dress, and he sticks his face right into the cleavage and he starts hollerin', 'Hello, down there,' and laughing. If it was my mother, I'd a killed him. No doubt about it. I would a grabbed him and thrown him on the floor and knocked his face to pieces. I'd be in a jail. I would. I would a killed him."

"And Larry didn't do nothin'."

"Nothin'! He didn't do nothin'! He stood there like a dumb fuck, like he didn't know what happened. I got no use for him either, anybody who'd let some asshole get away with that with his own mother. I mean he stuck his head right there between her tits and started hollerin'. I'd be in jail now if it was my mom. He'd be dead. And if I didn't do it, my brothers'd do it. First, to get to him, they'd knock the shit out of me for not doin' nothin', then they'd fucking kill Bobby. I mean, your own mother! Lettin' that go by. He'd be one dead motherfucker."

Outside, the muted tones of neon, red, blue, green, yellow spread along the street, across storefront windows, brick walls, and a white cop-car on the prowl. A bus glides by with a single passenger asleep. The bent lady with the clawed hand stands on the curb trying to light a cigarette. The sky, imperceptible above the cross-streets, stretches all the way to Door from here into stars, while men in the next booth talk mayhem and murder. There is no Escape To Wisconsin tonight.

September 19   *Déjà Vu*

Standing on my father and mother's backporch, overlooking the garden where transplanted pine trees from Door County, my own woods, grow on a well trimmed lawn. Deja vu. Years ago, an apple tree grew near the same spot. That is all I remember of the yard. An apple tree, grass that grew all the way to the alley. A vegetable garden during war time. A victory garden. This porch—the same. Fences. Mostly, a very large apple tree. I remember the bark. The apples all over the ground. Before visiting my mother at the hospital today, I take my father with me downtown on Michigan Avenue where I deliver a book review to the office of *Chicago Magazine*. I show him the newspapers (the Tribune Tower, the office of Chicago *Sun-Times*) were his son has published a lot of work in the past years. Deja vu. I show him the *Sun-Times* courtyard, so beautifully landscaped with flowers, trees, benches, a perfect, peaceful setting near the river. I show him the presses inside, preparing to roll the next edition. Chicago is beautiful, warm, alive in September light. I show him the Billy Goat Tavern down below and wish, for the moment, we might sit at the bar and linger awhile over a beer. I wish still, alongside of him, for some kind of identity. Something for him to take home to the relatives and friends in the neighborhood. Something for him to tell Ma when I'm not around. To meet on the street, some newspaper writer I know from the Trib. John Blades, perhaps. Or to run into Henry Kisor or Herman Kogan from the *Sun-Times*. Or Mike Royko. Royko would truly impress him. Somehow, in some way to connect his son with the places and the people who work with words and feelings for this city. We walk Michigan Avenue to Water Tower Place, which he has never seen. He is impressed, I'm certain, but keeps it to himself. He can't believe the quiet waterfall that cascades between the escalators. I ride with him on the glass elevator to the top floor and then down again. On the way back to the parking lot, I ask for a few minutes longer to step into the Museum of Contemporary Art, where I would like to look briefly at the exhibit "The Portrait Extended" which includes the work of a friend of mine, Meridel Rubenstein, from Santa Fe, New Mexico. Deja vu. He waits quietly on a starkly modern black bench in the lobby, while I pay $2 and walk in. The portraits of Meridel seem to find me. I smile at the faces, the words, the landscape of New Mexico. I find it enervating, sad, comfortably warm to be among these people once more—there's Grandma West (Mildred) with one

124

of her granddaughters. And there's Jerry West, her son, an incredible human being, and friend. Jerry and his best friend, Charley Southard. My knowing the love of these two men for the land, for each other, for life, extends Meridel's portrait beyond words or vision, holding us all, everything together in spirit. My eyes beginning to well, I leave, remarking to my father outside while we walk to the parking lot how very strange the feeling was. How I knew almost all the people in her photographs, and here we all are in Chicago. Remarking quietly to myself how good it felt to be near all of them again. How difficult it was to keep from speaking to them in the photographs, welcoming them to the city, wanting to take them all out—and my father, and my mother—to stroll down Michigan Avenue, to have a beer in the Billy Goat, to sit on my back porch in Cicero and talk about pine trees from Door County, the transplanted soul, and the nature of all things in general.

September 20   Land's Return

Overcast. Driving back to Door after a week in Chicago of highs and lows, and nowhere, nowhere to retreat to the solitude of the land the way I do in the North, in the Southwest. In the absence of that kind of quiet communion I rely instead on family, food, friends, movies, long neon nights in a bar where the women, the music, the conversation sustain one's

spirit, yet never completely satisfy.
Gray skies . . . the threat of cold,
of winter, of little sun. I wait for
the time—some distance beyond Milwaukee—when the land opens up,
hurtling myself into an horizon that
can only extinguish me.

September 21   Garden Dying

Corn stalks shrivelled, rattling in the wind. Onions, as big as baseballs, pulled and left on the earth to dry. The weeds have taken over between the rows; sunflowers hang their huge round heads in seed; the climbing vines of snap beans have turned a scaly white. The garden hardens. There is dying all around in the garden, but for the tomatoes, still red, and peppers, and early yellow squash. Red cabbages still forming round heads, and best of all, pumpkins swelling in gold and orange. In the back garden, I pick and swallow a private sweetness of silvery coated purple grapes.

September 22   Sweater

The chill returning, this first day of fall, entering the body late evening: tired body and the rocking chair. I refuse to resort to the sound of the furnace going on. I dismiss the chill—for yet another hour. Weakening, finally, by 9 o'clock, the chill lodged somewhere in my shoulder bones, I walk reluctantly to the small chest near the kitchen door and from a pile of clothes, dislodge a woolen sweater from last winter. In moments I am warm again, comforted, though the inevitability of winter gnaws at the back of my head, lodging clear slivers of icicles into my brain.

September 23   Crow Moon

The roadside filled with the tiny star-like clusters of light purpie asters, mixed with a deeper, violet-colored clover. In the garden I remove the trellis for the snap beans. I pick almost-red tomatoes in the event of the first frost tonight. I roll up some 30 feet of chicken wire, right down the center of the road. There is no traffic at this time of the year but for the sound of three crows cawing overhead. Some nights the full moon rises, spills its light, and the vision of crows, white in the woods, comes back to me.

September 24   Apple Tree

I will go to the line of round stones in the field, pressing the body in the long, dying grass. Drink coffee. Eat fruit. Feel the only warmth of such time which is flesh. By the large wild apple tree, unpruned, free to embrace each body it beckons, I nestle inside the giving branches taking nourishment of the fruit which is ours.

September 25   *Rooster*

Though we live in the interiors of this county and seek the peace of space, others keep coming, dividing the land, carving up farms into lots for citified homes. One of the things sacrificed is the realness and strength of rural sounds. I think of this this morning on the road, 6:10 a.m., the full moon diffused in mist and cloud cover like a watercolor, wet on wet, a creaminess running, spreading into gray. Let a cock crow in the quiet of this morning, I say, in an almost Indian way. Let that sound not disappear. And from somewhere to the north (Maynard Smith's farm, I surmise) comes the rooster's first call, sending a fire through my legs, warming the arms, the hands, the very fingertips. And from the west, a chorus of cattle mooing the morn. A gauzy yellow light seeps in the eastern wooly sky, while the moon dissolves itself in common cloud. The rooster crows again. My morning incantation is ended, though I carry home with me the cry of a red-combed and iridescent feathered rooster in my throat.

September 26   *Frost and the Bog-Man*

Beginning in the late afternoon of yesterday—frost warning—moving into the cold, wet garden like a bog-man, the elements just dripping from me, the earth itself clinging to hands, pant-legs, sweater: vines, leaves, roots, wound around button holes, stuck in the eyelets of workboots. Cold rain and perspiration. Flinging old bedspreads and blankets over large patches of green tomatoes, musk and watermelon. Twisting big orange pumpkins from the prickly, hollow stems. Snapping off hard orange squash. Carrying handfuls of rotting straw to cover whatever tomatoes and melons won't fit under bedspreads. There is too much left to sacrifice. I whirl around in the center, hating to give it all up to the inevitable frost. I would cover it all, if I could, keeping it alive and in color in the heart of deep white winter. Yellow peppers still growing and blooming. Must I forsake those too? And the beans? And what of the celery, the red and white cabbage? The broccoli? The kohlrabi? Under the earth, the red potatoes and thick carrots lie safe. But what of the eggplant, just now coming around? Must those too be lost? I rush for two empty bushel baskets, crowning, attempting to save at least two plants in that way. The mud oozes above the soles of my boots. The cold drizzle tingles and tears through me. The bog-man retreats in a shadow of death, plant life losing color before his very eyes, the garden awaiting the first frost. Tomorrow he pictures its black, strangulating handiwork and recovering whatever survives, hoping for a few more hours of sun. His sleep that night is marked by the intricate delicacy of the white flakes of frost. His mind clings to the firmness of a sweet orange.

DOOR COUNTY.
SEDIA
6/12/

BUILDING A
STONE HEDGE.

—Putting the heat on in the coop this morning for the first time this season. The burning smell of the damp and woodsy interior transforming into warmth.

—The porcupine in the woods out front, staring me down, less than five feet between us. Docile? Dumb? Vulnerable, certainly. I think of the old man across the road who has killed them with a baseball bat. Such innocence upon the earth in the face of blind rage. A gentleness in unsuspected dying?

—The woman down the road who protects a beautiful, huge, red dahlia from the frost each night, in a clear hot-house plastic covering. Inside, a blur of red glows like a watercolor running wild. In the next day's sun, uncovered, the perfect petaled flower catches the eye of the passer-by, holding one's gaze to the center of the mandala, the light, oneself and the center of the universe.

—The small, dying mouse my daughter brings to me on a leaf . . .

—Night games of the moon flooding the Door fields at midnight, setting down a shimmering path upon the lake . . . the water's way. We enter it all and we are it. Or we stand outside, feeling cold, fearing death, securing life, mourning the way of all living things, yielding to the moon's pull.

Their silence above all. Their surprise underfoot. Shaggy mane mushrooms this morning, tucked into the earth. Now rising, moist. Conjuring thoughts to the underside of things . . . white, deadly thoughts. The smell of decay, soft as old flesh. We people this world in fantasy, make ourselves small, find faith in fairies.

Two horses, a black and a chestnut, stand still in the rain. Nothing moves. Autumn. The barbed wire fence gleams through the middle of their burning coats. I fix a red heart to their flanks, make fetishes of such standing, perfect life.

In the humid morning, the earth abounds in decay, exudes a rotting stench that holds all life at bay. One disintegrates in steps, moving across the field. Birds are held fast. Plants are sucked in. Deer disappear whole. There is a moist sadness in dying.

October 1   *Geese*

Mornings and afternoons, their noisy, patterned flight above these woods, this coop, takes on ritualistic overtones in fall. How to explain the stillness first and then the sudden distant honking sound above the clacking of the typewriter? I hurry outside to catch a glimpse of them. Though they are beautiful in the clear and sunny skies, the dark and deep mellow grays seem their purer element, most inviting, as the neck pains from bending back too long, and the eyes strain to be with them as their continually ragged, continually perfect V formation loses wings, loses sound, transforms to gliding periods upon a blank page, then disappears in solitariness that leaves the earthbound gray in his own unsteady footsteps, his head a mirror to the October sky.

October 2   *Bushel Basket*

Picking, pulling, snipping the garden remains. Frost warning again. The garden cold. The plants, many of them still green, seem to pull into themselves, prepared to take on brittleness, to crack, disintegrate. The old bushel basket I fill and carry to the road sits there in warmth and laughter. Green striped, small watermelons, long yellow-green peppers, orange and gold winter squash, rough silver-green-skinned muskmellons, pale green-white kohlrabi, purple-black eggplant, and tomatoes so red they defy the threatening cold gray sky. The basket glows in its own light.

October 3   *October Morn*

You scrunch your shoulders in on a day like this. The trees, the sky, the very air seems made of the coldest, thin metal, reflecting the light of stainless steel. As I walk, the pelting rain turns partly ice, partly snow, then rain again, as the day indecisively works the magic of the northern air in early fall.

October 4   *Still Motion*

The sunflower fields, sad in the weight of their seeds. Canadian geese hovering and honking over a dry cornfield, stalks askew, leaves rattling like broken wings. Nineteen mourning doves upon a wire. Eighteen . . . seventeen . . . sixteen. . . .

October 5   *Lovers in Sand*

Sevastapol sand dunes and Whitefish Bay Sunday, a fall day of such brilliance, such silent knowing, the sky and the water vying for a brighter blue, the sand carrying and losing us down to the water and back up the trail, back to a stony trail where the woman who is wife wraps her arm over mine and both the goodness and the strangeness of our years abate in the wonder of our October walk. The intimation of making love in the dunes, the feel of old forgiving hands upon the body electric, the comfort of the past. An expedition through old ways. A nostalgia for certain weeds, delicate and golden in fall, that will grace a winter's room and hold us in memories of mutual acts, unspoken, held fixed in autumn love.

October 6   *Milkweed*

Milkweed pods drying to their teardrop armor, some of them opening now in the fields. The silken seeds puffing out along the seam, awaiting the wind and first flight. I draw a fingerfull from the pocket, lay them gently in the palm of my hand, watch the wind, in a gentle updraft, lift, sail, scatter life in acts that defy man's manipulations of seed. Gardening in the wind.

October 7   *Riversong*

The trees . . . green, golden, red, running river in the wind, running light . . .

132

October 8   *Electric Light*

Walking into a daybreak sky, cream-colored and orange-rimmed along the spreading edge, pouring, filling, running into the leftover, gray-blue last night sky. The crows, ah the crows, three of them cawing the treetops then into the air in a single shot, scattered wings, scattered flight. The leaves on the little birch tree, how they glow in autumn beech-tree light. Returning to the dark kitchen, flicking the switch . . . the artificial ugliness, deadly electric light.

October 9   *Carved Heart*

Peeling the layers of bark from a white birch tree, inscribing with a penknife, a heart left over from childhood days. I have no name at this mid-stage in life. Only the strength to cut deep into the spongy life of the tree, beyond the bark. A sun and a moon should do. With a single ray touching, bridging the emptiness. A love of the universe . . . this and these lives. The blue water laps the sandy beach. There is fire in the trees. This carved heart will grow and spread and be resolved in scarless emptiness and memory.

October 10   *Horse Lover*

The horse, Gypsy, nudging my shoulder, nuzzling my hand, gently opening the fingers in search of food. The love of an animal, so simple. While the love of a man and a woman, so fraught with despair.

October 11   *Birds of No Name*

I prefer the namelessness of birds in this time of the year. All of them gray and on the wing. A cloud of them this day, tiny ones, swarming above a field, their direction determined by no force I know but the seduction of space, the feel of pure flight.

October 12   *Country Church*

The white siding and blue roof. The sun on the windowpanes. The small graveyard alongside. Nine cars in the parking lot. The line of maple trees

out front, gold, yellow, and red. The land extends beyond the church in all directions. Fenceposts lean, refusing to hold the line. There's a gentleness about the land this Sunday morning, and an absence of people but for their voices singing a hymn of praise inside. If God is anywhere, he hovers somewhere in the midst of all this.

October 13   Rose-Hips

The flowers along the roadside I miss most of all. Their colors fade fast. Occasionally, a late growth of the tiniest of Queen Ann's Lace makes its presence known. Knapweed, a soft lavender, grows low in a last little burst. Once in a while, a very weathered Black-eyed Susan, scrawny, bent, unsure of its place upon the earth at this time. The reddest of rose-hips punctuate the flow of this gnarled, dying earth, lifting this October heart at times to joy. I recall then the vision of the same plant in spring—Prairie Rose— and how more in tune with time I was then. There were no limits to the bloom. And the color of the petals was the color of the lips of a girl I loved long ago one spring. I hold the bright red rose-hip in my fingers like a stone.

October 14   Dream Window

In this gray and deadly day, the embers of falling leaves, the chill that slashes through the body in glinting blades, the birds flying backwards in the heavens, pushed by fierce winds . . . I rekindle all the desires inside of me—poems, paintings, places, people, books, all the images that speak of joy and love . . . then go back to sit before this desk, see what I dream outside the window, and once again remake my life.

October 15   *Harvest Letter (R.M.)*

A letter from a close friend brings the seasons of men closer together. Three pages of comments on the story "The Landscaper" he puts in my hands—the fruition of his own garden of thinking, feeling, being: "This is the most Zen story you have ever written," he says.

I bite into his letter with a taste for hard, tart apples. Savor the sweet unexpected juices. Chew, with satisfaction, the hard thoughts I never fully understood, but were part of the form, I shaped and placed there, like the tautness of skin, the darkness of seeds, lying in wait for the revelation of readers and seekers to match my appetite.

October 16   *Picking a Garden Clean with Love,*
                                        Grandma & Grandpa

The earth makes loving sense in the hands of the old. Grandma and Grandpa this morning, rummaging through the cold, gray garden with their daughter, digging potatoes, picking damaged, ripened tomatoes, pulling carrots and stalks of celery. "These grapes are still good," says Grandma, tasting one between her wrinkled fingertips. In the kitchen, late morning, the windows are all steamed. Grapes, cooked to a froth, now hang in a gauze sack, tied to the back of a chair on top the table, the juice dripping clear into a bowl, in preparation for a final metamorphasis of jelly. In a large pot on the stove, Grandpa lifts the lid and calls for me to take a look at maybe two gallons of soup: "See," he says. "And all of it from the garden," smiles Grandma. "Tomatoes, carrots, celery . . . everything, fresh." There are still some apples on an old tree out back, I remind her. "Good," she says. "Tomorrow I'll make a pie. Nothing wasted."

October 17   *Wind Thrasher*

All through the night it blew out of the northwest, leaves, most of their life gone out of them, churning on the branches, blowing past the window, clicking against the glass. By morning much of the world looked new again in its age—branches bare, new light and distance opened between the trees, the earth covered in a Persian tapestry.

October 18 *Overcast*

Walking the gray day, much of the world around me still asleep. Intimations of the only man breathing, but not for long. The tops of birdhouses blown off. The tips of trees scripting a message I cannot read upon the air. Death is delivered on the wings of crows. Gulls stare the sandy shoreline into traceries of ice. Mornings like these have kept me alive. I skim the surface of the dying earth.

October 19 *Tree Talk*

Conversations enroute to Chicago with Grandma and Grandpa:
Grandpa: "I think the trees are brighter here in the sunlight."
Grandma: "Of course. They need the sun and the rain. The rain gives them more color."
Grandpa: "In Chicago the trees aren't so pretty."
Grandma: "There's no color. There aren't any sugar maples like here."
Grandpa: "Oaks. Oaks don't have any color."
Grandma: "Not like sugar maples."

October 20 *Swamp*

Pulling off the highway onto a dirt road, on the trip back. Large cedars, brush, swamp, the air alive with bird cries, branches and sky filled with red-winged blackbirds, their tiny flash of red the only color in this late October scene. Swallowed by this swamp, my whole history of the day is gone. I live here amongst the trees, the water, the red-winged blackbirds, answering the call.

October 21   *Clear Vision*

Just gold leaves stuck to a blue sky.

October 22   *Squirrels*

There is a frenzy of them now in these late, desperate hours of autumn. Sleek, sinewy, tough, they encircle the girth of large trees in a crazed chase, shoot up to the branches, swaying, flying, hanging to the very tips, dropping down again to branches below, following limbs like forked and junctioned mapways with a wave of a tail, a downward scratching of claws along the tree trunk. Skittering through leaves, pausing to stand upright, take in the gray of the day, they explode under stacks of wood into hollows of old logs, up the trunks and branches of closest trees. The skies are alive with squirrels. I stand, looking up, suspended in the madness of their just-holding-on.

October 23   *Morning, Noon, October Night*

Morning, and the gray sky puckered with the tiniest of clouds. A textured sky—a rarity in these parts. From puffs to long streams to wave upon wave —all gray, gray blue, a hint of white. The sun, rising now behind Carlson's house, seeps through in a splotch, lines extending upwards and across both sides like the Zia, the symbol of the New Mexican sun.
Afternoon—we tighten the house for winter, exchanging screens for storm windows, holding in the warm air for winter. Late afternoon and night, the sound of distant thunder, a fleeting memory of spring, though the time is certainly October. Looking north in the night's blackness, lightning fills the skies with gigantic white flowers seen only in the paintings of Georgia O'Keefe.

October 24   *Cows*

Cows . . . caricatures and comic . . . coathanger hips and hatracks . . .
heavenly holsteins . . . bovine bellies, a bag of balloons . . . Mercator
mapped hides in black and white . . . The cows sway over the highway in
comic routines . . . chewing cud . . . sloshing milk . . . hindends high . . .
swishing . . . plopping . . . mooing morning moons, the laughter turned to
sadness of creatures who don't see our world in their liquid eyes.

October 25   *Hard Shake*

Black wet limbs of trees in the morning, after a cold night of October wind
and rain. Black, wet limbs and the gold leaf confetti strewn under each
midnight tree.

October 26   *Inside Out*

Feeling "outside" of things again: outside the leaves, the trees, the birds,
the fields, the sky, the water, the stones, outside in the way that I travel
today with the family to Green Bay. I drive through a landscape of some
intensity, yet it moves through me like conversation, the music on the radio,
the traffic going the other way. Living outside of it all in such a way is not
living at all. I wait for the way back in knowing I cannot look for it, force
my way inside. That moment will come, unexpected, when walking, sitting,
driving, working, I shall dissolve—looking out from in, being part of that
life of which there is no other, like the act of love. The time has changed. It
grows darker earlier in the evening now.

October 27   *Storytime*

A day, a perfect day, for living a life I never knew, or knew only partly. A
day for peopling these woods or other places . . . Chicago? New Mexico?
Greece? To live now for a while in whatever setting or scene presents itself.
A day which may last for months to come of going through the motions in
my ordinary life. A time now for making stories.

October 28   *Flash*

This was all the color in the world today—one red cardinal.

October 29   *Quiet Acts*

Working sunflower seeds with my fingertips out of the huge, dry hanging head in the garden this morning, cracking seeds open between my teeth, tasting the winter food of stray birds. Looking on the slightly frozen ground for the patches where I planted the fuschia, purple, pink hollyhock seeds, envisioning the tallness of flowers in the springs to come. Then on my knees, feeling for warmth of a wide nest of tall grasses, pressed down in the secret sleep, the stillness of deer in the moon-drenched night only hours past.

October 30   *Games Upon the Road*

I've played these games upon the road with my son for more than 10 years now: baseball in spring, football in autumn, hockey in winter. In fall, especially, I've watched his shadow grow into mine in the always setting sun behind his back, felt his arm strengthen and his pass aim sharpen. He plays to win, to seek a perfection beyond the old man, while my passes grow shorter, and my runs are all too soon out of breath. I play to be outside in these dwindling hours of autumn, to hear the missed pass rustle through the leaves, to consume the sky above his head in such a glow of gold and lavender, the softest flush of pink. We toss passes till the light is gone, till the ball must be arced considerably toward the receiver's hands. Till I call "time to go in," knowing this fall in particular may well be our last chance at autumn games, the shadows having merged and boyhood disappeared.

October 31   *Halloween*

Not the pumpkin that is carved into a jack-o-lantern, but pumpkins in the field like scattered suns. Cornstalks rattling in the night wind. The sky deep and lost with stars. Fear only what you love.

November 1   *Potatoes*

The secrets of the earth: pulling a carrot, a radish, a turnip . . . who *knows* what the earth will deliver? The color is certain, the size indeterminate. And the digging of potatoes, a special delight. Shoveling deep, lifting and turning over, the anticipation and uncertainty of just what the earth is prepared to yield in size, shape and number. There's one! And look at these! Here's another in this clump of sod. Rubbing off the dirt, feeling the skin, the bumps, the roundness in one's hand. How well it sits in the hollow of the palm. What delicate weight. Oh, the deliciousness that lies in winter suppers ahead, boiled, baked or fried. Steaming potatoes in slightly faded pink jackets, cutting or breaking them with a fork, dolloping the butter, shaking the salt. The sweetness of white potato meat. The chewing of slightly bitter skins. The taste of earth. The mud still lodged beneath these fingernails.

November 2   *Landkeeping*

Turning over the garden one last time for winter now. The sky, the wind, the late hour of afternoon all in layers of gray. A man alone with one machine, pulls the starter, breaks and churns the darkest earth for one last fling, as if power can save him from this dying time. There is comfort, though, that this way puts the earth to gentle sleep. Comfort, that in the way of the woman, his wife, who now strews bags of dead leaves in the path before him, the earth will be fed, and the land kept.

November 3   *Gulls!!!*

A hundred plump seagulls nestled on the dock near the library in Sister Bay, reading the wind . . . gray, white, and cobalt blue. They rise in exclamation marks.

November 4   *Doing Things*

The balmy day, the blue sky, the bright sun, and the mania to make things complete about this place for winter. How the frenzy comes upon me.

Unexplainable. Possessed. This afternoon in a fit to fix a broken washing machine, draining it (filled with clothes) in a bucket, fixing it, refilling it, then moving to the outdoors, sweeping the garage floor filled with leaves, removing the bikes, straightening out the second stall in preparation for the storing of summer tables and chairs, hauling those on my back, rearranging the stall (methodically) so everything fits. Placing one table down, another on top of it, benches on top of that, bushel baskets and the wagon underneath, a place "perfect" for all odds and ends. The huge summer inner tube moved to the upper rafters. The moving of bikes to the cellar, making room and arrangements there. Back to the outside to collect the various front lawn decorations, the bird bath, the Italian masks, the nude statue of a woman, the swing. Carrying all this to the cellar, and once again finding room. Do I fight the coming winter, or a fear within myself? My head in a thousand directions, all of them tasks unfulfilled. The roof . . . will it be able to withstand a hard winter? And what of the building-up of ice along the edges? The possibility of water once again leaking inside? Will the insulation hold? What of the moisture problem? Venting. That should be done. Still putting things away, still thinking of the next task I spot the old row boat and move that to the rear of the garage. She will want to hang out the wash now that the machine is fixed. I move the car out of the way to give her freer access to the clothesline. I put her car in the garage. I hang up an old painting on the side of the garage. I run to the coop to answer a long distance call: a university across the state calling to verify my appearance there next April. April! Jesus! And what of the writing? Can I get back to it now? Sometime this afternoon. The garden . . . the garden is still unfinished. More of the garden should be turned over. Turn the heat off in the coop, move to the garden, clear some of the still-standing cornstalks, clear another patch of tangling dead tomato vines, start the tiller, once again begin my back and forth working of the rows like some surreal seamstress' sewing machine, stitching the land up for winter. The neighbor, Mrs. Carlson, walks by with a jar full of pickles she has made for us. I thank her, smell the sweetness of the contents, and go back to the work of the earth at hand. The sun is setting. The day is beautiful in its fading, the sky the color of Indian turquoise set in silver. The dog sleeps in the weeds. Soon I will go inside (these fingers of my left hand ache from holding the clutch handle of the machine too tight). I will eat dinner as the day darkens.

I will sit in my rocking chair. I will watch the national news, read the New York *Times,* stay up half the night watching the election returns. Sleep will invade this body, this anxious mind throughout the vigil. I will climb the stairs and put all of this to bed. And in the morning, whatever awaits, whatever is, I will for certain write again. Winter will be one day closer.

November 5   Spotters

They have begun a steady surveillance up and down our road for well over a week now. In my rocker at night, I see the glow approach of their headlights out the west window. The dog, sensing my concern, begins growling. As they drift past my house, I watch the powerful beam of their light sweep the woods across the road, see the light reflect and break upon the trunks of birch, maple, beech and ironwood, an invasion of the privacy of woods and peace in a country night that I equate with an act of violence. I pray that the eyes they are looking for (the deer they are tracking to kill in the season of blood that begins just weeks ahead) do not look back at them. That the beautiful eyes of the deer should reflect the light ending in their own inevitable demise remains intolerable to me. I walk the woods later in darkness, exulting in the secret presence of deer, in the saving light that only night reveals in a dependency of moon and stars.

November 6   Animal Dawn

The sky opening like a slash of a child's vermillion crayon this morning. Layer of muted, coral light above it. While all in front the open color passes a parade of silver-blue cloud creatures in steady procession; a bull, a panther, a whale, an ostrich, a horse, a woman lying on her side. Back on earth, a deer the color of dawn crosses the road, stops, holds us still in each other's eyes.

November 7   Inner Forecast

Rain changing into snow . . . so true of this day, as snow—wet and fast and melting upon the ground—once again becomes a presence in this air, transforming the rain man, the sun man, the sky man, the garden man, the flower man, the water man into a hollow body filled with flurries, the head layered in welts of white.

November 8   *Meditations on Swift Changing Things*

First, the frost upon the few remaining cabbages this morning. The garden earth so still beneath my feet.
Then the wind, the blade of it, the teeth of it, the talk of taking and not giving.
Followed by rain to sleet to snow.
And only one small patch of it, by early afternoon, sitting like mold upon the leaves.
The wind, changing its course northwesterly in the hours to come. Changing its talk to chorus, to cry.
Clearing the skies in sudden bravado, applauding itself, in light.
Then rushing the clouds, the rain, the coming darkness of the late hour.
Till the trees now wave like scolding fingers, blue and black and white.
Drops hang outside my windowpane questioning the time to fall or turn to ice.

November 9   *Hard Fire in the Field*

The burnished fields, wet and dry—each thin stalk like brass welding rods. To weld a field now of molten brass, glowing within itself. So unyielding, touched in a moment's snow.

November 10   *Secret Spaces*

Why is it they appear so visible, so unafraid now that the season for them draws near? The deer are everywhere: on the road in the morning, resting in the fields in late afternoon. Early this morning, from the dining room window, a doe could be seen nose to the ground at the very edge of the woods across the road. I think of tameness first, then of beauty, then of death. Not death itself so much as that instinct for the space of time preceding the last breath. Watching the deer gently, visibly move its sleek form past birches, in between maples this morning, I thought of fish in the bay, coming in, coming home to die, the loss of privacy within the perfect habitat. And in the loss of that, the secret presence, the gift of what we are in death. The true life form, though, the mystery and mystique, the presence—untouched, unbounded, unknown—of our breathing, of our skin, of our form, be it woods, be it water, be it the darkest spaces of our minds, the light within our bones.

November 11   *Walking In*

There was a morning weeks ago (days ago? months ago? years ago?) when, because of the "rightness" of that moment, because of the innerness of the morning, the trees, the fields being me, I was reminded that I must truly walk again soon. That I am in need of those solitary meanderings so close to me in the times past, that unexplainable movement of finding myself taking to the woods and fields. And this afternoon, an answer to that calling. Breaking through the dead and fallen branches behind the coop, the dog out front of me, my steps in and out of hollows, cracking branches, scattering leaves. Through the field behind these woods, eyes feeling for the pattern in these weeds—why the circle of such low growth all around this tree?—which way, now, did I proceed in winters past on skis? Around this bush? Under this tree? A pause to inspect one golden apple hanging from the leafless branches of one tree. And Charley's stone fence, where I come to rest in the warmth, incredible oven warmth here, against these stones. Then down the line, to the opening, into the area fronting Charley's house. The thorns, the size of these thorns piercing through my pant legs, scratching a calligraphy of wounds upon my hands. Charley's old "Dutch Apple" tree he called it, the golden apples of the sun hanging against the black tracery of branches. Then down his old logging path. The dog free and anxious, and far ahead of me now, sniffing the earth in helterskelter movements, picking up the paths of deer. The silence astounding. Few birds. One downy woodpecker I see, disappearing into a high hole of an old beech tree. The sun at my back. I gauge the time for my return, expecting the full flush of its descent to pour out of the sky, over these trees, into me. To want to lose myself in all of this. Pines—take hold of me. Path—turn, twist, lose these steps. I want the mind clear of the shards of this day, the day before . . . family, friends, duties, money matters. Disappear. Leave me in all this. But no matter the depth and darkness of the woods, the light at my back and held in the tops of trees ahead, the outside world remains, waiting to be felt, if not heard. One proceeds, then, with that echo. Waiting for surprises, whatever lies ahead: like now, the water of the lagoon, the old dock, the absence of fish, the opening to Europe Lake as magical as fairy-tale reflects the sky, showing the way, the tracks of deer who have come down to the edge to drink. And the beginning, the thinnest skin of precious ice floating free. I reach in with a hand, gently lifting a piece so pure, so crystalline, and marked in a complex delicacy of lines that capture the mind like a transparent mandala. Returning, with the lake on my side, just past a thin barrier of trees, the earth's floor is speckled in wet, heart-shaped poplar leaves that shine like brass jewelry. Lifting my eyes, I steal a parting glance through the darkness of trees, and see the entire lake, the other side, held in the softest light of golden sun, that I cannot believe the darkness of the path I trod, these black and midnight steps, while the light just beyond my shoulder holds this all in a nimbus.

November 12   *False Snow*

A teasing of snowflurries today. But no smell to them. No real scent of snow. The sound of first snow, almost right. Tickling the dry leaves upon the earth. Pattering them. Pecking. But soon melting. Again the white turns rain. The day lies dumb with regrets.

November 13   *Mitten*

No color to this world anymore. The tones of rain hue the day. And the deadliness of earth in all its forms of rotting brown, spared, occasionally by the testament of tall birch trees and the history of stone overturned in fields. In this polished day of black and gray, a child's single lost red mitten opens like a roadside flower, closing the heart to summer things.

The water dream last night. The figures (man and woman?) statuesque, standing upon the water on each side of me. Something circular—the turquoise sea itself? No, the entire setting, circular, like a holy image set inside a stained glass window of my childhood church. The sky, white, with a radiance, an horizon the Hopi call the yellow line. And I am in the water, submerged half-way, and filled with fear and anxiety—but not of drowning. A fear, instead, of some undefined force that may get me unless I somehow enter a burnished, leathery colored bag or sack. Since my lower half is safe (in water? the submerged other half of the bag?) it is only a matter of covering my upper half to execute some act of completion. But the bag or sack will not open, cannot be spread apart in time. In the knowledge of this fear that I cannot be saved—I awaken. "Pain," (I am reminded by a friend of a quote that may help to explain) . . . "you can't escape it, so you got to go into it . . . it comes back to you when you're not looking, *whoosh,* it jumps out from behind the stove and grabs you. I shut up, active silence. I bear it. I stand before it. I call the pain out. After you go through this, you got choices."

The Hartman house of summer people, summer times, summer friends. Passing it at least once, almost every day of the year, in journeys to and from town. The white farmhouse, off in the distance, the field before, the long lawn in front, the border of trees along the driveway, the cherry orchard on the west side . . . all speak a special place in time, of warm friendships and good memories. The house becomes a roadmark in my wanderings, real and imagined, past and present. Seasonally—April, usually—I watch for signs of their arrival. The work of opening up the place once more to summer. And summer itself, I find myself turning down the long driveway to visit with the Hartman family, and, in passing, often see Willard and Mary working in the garden, the children cutting lawn—the scene both serene, consoling, and continually active. In fall, a sudden quiet falls upon the place as they return home and visit only occasionally, on weekends. And then the final visit, which is now, the weekend spent in closing up the place. Something sad in the slow process of reducing things—only part of the family here, only one of the cars parked near the house, the garage door itself, only partially opened, barren trees, garden still, a single light in the upstairs window when I passed the place last night. "The Hartmans are up," I say with a longing for the tumult of summer.

"Well, at least someone is here." I talk to myself. Realizing that after Sunday morning it will be only the Hartman house and me in the days of wind and snow when the house appears to rise in drifts, and in the long nights of the tall trees and empty orchard and the only light, the white of the empty farmhouse in the stillness of stars.

November 16   Reading the Trees

The pines this morning, planted in Charley's field, how many years ago? Five? Six?—less than a foot high. I stare into them this day and gauge their height the same as mine. And where have I been all this time? Have I really grown that old? I feel the lines around my eyes, feel the wind rustle my hair and cast before me a number of silver strands. Turning back home on the road, I face the eastern edge of my own tall trees, thinking in the peculiar warmth of the day, what a beautiful morning, and reading in the dark yet sunlit thickness of my woods, the white calligraphy of birch trees.

November 17   Twilight

Saucer-of-milk moon over my shoulder in an eastern blue-green sky. Twilight time. All the light in the very tops of trees. Pink flush of a woman's skin just after love—the sky of the west. I move with crow feet on the dark edge of the night between these things, loving the blackness in my loins, the white moon and the woman's pink thigh in these hands.

November 18   In Place

A 5-in-the-morning calling again, I settle into the last frame of darkness, a delicacy of night sky strewn with stars. Oh, the clarity of death and blackness at such times. The morning light adjusts itself over the eastern edge. I wake inside here with words, letting the day bid itself in creating the trees and stones and sky outside my windows. And an hour later, in a daylight colored in the hollow of sea shells, I answer the morning's beckoning, stepping out into it once more. The hell with words for now. I am here and will always need this peace of land because of this. The city will call, and I will answer, but always I must return to the inner reaches, the

147

silent light of the earth in its own way. If not here, the desert then, the mountains, the sea. The solitariness of place is where we best sing. Reading the Navaho medicine man, Rolling Thunder, late last night: "This we know. The earth does not belong to man; man belongs to the earth."

November 19 The Nakedness of Women and Their Jewelry

Found: One faded purple wild aster along the road's edge; one dry plant in a ditch, speckled with the brightest of red rosehips; one naked apple tree in the distance, necklaced, bejeweled in golden delicious. I am reminded of sad, beautiful women after lovemaking, in the presence of all this.

November 20 Birdfeeder

Putting the large platform feeder for the winter birds in place by the kitchen nook window. Filling all the feeders with sunflowers. Stuffing the wire basket with suet. Come woodpecker, come chickadee, come all the color and life that is out there. Fill the winter, these snow eyes, with the watercolors of wings behind glass. Outside, I will listen for your calls and restructure the song in memory of another season.

November 21 Moonset

A primitive night of the moon, the light so beguiling, it spills into the bedroom window onto the walls and furniture, into mirrors, upon the forms of sleepers, the woman lying on her stomach, the man on his back . . . light pouring into his eyes, stealing his dreams. He rises to the western window, the wondrous sight . . . his body translucent. Dressing quickly, he leaves the downstairs kitchen door ajar, making his way toward the road to meet the moon, his body now broken in light, his shadow displaced. On the road's way, the pavement has turned liquid light as he steps, treads, absolves himself in an urgent buoyancy of a river alight. The moon, first nestled and tossed in the grasping fingertips of dark branches, is then tossed free, bolder, bigger, rounder, yellower than anything conceived by man. Finding his legs once again upon the earth of a far field, the sleeper, the walker, the dreamer, now supplicant, asks for the continued revelation of such magic in his life. This is the veld, he knows. And I am African. This is the Russian steppe. This is the moon of Iowa, Navaho, Menominee, Hopi. Let all the spirit of a life's wonder, all ritual, celebration, imagining, be this moon as I divest myself of the final shadow, and step in.

November 22   *Opening Day*

Approximately 7:12 a.m. The first shot in the woods across the road. Men dressed in fluorescent blaze orange jackets and pants intensify the vertical darkness of the trees like a painting by Klee.
Flocks of yellow-black-white evening grosbeaks return to the winter feeders for the first time. Deer run with the color of trees. Blood settles on the forest's floor.

November 23   *Deer Dream*

All night long, not the deer themselves, but the movement of deer in dream, filtering through the midnight trees, cracking twigs on the forest floor, imagining, in my own sleep, the sleep of hunted animals, hind-quarters twitching, forelegs flicking, the dreamy-antlered head rising, hovering in watchfulness and wonder.

November 24   *Distant Sounds*

The shots resound through the woods all day in hollow echo, tearing through a raiment of bark and fur, sometimes answered in the distance by the savage cries of men.

November 25   *The Eyes of the Deer*

Thirteen men glowing in their orange garb along the road's edge, large numbers pinned to their backs, rifles cradled in arms, balanced over shoulders, barrels spent and hanging toward the earth. Laughter, small talk, cigarettes dangling from their mouths, while two men, kneeling over the buck's carcass, dispense with the entrails in a moment of butchering. There is life yet in the eyes of the deer, and a beauty beyond weapons, its color of blood truer than the color of clothes the hunters must lawfully wear.

November 26   *Deer Trees*

Outside Sand Bay, on a local farm, three bucks hang by their hind legs from a tree. Their bodies slit, cavities opened and exposed for curing of cold air and sun. In their eyes they are still running.

November 27   *Thanksgiving*

The first real snow of the year falls. By phone we extend messages of friendship, more than thanks, to mothers and fathers and grandparents. Gray and white the morning . . . a study in silence and wintery foreboding under glass. In the kitchen, the smell of pumpkin pie in the oven. We journey down snowy, slick highways in mid-afternoon, to a homey restaurant where we will eat our Thanksgiving dinner amongst some of the townspeople and some of the visitors. The meal is delicious, and more than adequate: turkey dressing, whipped potatoes, squash, cranberries, creamed onions, lima beans and corn, assorted relishes, homemade muffins and bread, hot cider, milk or coffee, pumpkin pie with whipped cream, mince pie, or Indian pudding. The taste of Thanksgiving still lies here—though the feeling, espcially in the hearts of daughter and son, lies back in the neighborhood homes and dining rooms of their grandparents. In our presence in the restaurant, though, sits one of the most solitary people in the county—Black John Henderson—eating his Thanksgiving dinner alone. The spirit of this day finally touches us then, and when he answers our wave of the hand to come over to the table and talk. In the darkening afternoon, and all through the night, light snow continues to fall. The fields begin to soften, and the woods possess a new low, earthen light. While the deer unknowingly track their own death, nodding their heads in the beauty of the night's first snow.

November 28   *Deer Crossing*

The hunter who sits in the woods at night, watching the deer pass in the moonlight.

November 29   *Dream Antlers*

"If you go into the dark, you come back with wings" . . . dream message fragment . . . the entrance to the woods is made of antlers.

November 30   *The Man Who Loved Deer*

Darkness and a crescent moon morning, 4 a.m. The deer and their last day in the season of their dying. All day the sun warms the leafed earth once more, and the tracks of deer disappear in the melting snow. By sunset, all the hunters have gone home, retiring blazing orange jackets and polished weapons, sharpening their stories for the wintry hours of telling. That night, the man who loves the deer gathers those that remained amongst the trees of the deepest wood, his hands full of apples, his heart beating for the sanctity of wild animals. It will be spring before he can see they are still here.

December 1   *Winter Lines*

The rhythm of snowfences being set in place in the open fields along the roadway.

December 2   *Winter's First Real Day*

All night, the arctic wind howling outside the bedroom window. At day's break, the scene transformed in winter's first stormy snow. Birds, fighting the wind at the feeder. The dog, nuzzling her way in a rush through the new

fallen snow. The wind of a new winter courses through this drifting figure of a bundled man, head bowed. His head dwells in the lashing branches of trees, the snow-flecked stubble of the changing fields, the angry waters of the shore, night-mared in ice.

December 3   *Snow Breath*

A world of pink snow, this morning's muted sunrise. The earth, the woods, the road cast in the shimmering, delicate light of a soap bubble . . . pinks, the rarest shades of violet. The world rises in a breath, turns, floats, colors. The movement of my hand, too suddenly, can dispel it all.

December 4   *Warming Spell*

Enter the warm again, the soft rain, the drizzle, the snow-covered earth slowly hollowed, opened, giving way to the realness of plant, leaves, gravel, mud again. A shininess persists. The world gone mild and wet again.

December 5   *Saw Mill*

No sound today but the whining of Carl Carlson's buzz saw down the road: the winter logging has begun, "Snaking cedars out of the woods with tractor and chain." The wood sings in the whirling blade.

December 6   *Black and Silver . . . the Passion in the Mist*

A monochrome morning: Chinese ink brush, the trees so black and alive against the silver mist, the branches reach out to be touched, to be held in dance. We turn in the Orient of ourselves, the dark tresses in my moist mouth, a way silvered in a passion that knows the orange sun muted under water, poised behind the mountain tops.

December 7   *The Curve of the Hawk*

They are more in evidence at this time of year—the edge of winter. Hawks. Perched on branches very near the ground. Sweeping the fields in slow motion. A low, lazy flapping of their large wings. The hawk before my eyes, uncurling itself from the branches like a scroll, gliding down in slow descent to the very edge of the field and the line of trees, curving itself up in the gentlest of unseen waves, attaching itself to a tree again.

December 8   *Snowy Owl*

A ghostliness about him in the cloud-laden December day. Perched there off the road on the hard silvered branches of the beech tree, his world is the stillness of why he waits, the wind, the quickened eye, the merest unexpected movement in the grand field. Snow's own shadow, the snowy owl contemplates the flying path.

December 9   *Ditch Water*

In the ditches alongside the roads this morning, this afternoon, this night, all the water has turned ice. Weeds and cattails, held fierce and beautiful between two skies.

December 10   *New Moon*

"Did you see the moon last night? At 5:00 almost dark, western sky, midnight blue, here and there black clouds moving swiftly and a slice of new moon glowing in the middle. The kind where the shape of the whole moon is barely visible—like a foreshadow."

December 11   *Winter Window*

Strange, dark luminous flower of a poem . . . frost on the window last night.

December 12   *Transparent Birds*

Chickadee, stone bird . . . forms merging beyond glass. Gone. But not gone.

December 13   *Meditation for the Son*

Incense burning morning, light of the golden dawn, all images, inner and outer, prayerfully for the path of one's son. Incantations of crystal rainbows, the ring of stone, the round pottery of Acoma, soft in these hands, the turquoise frog, the horse, the window looking in. Reflections of Zen pebbles, piled, their spirit swinging back to me. Reflections of the prism's stillness, the quiet love we know out there. Circle widening. Smile. It is here.

December 14   *Meditation for the Daughter*

The little lake, frozen at the end of the road, calls her this sunny, frosty Sunday morning. With skates in hand and dog beside her, she walks in anticipation of the year's first solid ice. There is an aliveness in her step, a joy to her being which even the dog senses and playfully responds to. I see her on the small dock, the ice glinting, blinding in the sun, pulling on her thick socks, pushing her feet into the white skates, lacing them. Then finding the balance on ice. The first hesitant, small, and anxious move. Ah, daughter, the innocence of the lake, the purity of this space is all yours this morning. The world is all ice . . . the blades cutting their cold hieroglyphics, sun flashing, fish silent in depth beyond imagining. There is a grace in your sweeping motion that sails like only a father's love. In a small circle, some distance out, the opaqueness of the ice gives way to a translucency of pure crystal. Here the movement stops in the wonder of thin ice. I circle the light of that ice with you, though I am not there. Crouching, we pray for stillness of white stones on the lakebed. Entering the silence, we await the vision of magical fish.

December 15   *Meditation for the Mother*

"There's a robin hopping out there, trying to find something to eat. The poor guy. He must be lost."

December 16   *Meditation for the Father*

Snow . . . snow . . . snow. . . .

December 17   *Love and Death in White*

Snow continuing. And with it, the wind, softly at first but as the morning wears, an intensity of near blizzard proportions. The road ahead disappears. The windshield freezes. Backroads, main roads, all one and the same. The journey is mystery, is danger, is oddly enough, a mixture of love lost but romance retained. In endings, immobility, as pure as this there is a beauty often blind.

December 18   *Blue Morning Calm*

Then, ah, the sun again. The clear blue sky. The calm. The snow settled in a blue stillness. Unexplainably, I mourn all the dying that was yesterday, languishing now in a day that is almost too bright.

December 19   *The Silent Loss of Trees*

Because of the spaciousness of fields and woods, storms move through the land in a sweet, destructive secrecy. Only days, weeks, months later does one chance to come upon the hunger of a winter wind. As this day, the evidence awaiting me on the snowy path ahead: the loss of a huge, egg-shaped pine tree felled by yesterday's wind (a tree often painted by Phil Austin), the jagged stump pointed toward the quiet sky, the immensity of the tree, bright fir branches, resting giant-like across the trail. The sadness, to me. My memories of how it stood so alone amidst a fence of stone. How I tracked the seasons by its relationship to sun. How it heightened the color of the sky. How it welcomed snow. How it harbored birds from chickadee to hawk to owl. How each branch grew black—like a woodcut against a blinding flow of orange falling light.

December 20   *Lovers in Ice*

Murmur to me in ice this morning, how it builds on the wave-tossed pilings, the bows of fishing tugs, stoney shores, and this heart this morning . . . thin layers of translucency to a thickness of china white, gasping, voiceless, in the darkest stranglehold of unsuspecting pain.

December 21   *Charley and the Christmas Tree*

Always around this time we would go, the old man (Charley Root) and I to find the place where the Christmas trees grow. "All balsam," he would say. "And so blue." Hatchet and saw, a ball of bailing twine, I would follow his old footsteps into a woods sometimes thigh-deep in snow. "There," he would say, "There they are," as if they were waiting for us. "Now let's find us a good one, a full one," he'd circle around the stand of pine in an old,

156

old dance. "These here should do." He'd saw, I'd chop. We'd work up a sweat in the coldest temperature. "Now, let's tie 'em up." Trudging out of the woods in the last light of day, exhausted, sometimes falling, I'd retrieve my ungloved hand, needle-pierced, from the trunk of the tree, spread my sap-stuck fingers before my face, and breathe deeply, the scent of pine. "When I'm gone," he said, "Don't forget where this is so as you'll come back and get your Christmas tree."

December 22   *Snow Crow*

How the wind and falling snow hold the crow's flight still over the white field like a sumi master's brush stroke.

December 23   *Journeying*

Leaving Door for Chicago for the Christmas holidays under the usual tension of family travels plus the inner burden of knowing one is losing the relative peace and isolation of life in the woods for all the turmoil of a long drive, a packed car, the uncertainty of weather conditions along the highway, and the certain frenzy of arriving back in the neighborhood and into the arms of the family for 5 or 6 days. Even in the car I cannot find my place in the land and water I pass, cannot retrieve that sense of isolation I need in nature to let me mind merge with the feeling of the landscape, or rest with as much solitude as that deserted barn. If I could but walk right into that dark entrance. If I could see the cracks of light seeping in. If I could lie there and know the night of all seasons.

December 24   Christmas Eve

Looking through the Venetian blinds late at night, the way I once did here in the house of my childhood. Here in the living room, here on the sofa where I was privileged to sleep only on those occasions when my bedroom was being painted. Now, as the visiting son, the living room has become my bedroom whenever I return home. And I still love and recall the adventure of it all as a child . . . a bigger kingdom at my command. A nearness to an outside door. Closer proximity to the front windows and the world outside. And so as a man? as a child tonight? I peek through the blinds tonight at the sidewalk, the street, the houses of my old neighborhood. I watch the new snow filter past the streetlights, covering steps, sidewalks, and trees of all my years. And I am a child again, waiting for someone to pass by and leave the first footprints.

December 25   Christmas

In the basement of father's house again this cold Christmas morning, here where I write on his workbench, type on his ancient Underwood, beneath a small window of frosted glass. Walking through the alley earlier, around sunrise, I saw the many chimneys unfurling smoke like spun glass, the backyards of gardens with covered rose bushes, birdhouses and benches upturned. My pathway to the sun was blocked by squares and angles of all sorts—the corners of houses, the lengths of gangways, brick walls, roof lines, telephone posts, the very height of neighborhood homes. Yet the air had the ringing clarity of crystal. Jets, to and from O'Hare, shattered the skies in their near but far freezing cries. Christmas carols could be heard behind the frozen glass of a backporch kitchen window. And though the full measure of the sun did not appear to me this morning as it does in Door, I saw windows in the east everywhere—basement, first floor, second story—lacquered in this golden day's glow, holding the hallowed warmth of Christmas light, heralding it, spangling it like holy candles at morning mass.

December 26   *Iron Birds*

Automobiles, exhaust, wheels whining on ice before stoplights, expressway
traffic, shoppers in the Loop, slush as the day warms, breakfast under a
fake tree at Marshall Field's, shoppers with armfuls of discount Christmas
cards and wrappings, the shriek of the El, taxi horns, busses creeping up
and losing power, crowds of children outside Field's Christmas windows,
Salvation Army Santas ringing bells, shoppers bumping their way through
. . . pigeons, only pigeons in their irridescence, free-falling, fluttering down
from their roost of girders, elevated trains and tracks above . . . iron birds
pecking on sidewalk salt . . . intimations of nature and the futility of wings,
the loss of sky.

December 27   *Neighborhood Ramble*

The warmth of the winter's day in my own neighborhood . . . the sun
shining on Cermak Rd., Cicero and Berwyn. I visit the Czech bakery shops,
a boy again, listening to the old language once more, smelling (and later
tasting) the oven warmth of freshly baked rye bread, fruit-covered
coffeecakes, crisp salty horns, kolacky, houska, poppyseed bread. I stop at
the Prague sausage makers to buy jaternice (Bohemian sausage) for lunch,
to breathe the spicy air of Bohemian butcher shops. Again, the lure of a
language I love and can barely piece together from my past—a butcher an
an old man discuss the day in crackling talk. A few blocks away at a
neighborhood travel agency, I place my reservation for a flight to New
Mexico, only a month or so away. Late morning, in the nearby neighborhood of Oak Park, I roam the bookshops in search of more answers, then
drive down Kenilworth to pay homage to the boyhood home of Heming-
way. In the evening, dinner with Willard and Mary Hartman in Wilmette
. . . our two families who have come to know each other in Door County.
Incense is burned in a small burner shaped like an Indian oven (a horno)
found in the pueblos in the Southwest. And in that scent of pinon, this
holiday night, I am transported once more to the streets of Santa Fe, the
pueblos drifting in woodsmoke, the same smell of pinon I burn in my coop
in Door, and memories of midnight mass in my old neighborhood church,
St. Francis of Rome. Such a journey of senses, this day, this night.

December 28   *The Art of Rain-Washed Streets*

Children, these neighborhood streets of mine, asphalt and concrete, now washed in midnight rain running rainbows of neon, merging floral patterns of reds and oranges, greens, yellows, blues. These were my early watercolors. This, my art.

December 29 *Going for Milk*

This world I leave behind me once again, this world of bricks and concrete, iron and neon, this world of nature parceled in small backyard patches of earth, I will surely yield this day, surely miss. But not for the moment. Not for the quiet ecstasy of the journey north . . . to see the first solid forest of trees, every trunk, every limb, every dark branch limbed in a nimbus of pure white; the burst of black birds ascending from a barbed wire fence lost in snow. The country roads and nights of ice that await me, lifts me from the very land itself, gliding, hovering in a dream terrain, all blue, all white, sculpted in swirls, transfixed in glass. I punch delicate holes in it, in my steps in the dark, moving now toward neighbor Gordy Nelson's barn where the cows, in their straw-smelling animal warmth, dream green pastures in

such obsedian eyes. I fill two gallon glass jars with sweet milk, extinguish the light, feel the darkness of the barn move with the swaying cows, and whisper-walk through the glass-white world once more, a gallon of milk gripped in each hand, hanging from me like lanterns of cold winter light.

December 30   *A Remembrance of Red*

On my road this morning, past Charley's, toward Carlson's, in this world gone white in my absence, one ribbon of red unfurls across my path, gathering itself like a bow in a pine tree. I praise the color of the cardinal to keep me through winter.

December 31   *The White Path*

I am buried in a nightfall of new layers and drifts of snow. Rising in darkness, I peer through the blue windows, waiting the light that reveals there is no path again. All that I know is old has disappeared. Fresh tracks must be made. Greater visions—the earth, the life transformed—await my eyes this day. Pushing an arc of snow outside my doorstep, I set out, deep in thought, deep in snow, familiarizing myself in a bewildering, beautiful emptiness that is the earth gone white in a dream of love that must be made path to know my way there and back again.

The Seasons

Doors that open on the countryside seem to confer freedom behind the world's back.

—Ramon Gomez de la Serna

Visiting Door in Winter

Visiting Door In Winter

As Door County begins to empty in late fall, after the last tourist has seen the last red/gold/yellow maple leaf fall, after the last bushel of McIntosh, Cortland, and Delicious apples has been picked, after the last white sailboat has been hauled from the last October harbor darkening into November, I sit here at my desk, or walk the quiet road nearby, studying the woods of birch and maple opening to new light, listening to an ominous wind of no regrets, watching a sky the color of weathered barn wood, and feel a mixture of envy, anguish, and even fear as the emptiness encroaches, filling a man, again, with thoughts of loss and loneliness as the long white days and nights lie ahead, when new boundaries of the heart are drawn or eliminated entirely.

I envy the summer and autumn Door tourists who have experienced the best of this place in full measure: the incredible 200 some miles of shoreline, rocky, sandy, blue-green and glistening; plentiful pure parks with trails, campsites, bluffs, and trees, trees, trees; beaches beckoning everywhere, clean, scenic, seldom overcrowded; good restaurants, lounges, gift shops, theater, concerts, movies, vacation classes and schools such as the Clearing in Ellison Bay. And water, water everywhere to please sportsmen, fishermen, windsurfers, and watchers of sunsets. The Door County most summer tourists revel in, love, and take home with them in memories, photographs, paintings, and promises to return summer after summer.

Some call it Door County. Others, God's country. Still others read the landscape—woods, water, fields, and village life—to decipher a private meaning in their lives, far beyond a summer vacation place.

I envy the summer tourist who has the best of both worlds: the quiet beauty of the rural in the green and gold warmth of seasons, then the excitement of city lights when the death of winter sets in. I lived both those worlds myself a dozen years ago, and I sometimes feel exiled now, abandoned here in the worst of seasons, waiting for a summer sun across endless white fields, ice-sculptured shores, a sun that seems destined, especially in February, to never rise again.

Envy, regret, fear, loneliness, isolation, yes. Yet sometimes I smile, a secret smile, the smile of the Frenchman who knows Paris isn't all of France, or the smile of the Greek islander who realizes there is more to Greece than Athens. Or the smile of the Door County native, perhaps, who knows that once "the season" is over, the place, in winter, becomes his again.

He doesn't have to fight bumper-to-bumper traffic in downtown Sister Bay while tourists in Winnebagos gawk at the goats on the grass roof of Al Johnson's Swedish Restaurant and Butik. (The goats are wintering on Al's farm.)

He doesn't have to wait to eat an hour or more at most of the popular restaurants. (Most of the popular restaurants are closed while Al's remains open throughout the year, closing only on Thanksgiving and Christmas.)

He doesn't have to take a ticket at Wilson's in Ephraim and wait for his ice cream cone. (There is no Wilson's in winter. There are no ice cream cones. And Wilson's itself resembles a giant sundae, wrapped in whipped cream snow, topped with a red, cherry-like Coca Cola sign.)

He doesn't have to do much of anything, really, as the county settles in layer upon layer of pure snow that piles up until spring, as natives and transplants (city people who have moved here) face the cold facts or bolt to Florida.

Winter *loves* Door County so it usually arrives in early November (sometimes mid-October) and hangs around till it wears out its welcome, and people quietly begin going crazy in April and May with ice on budding birch branches, crocuses trying to find light, and robins going snowblind.

Door county people talk and live winter all year long. Next to the goats on Al Johnson's roof, it's the most frequent topic of conversation: "What do you do here all winter?" goes the refrain. Natives suffer this question continually from visitors, smiling their way through answers that include everything from "nothing," to skiing, snowmobiling, knitting, and just plain serious drinking.

The truth is there's nothing going on. The truth is that is the real attraction. The only way the summer tourist will ever understand it is to come see Door county himself in winter—for a weekend, a week, as long as it takes to see if it's only a summer love affair for you, or true love after all.

I won't say you have to be tough to brave the winter up here, but toughness helps sometimes, shoveling a long path out of your house every half hour, just to keep a trail open to the garage or woodshed or road. Madness helps too, when you're driving a maze of ice-coated or drifting back roads *just* to go to town for a cup of coffee, because if you're in the house another day without more human contact, you're afraid you may lose it all and begin babbling to the snowmen you've built around the house for companionship.

Truth-to-tell: the major highways (57 and 42) are always open in Door in winter, and in better condition than most city streets. But the back roads here can be an adventure.

Truth-to-tell: some of the serenest cross-country anywhere is to be found here in Door in winter.

Truth-to-tell: you may know Door County in summer, but only in winter does an older Door County emerge, a Currier and Ives place, a primitive landscape acquainting our minds and imagination with a visual history of the past: how Anderson dock, the bay, the bluff must have looked to settlers in Ephraim long ago; how beautifully distant the fields and woods must have been; how cold the harbors locked in ice; how vast the Lake Michigan horizon; how the natives must have fished, felled forests, cut ice from the lakes, hunted deer, just to survive the winters in this place.

I often think of friends or strangers coming up here for a weekend in winter, and sometimes even visualize myself in their place, knowing what I know now, after living in this place. How they or I might do it, coming up, say from Chicago, on a Friday night.

I'd tell them to cross the new Sturgeon Bay bridge, checking the beauty of the lights on the channel, and checking their gas as well. (Winter nights and Sundays in Door, it's best not to be caught beyond Sturgeon with an empty tank.) Then I'd tell them to quick head on up to the northern part of the county, where I live.

Oh, there's much to do in Sturgeon Bay, I guess—the county's only year-around movie house, the Donna, is found there—but city people don't come to Door in winter for movies. There are also larger stores, gift shops, restaurants, and bars within the city limits, even something like a shopping mall. Also, there's Potawatomi State Park, over 1,000 acres, downhill skiing slopes, and miles of cross-country skiing and snowmobiling trails.

Still, Sturgeon Bay (the shipbuilding capital of the Great Lakes) just ain't my kind of place and I aim, always, for the Door that opens just beyond there. Just about where highway 42 splits, and you either proceed north on 57 along the lakeside (Institute, Valmy, Jacksonport, Baileys Harbor), or take 42 north along the bayside (Carlsville, Egg Harbor, Juddville, Fish Creek, Ephraim), coming together again in Sister Bay, with 42 alone coaxing you further north into Ellison Bay and Gills Rock (the end of the world, the Top of the Thumb) where you may further ferry (via Northport in winter) to Washington Island, where you can really find winter in Door, where all 500 some residents (or no one) might meet you at the dock and wonder what you're doing there, and possibly toast you with a drink of bitters at a local bar (bitters being an islander drinking tradition). And be advised to check the ferry's daily schedule, as winter crossings are few and far between.

So say it's still Friday night, the temperature is freezing, the sky is cluttered with bright, winter stars, the snow is violet in the fields and ditches, and you're coming by way of 42 out of Sturgeon Bay. There's the Carlsville Bar for refreshments, if you're so inclined. Carlsville is hardly on the map, rarely in any guidebooks, and there is serious speculation among some that it exists at all (kind of like the mythical Juddville a few miles more up the road). But the Door Peninsula Winery's made a name for itself there, just across the street (tours December 1 through April 30th from 10 to 4), and I know for a fact Carlsville Bar does exist, though I've met only one Carlsvillian in my time, and he's never home.

In Egg Harbor there are a few more bars to choose from (which may or may not be open in winter depending how the owner feels this particular winter: whether he cares to open and stay in Door this winter, whether he cares to close and stay in Door this winter, whether he cares). The same goes for restaurants, though usually Casey's is open. And for sure, if you're hungering for a spicy hot pizza, I'd check out Tony Demarinis in his new place, Olde Stage Junction, where Tony and family will never disappoint you, unless he happens to be closed.

Coming up: Fish Creek. (That was Juddville you just passed through.) There's Omnibus on your right, once Door county's only downhill ski run, now just pure cross-country skiing, food, entertainment, and a fine bar of imported beers.

Fish Creek in winter may come as your first big shock, if you know Fish Creek in summer at all. Where has everyone gone? Nobody's home. Fish Creek in winter is my kind of place. The Bayside Tavern's open year around, good eating at the Cookery (mostly weekends through March with a Sunday winter brunch), and the popular C & C Supper Club, weekends as well.

But the pride and warmth of Fish Creek in all seasons, especially winter, is the White Gull Inn, just cozy as hell in a country inn sort of way. A good place to put up for the night, and a great place to rise (or visit) in the morning for a superb breakfast, basking in Door's early light near the warmth of a fireplace.

Gliding into Ephraim on a winter's night, you'll find the village mostly asleep, picture postcard perfect. *This* is what you've come to Door County in winter for. If Ephraim in snow, night or day, doesn't tug on your heartstrings, you belong on the Eisenhower Expressway in a snowstorm in rush hour traffic.

One of *the* places to be by far on a Friday night in northern Door in Winter is the Sister Bay Bowl in downtown Sister Bay. If Wilson's in Ephraim is the place where young and old meet in summer to speak and eat of ice cream cones, the Bowl is where young and old and everyone else gather for the Friday Night Fish Fry, especially in winter.

Now the famed Wisconsin fish fry has been much maligned lately by uncouth unWisconsinites, but who cares? Let them eat hardboiled eggs at Chicago neighborhood bars, and those terrible tiny heartburning salamies. Whether the fish (perch, whitefish, shrimp) are fresh or frozen, no matter their origin, they are fish nonetheless, fried to perfection this winter's night in Door, warm to the palate, and utterly irresistible when chewed with cole slaw, pummeled with potato salad, and washed down with cold beer.

This is *one* of the things people do doggedly in Door county in winter, and one of the reasons people bolt for the Bowl on Friday night to compare snow depths, discuss the thickness of ice on the bay and commiserate with friends over fried fish and beer.

I'm aware of friends, strangers, and winter tourists who drive nonstop (Chicago, Madison, Milwaukee, Green Bay, etc.) in the Friday night dead of winter, braving all kinds of blizzardly conditions, just to hit the Bowl when everybody who is anybody is there, and mingle with the masses, feel they belong, feel they have reached their destination in spite of all obstacles, and can now reap their first winter weekend's reward.

There are accommodations enough throughout the entire county, in and around Sister Bay, and all the way to the top. Most of them offer winter rates. All of them are convenient to whatever it is you've always wondered about winter in Door.

But I'd further advise friends and strangers to pick up both a *Door Reminder* (free . . . circulation 12,546) and a *Door County Advocate* (25¢, circulation 12,904) immediately, just to find out what's going on.

The *Door Reminder,* a weekly ad-rag, a local necessity, is filled with shopping buys, notes of thanks, garage sales, dining and entertainment info, occasional poetry and prose, and things like: FORE SALE: 2 Guernsey heifers, 1 due to freshen in Nov., & 1 in Dec., 100' snowfence, $40; HELP WANTED: Handyman needed. Steady work; FORE SALE: Feeder pigs & boars; WINTER HOUSE SITTING: Responsible woman looking to care for Door county home Dec. 1 through May; RABBITS, RABBITS, RABBITS FOR SALE; SERVICES: Will buck, split & pile your firewood; WANTED: Woman to share nice house on wooded lot (there's a lot of wanting that in winter in Door); HEAVY THOUGHTS CLOUDING YOUR DAY? Talk things over anonymously & confidentially with a HELPLINE volunteer (that's a number to keep handy by the phone till spring).

The *Door County Advocate,* published twice a week, keeps one in touch with local news (confirming the gossip or feeding the flames): sports, politics, features, events of all sorts, weddings, deaths, divorces, deer kills, drunken drivers, and just about all you need to know about the county on that particular day.

There are local columnists, such as Sarah Magnusson from Washington Island, who will tell you: "Ione Davison went to New London, Wis., to see her 14th great-grandchild, Amber Lynn Anderson, born Oct. 21 to Mr. and Mrs. Alan (Anne Davison) Anderson. She is the first grandchild of Mr. and Mrs. Arlie Davison. The other 13 great-grandchildren of Ione Davison are grandchildren of Verl Davison. Congratulations to George Johnson on his 86th birthday Nov. 7 and to Alfred Anderson (brother of Lawrence) on his 82nd birthday Oct. 30th."

There's even a column from Hainesville-Idlewild, a place I haven't even located in Door County yet.

171

There are photographs of a 17½ pound rutabaga, a kid holding a 2 pound 14 ounce carrot, and a lot of pictures of a lot of guys holding a lot of fish hanging from each hand.

There's even a Letters to the Editor column, which can be more entertaining than most of the editorials and all of the TV programming found in these parts on a snowbound winter's night: "Pastors—shake loose the cobwebs, hit those pulpits, and begin the revival! Forget the booze, don't compromise, lay out the facts, but again, I guess not. I like my booze, I compromise and I don't make waves. I give them a good once-a-week 20 minute sermon. They are happy!" (Excerpted from a long letter by E. W. Bojko).

What do people do in Door County all winter? They read the *Advocate* and the *Reminder* religiously by the homefires, sometimes smiling to themselves.

Saturday morning, perhaps after a beautiful early morning ski through Newport State Park (east of Ellison Bay), the most prime and pristine skiing experience in all of Door county (or Peninsula Park, between Ephraim and Fish Creek, another favorite), there's Al Johnson's Restaurant in Sister Bay for breakfast (lunch or dinner) of Swedish pancakes loaded with lingonberries (or strawberries, whipped cream, ice cream) and a side order of Swedish meatballs (a cheeseburger with onions or a thick beef sandwich on limpa for lunch; pike or pan-fried perch for dinner).

Al's in winter (especially at coffee-break time) is a gathering of the faithful, the friends, the fools who couldn't get away for the winter, who tell stories they don't believe themselves about how rough the winter is everywhere else, especially Chicago.

The goats are gone from the grass roof, now thick with snow. The restaurant reverts to a place where locals can linger over their limpa and lingonberries, talking politics, people, illness, gossip, death and taxes, and where even Al himself can be seen sometimes quietly standing (and sometimes actually *sitting*) with a coffee cup in hand, shouting (sometimes even *talking*) about politics, sports, how many miles he skied that morning, and complaining why his Chicago *Tribune* never arrives on time. (Or he may even tell you his favorite Belgian—the Poles of Door county—joke again: "How can you tell when it's spring in Brussels? When you see the Belgians hanging maple syrup buckets from the telephone poles!")

It's worth visiting Door in winter just to get a chance to listen, maybe even talk with Al.

"The winter business has been up 1,000%," he'll tell you. "I've been here for 34 years, and I remember when after Labor Day there was nothing, nothing till next Memorial Day. The big thing here now in winter is cross-country skiing. The snowmobile never really took hold. Cross-country skiing makes it easy for the family to do something as a unit for little money.

"Here it's like Sweden in winter where every little town has its trails. You can ski almost anywhere here. Our trails are similar to those in Sweden. The landscape's similar. Newport State Park is equal to anything I've skied in Sweden. Peninsula Park is also good, although it can get pretty crowded on weekends.

"Winter here is just a slower pace. And the tourist is a lot different. The winter person is upper-middle class, secure in his job. Maybe even works only a four-day week. The trend now is to come up here on Thursday and go back on Sunday. Mostly it's family, very close knit. People do things with their kids. There are even some families who've changed their whole routine and vacation here in winter rather than summer."

When it comes to aesthetics, Al, a very physical person, may have a little difficulty explaining just what's beautiful about Door County in winter to him: "I never miss a day of skiing. If I don't ski twenty miles a day in winter, something is wrong. Listen, I can take you to a place and show you what Door county looked like a 100 years ago. That's something to see. That's something. I've skied in the city, brother, I know what that's like. If anybody doesn't think the environment doesn't make a difference like skiing here in Door, they don't know what they're talking about.

"Rim frost. That's something to see. Rim frost on all the trees. And a moonlight ski. We go out at night when the moon is high, me, my wife Ingert and Bill Bastian. You can't believe it, especially if you can get out by the Lake Michigan shore. The temperature, say, is around 28, and the silhouettes of the trees, now *that's* really something!

"The snow is whiter here. The air is fresher. It's like Donnie Erickson said here one morning when they were arguing about taxes. 'What do I get for my taxes?' one of the guys complained. 'Go out and take a deep breath,' Erickson told him. That's what I mean."

So it's cross-country skiing as the major attraction for winter visitors and locals alike. There's snowmobiling too, though most of the ecology-minded folk and true lovers of Door would prefer snowmobilers trade in their vehicles for skies, snowshoes, or a good pair of hiking boots. There's sledding and tobogganing as well on Hill 17 in Peninsula Park, and skating here and there in various villages, bays, and some of the inland lakes—if the snow cover is light, if the wind is in the right direction, or if you can find a native with a plow to clear a space for you. There's occasional ice boating on the bays. And ice fishing for those intrepid fishermen who can handle the wind, ice, snow, sans shanty, or find a friend's shanty to settle into, build a fire, ream the hole in ice over two feet thick, pull up a camp stool, sip the brandy, drink the beer, and wait for the fish to find you. (Or, as a local once said, "I don't care if I catch no fish or not. She's back at the house, and I'm here all day, feeling pretty good.")

Sister Bay, as any visitor soon learns, is the center of the northern Door, and certainly so in winter. Though it can't compare to an urban downtown or even a shopping mall, it is just about the only place with a bank open, a hardware, a barber, beauty shops, feed mill, gas stations, doctors, dentists, a lumber yard, supermarket, drug and department store, plus Kenneavy's Kitchen & Bakery, run by an exiled Irishman from Chicago's westside, occasionally dressed in green, trying to survive in winter serving soup and sandwiches, fresh bakery, Chicago pizza, Italian beef sandwiches and meat pies in this land of limpa.

So if shopping, from goodies to gifts, is on your mind, this is the place, including the Walkway Shops, a number of which are open winter weekends and more, such as Passtimes Books, Door County's major cultural resource in winter, where one can find an extraordinary collection of good books to wile a winter's night away.

There are small, Ma & Pa food stores scattered throughout the county which are rather remarkable for all they contain, even in winter, and the services they provide. The Pioneer Store in Ellison Bay, for one, has become a bit of a landmark for its old fashioned general store presence and peculiarities, with its big pot-bellied wood stove to warm the winter shopper, skier, kibitzer, tourist; it's likely to be open just about anytime you need a store, including holidays and winter nights.

A winter visitor to Door will soon discover that a weekend here is not enough time. There are whole establishments, parks, back roads, bars, and ways of life to explore.

The Wagon Trail, five miles northeast of Sister Bay on County Z, a one-stop place in itself, might so occupy a person's attention (restaurant, bakery, lodge, swimming pool, sauna, ski trails, etc.) that he'll miss the rest of Door County entirely, which could be a big loss.

Not to check the Anderson Dock in Ephraim in winter. Not to venture on any of the back roads to see the beauty of the rural countryside waiting there. Not to travel south out of Sister Bay, highway 57, just to see Baileys Harbor (and visit Nelson's Shopping Center and Paul's Glass Bar), Jacksonport, and the Whitefish Dunes State Park under snow.

And if you're headed to or from a ski at Newport State Park, certainly to call on Uncle Tom (the corner of Timberline and Europe Bay Rd.) at the old Newport Schoolhouse. Uncle Tom, pancake man, candyman, popcorn man, Greek, minister to the human spirit, ambassador to America at large and Door County in particular—he'll warm your heart regardless of the temperature. "The Chamber may think Door County is all tourist industry and business and more business," he'll grab you by the arm and look right into your face, "but Door County is people! People, buddy. You better believe it!"

Dressed in baker's white with chef's hat (Pancake Man) and red bandanna, Uncle Tom is a throwback to good old fashioned hospitality. (He's not selling pancake mix and homemade fudge, he's *giving* Uncle Tom!) If you can walk away from Uncle Tom still feeling blue, you're a hopeless human being. During the cold, dark months when all his summer visitors have fled, he deliberately keeps a light in the window, keeps the old schoolhouse open for winter wayfarers, in the true spirit of the Greek word, *xenos,* meaning both stranger and guest.

"Hospitality place this is," he says, opening his arms to encompass his whole schoolhouse and kitchen. "You want some coffee? Here, I just made these muffins. Hospitality, yes indeed. Al Johnson may have an elaborate layout, but I'll match him any day for communication between people.

"I have so much enthusiasm right now. My body is 78 and my outlook is 30 going on 25. And everybody can have that! I don't know any ingredient that can activate attitude as much as gratitude. Gratitude for everything! Everything! You remove the pettiness, the trivialities will disappear.

"I'm here all winter, yes, anytime. The coffee pot's always on. And the price is right—no charge. Pancakes, pancakes," he begins laughing at his own success." It's been quite a life.

"The winter, ah, the winter here is paradise. Paradise! Michigan advertises, "Say yes!" Door County, yes! Door County, say yes! If you love Door County, tell her so! The wind, the snow, the sunshine, the crystals on the evergreens. These places that close for the winter, they're crazy! Everything's here. In full measure. Winter, oh yes, winter.

"The winter people who come here are really nature people. It's a special breed of people. They'll even camp out in tents in the snow! Summer tourists, I tell them, please hurry back in winter and we'll talk it over. Unspoiled out here! Cross-country skiers . . . great people. There's more time to communicate with people. It's been a spiritual revelation in this place. People bring their sons and daughters to talk to me. After your minister and your priest, you come to me, and I'll tell you how to make it work in the world.

"By all means come now and look into the heavens on a clear winter night. The hour of affirmation. I think the hour of affirmation comes in the slumbering of winter. Everything's sleeping, everywhere sleeping. And Door County is fast asleep. And people are better able to put themselves together."

What is there to do in Door County in winter? Visit Uncle Tom for sure.

If you've been breathing the precious pure winter air of Door county all day, if you pushed yourself exhilaratingly beyond your physical limits skiing, skating, hiking, shopping, etc., you'll probably find yourself falling asleep by 7 or 8 o'clock.

But if you insist on a Door winter's night on the town, the pickings are slim at best. Most any bar you happen to find open will accommodate you with a drink at the bar, maybe some TV, and perhaps some local conversation, if a local feels prone to conversing. Mostly it's meditation time: each man or woman, head bowed, staring into his beer. Probably wondering how long the winter will last.

You'll want to try Husby's Tavern in Sister Bay for certain, for no other reason than it's there, has always been there, and hopefully will remain forever. Husby's is a kind of Wilson's for people who prefer beer to ice cream in an authentic surrounding. It's one of the few working bars left in the northern end of the county, though those who are in there every day are probably not working, and wintery times can mean a crowded bar. Daytime, nighttime, bedtime, Husby's sort of leans there aiming to please.

Then there's the A.C. Tap on highway 57 between Sister Bay and Baileys Harbor, another local landmark, where you can drink yourself silly for less than five dollars. Where the conversation can get loud and the stories get wild. Where Freddie Kodanko, local legendary farmer, holds his birthday parties, advertised in the *Door Reminder*. Where Freddie will dance for you or sell you some potatoes. (That's his baby picture hanging on the wall in the gold oval frame.) Where every class of Door County's laboring men—fishermen, farmer, plumbers, cooks, the unemployed—can be found, at one time or another. And where the *only* game in town (at least at the A.C. Tap) is bean bag. Which they play with a vengeance.

Sunday is a sadness for most winter visitors—trying to catch up, trying to enjoy, once more, all the things they did the day before, plus all that there was never enough time to do. Sunday sadness seeps into the bones, for Sunday is the time for going home, and few people, regardless of how ornery the winter weather may have been, are that anxious to return. They've been so graced by the beauty and romance of winter in Door, they want to remain and live happily ever after in such a place, never quite understanding that their freedom to come and go enhances the desirability of each place and may be the real saving grace. Those of us who have lived in both places, slowly come to terms with that.

And those of us who are left to live all winter in Door understand and share some of the enthusiasm of the winter visitor, yet know deep down in our snow-covered hearts that the joy of skiing soon wears thin, day after day; that such a monotony of same people, same places, same everything sets in that one grows quietly forlorn, desperate for desire in any form; that one can only be surrounded by so much beauty and quiet that one grows blind and deaf to it; that winters at best in this landscape are solitary incursions into the self, and at worst can be interminable and self-defeating. So much one could do, but can't because . . . because it's winter.

Still, when you get right down to the rudiments of existing in such a place at such a time, it's really the universal theme of man vs. nature after all. And it's why some men choose to live here and others only visit. Each, knowingly or unknowingly, touches upon or responds to those primitive forces—be they trees, fields, animals, birds, woods, waters, wind, skies—miraculously transformed by winter, and each feels the spirit of this place, at home in the universe.

Ask the artists who live here and paint winter. Ask Charles Peterson in Ephraim who will tell you, "I love painting winter landscapes as there is a much sharper feeling of structure and form. The foliage is all gone. Rock forms seem sharper. The snow has a great advantage, from the opposite standpoint, in that it tends to unify very complicated landscapes.

"There's a much lower angle to light. I prefer what I see in winter over summer because of its more subtle tones. Even evergreens are more subtle in tone. Much grayer. I like the more subtle gray tones of winter landscape. It's much more emotive. I like the harsh threats of winter which are implicit in its colors."

It may all come down to this: You can't cross-country ski at sunset time in Door and not feel the color of snow and sky and trees and ice.

You can't walk a back road past endless fields of white, or near a woods at 10 below, the branch of every tree sheathed in ice, tinkling in wind, sparkling in morning sun, and not realize the need of space and form in a man's life.

You can't stand on a winter-etched shoreline and watch fishing tugs brave the steely Lake Michigan waters against on undiscernible horizon first touched by snow, then defined by sunrise, and not feel part of a place that overwhelms and justly diminishes a man in a world beyond his doing.

Door County in winter lends that distance and dimension to every wayfarer's heart once again.

Waiting for Spring in Door County

Waiting for Spring in Door County

I stand here, on what I recall as my road, sometimes knee-deep in snow on January 1st, awaiting the faintest suggestion of spring. Of course it's still winter, but it's been winter in Door since the middle of October, and come January a man has got to start looking for signs of rebirth. What I'm waiting for, perhaps, even here in the dead of winter, is nothing more than that rather mournful call of the chickadee (not the "chick-a-dee-dee-dee" of spring, but those sad notes that sound like a sigh) on a bright, sunny, wintry day when there is no other sound than the sound of snow growing deeper. If I can *just* hear that at a time of the year when all of nature sounds hoarse, when there is nothing to suggest song except the moaning wind at night, that little lilt of the chickadee lifts a man's heart considerably to the possibility that, yes, all is not dead in Door. Life, though obviously elsewhere, just might return.

On January 9th the temperature drops to 10 below zero, followed by 18 below the next day. Wherever that lilt of the chickadee may be (and it's usually heard in early January) it's lost in gusting winds of 40 miles an hour, clouds of crazy flying snow drifting to horrendous heights, trees creaking, snow squeaking, wind whistling a dirge you don't care to hear again. "Sometimes monotony can be irresistible," someone who never lived in Door once said.

Then the plague of cabin fever sets in and spreads and spreads and spreads. Lethargy is the word for the day, followed by torpor and atrophy. Cabin fever can be explained as a kind of a reverse boredom: you know you're bored, you're anxious in your boredom, and your only desire is to wallow in more and more boredom till you could scream, only you can't hear yourself scream and neither can anyone else because they're doing the same thing. You're sure that this is a dress rehearsal for the deathbed scene, but you're vaguely aware that this may not be a rehearsal. You just don't want to do anything, and you're angry with yourself because everything you may want to do is a deadend since the weather will not permit you to do anything anywhere anyhow.

Bang!

Spring, if it comes at all in the deadliness of these moments, comes in seed catalogs with visions of fruits and vegetables and flowers you can barely recall. It comes in the realization that, hell, there is *only* February to get through. And it comes with the feeling that the days do *seem* to be getting longer and lighter, though at 5 p.m. in the dark you're as dead tired as 6 a.m. in the dark when you got up.

Ah, spring—it can't be far away, goes the refrain. A sign, please! Any sign, even if it's wrong. "It can't be far away." But no one has ever attempted to measure the distance between the return of the robin and the long walk of Al Johnson's goats from a nearby farm to the grassy green restaurant roof.

Winter dies hard in Door, and the January thaw usually arrives one afternoon in April.

On an abnormally mild day in February, if men can make their way through snow into the apple and cherry orchards to prune the trees, one might take this as a significant herald of spring. Skunks, too, just might make an appearance, squirrels begin to chase each other, while ground hogs dig deeper, holding on to their shadows for dear life. Something may be in the air besides more snow, though it's still the season of down vests, cross country skis, and woolen caps pulled down tight over the ears.

Most of the birds at the feeders still reflect the colors of Door County winter: gray, white, black, tree bark brown, and jays as blue as the color of ice hanging from the roof. Evening grosbeaks are pure fantasy. You just *think* you're seeing a bit of spring color. "Harry, I just saw a bright yellow bird like a fat canary at the feeder." "Mabel, put your galoshes on. It's best we visit the clinic again." As for a red cardinal smack against a world of Door County white . . . that'll send you to the bottom of the Coronet brandy bottle for sure. Robin red-breasts and spring fever aside, red is the last color a native Door County child learns. It's the most difficult color of all to identify, for it does not exist here but for cherries in July and apples in August.

April may be the cruelest month, according to T. S. Eliot, who never spent a month of April Fools' Days in Door, but January, February and March can be damned merciless.

Enter March and all its madness of lions and lambs . . . and another step closer to spring. You're beginning to really crave it now. You're tired of feeling woody, tired of wet feet, sore backs, nowhere to go, nothing to do. Tired of being snowblind. Tired of snow shovels, snowblowers, snow rakes, snow tires, snowshoes, snowsuits, snow goggles, snow chains, snow scrapers, snow mittens, snow masks, snow plows, snow days, snowflakes, snowballs, snowdrifts, snowstorms, snowmobiles, snow reports, snowbirds, snowfalls, snow banks, snow sleds, snow depths. Tired of eating frozen vegetables or tasteless, anemic "fresh" ones. Tired of viewing dull weathermen frozen in their dire, dumb predictions. *Anyone* can predict snow and cold temperatures in Door tomorrow, but can someone please tell me where the hell is spring?

"Harry, the weatherman says the freeze will be with us for the third week in a row." "Freeze my _____, Mabel." "Yeah, that too, Harry."

Perhaps there is evidence on the road, March 2nd, when half of it appears to be melting in the sun and half of it frozen in the fierce wind of a day (mid-20's) trying to edge toward spring. Or reports of Canada geese, the very same day, touching down at Horicon.

There is also the lingering light of dusk and a sunset that runs and flows like a watercolor wash, spilling over the white fields and ice-locked bays. People are coming around to themselves, beginning to feel their own strength again, their own individuality, flexing their muscles in a way, no longer intimidated by the power of winter, the death rattle of the wind. They *know* winter is losing, that time is turning in their favor, and they are finding their way out of houses and barns into town, into Al Johnson's, into the first mild, sunny, wintry days, smiling more, laughing occasionally, wearing fewer layers of clothing, almost cocksure that things are changing. The snow *will* disappear. The ice *will* break up and float away. Windows will rid themselves of Jack Frost. Birds will return in living color to leafy branches. Tractors and power mowers will be resurrected. Snow blowers abandoned. And the waters of Door will run free once more, and men, women, children, and tourists will greet the earth and the clear, warm air.

But wait . . . Just wait . . .

Spring in Door County is the season of false hope. That is the great lesson to be learned here, the essential ingredient of Door County character. Abandon all hope all ye who wait here for spring.

It's the season of anger because nothing works havoc in a man's soul like anticipation. Always the persistent tease, but seldom the real delivery. Never what you really need, what you're really dying for. (We had a name for this classic boy-meets-girl condition in high school.) And I don't know what the hard facts are in Door County during the long tease, but I'd say alcohol consumption reaches new heights at this time, and even the grass grows higher and higher, no thanks to the sun that never sets since it so seldom shines.

But I speak of spring's approach in Door County . . .

March 8th brings yet another snowfall, although a light, powdery snow, easy enough to handle, to live with, in spite of the fact you're feeling, tasting, wanting, sorely needing more evidence that life returns. How *long* does it take for winter to leave? Just a little while longer yet as winter hits you in the back of the head with a slug that makes for a craziness even beyond cabin fever, because you're outside the cabin now, but inside an even larger cabin of more snow and ice and an occasional tease of the sun.

Things have *got* to change! It's March!

"It's March, isn't it Mabel? Did you turn the goddam calendar?"

March 12th: the first rain! A heavy downpour that lasts for hours. Not quite a spring rain, not that warm aroma of it, but a clean hard rain that breaks from the skies as if to has to, it's time to . . . time to steadily wear away at the snow cover, to loosen it, to open it, to bare the earth and let it breathe again.

March 13th: Patches of the fields, furrows of black earth overturned last fall are now visible in the snow-covered, rain-washed fields. An aura of mystery and miracle to their presence. Something lurking, something rising from the deep. The abstraction of their forms brings an abstract expressionistic joy to the heart. Then, sunset time, and how, over all the landscape, one sees and feels the burning of a summer sunset in Door, though the fields are mostly white and bays all ice. Still, the sun is *moving*. Moving. Something is going on.

March 15th: the first sign of maple trees being tapped. Now there's a joy, maple syrup time. A sure sign of spring. "Mabel, would you tap that line of maples along the fence this morning, then start the fire, collect the buckets from the other trees, boil it down to syrup, can it and take it down to the stores to sell? I've got some important work at Husby's."

And March 20th, at 5:30 p.m., the "official" first day of spring.

It's "official" because the first day of spring in Door County is usually authenticated with snow. And the next day a nice, fat, wet snow plops steadily from the sky. "Mabel, the snow's so wet I can't shovel it. Guys all over droppin' like flies liftin' that heavy stuff. Mabel, you hear me? Mabel, put that brandy away. It ain't but 8 in the morning yet."

But March 22nd . . . ah . . . is bright, sunny, it is *warm*. The snow has begun melting again, and there is *definitely* the sound of robins in the air. It is the kind of day so tantalizing, so filled with expectation, that everyone you meet in town smiles and says, "What a beautiful day." And you agree. You can almost see the goats romping on Al's roof.

Two days later you sight three robins on the front lawn. "Mabel, the robins is back! Hang up the snow shovel, get the seeds in the flats. I'll see if there bes any onion sets at the Co-op on my way to Husby's."

The remaining snow is beginning to honeycomb. Soon all of it will be gone. And on March 28th, meadowlarks glide in and begin firing themselves across the roads and into the fields. Meadowlarks mean maybe.

March 29th: the first real *smell* of spring. The morning air like it was freshly washed. The earth sending off scents, sharp soil scents, pungent matted leaf and weed scents. The aroma of cedar from the woods is so overpowering, a man's sure he has been just about raised from the dead. In the fields, patches of snow the shapes of clouds that have fallen and lay melting on the earth.

In Sand Bay, the sound of thin ice cracking, shattering like glass. The ripples in the sand left by ice retreating.

Flies are aroused and dumbly buzzing against windowpanes.

The earth, spongy but slowly drying out, grows beneath the feet.

March 30th: Ah, lightning! Ah, thunder! Let 'er rip! The sky convoluting, turning into and upon itself with sudden explosions of muted yellow sunlight unexpectedly opening up the gray heavens here . . . there . . . over there . . .

March 31st: to be able to freely walk upon the land again—from here to there—without stepping on snow. The land sort of unleashing itself, the joy of being able to walk out of the house and into the natural world, the sight of water in the ditches along the roadway and low fields filled with small lagoons. To see the wind rippling this black water silver in sunlight.

Then walking around the garden the first time. All the snow is gone. There are only the neatly tilled rows from last fall: the lettuce that was left there and cornstalks standing and falling to decay and become earth again. Rediscovering the garden in these first days of spring: this is where the beans were, this is where the crows and coons ate the corn, over there the tomatoes tied to tried to turn red. Check the outlying birdhouses for winter occupants, around the garden once more and then into it to feel its resilency, its freshness underfoot. Goddam, I'm gonna make me a scarecrow this year!

April means showers and May flowers, crocuses and violets, wild leeks in the woods, the smelt beginning to run, the fields slowly yielding to green, snow fences rolled up, Al Johnson taking down the wooden storm door and entrance to his restaurant. My wife's familiar spring call: "AHHhhhhhhh, a snake!" Daylight saving's time. Easter.

April means, sweet God o'mighty, spring at last!

Sort of . . .

April 3rd: the barometer drops to 28.6, one of the lowest recordings in northern Door County history. Early morning, wet and cold. By 2:20 in the afternoon, the wind has kicked up and is howling angrily, snow is falling, twisting crazily, blowing in from the northwest in great sheets. All the day long the wind howls. So do the people.

By next morning the ditches along the road have once again turned to ice. But the sun soon returns to begin melting the snow that has blown all over the land the night before. In the circular flowerbed beside the house, tender tulip sprouts are shooting up, dreaming of brilliant color. One silent, songless wren sits on top the wren house perplexed. He came all the way here to do something but can't quite remember what.

It's wintry cold in early April. Eighteen above and snowing again the next day, though you can almost feel the dead fields trying to expand, to force a green upon the landscape. On the forest floor and in the fields, very close and tightly packed amidst last year's leaves, twigs, stones, the tiniest stirrings of green blades, patches of tiny plants pushing their presence through. And by April 9th, a truly warm day, the warmest day yet—high 30's, according to some thermometers, maybe the 40's. (The thing about people and thermometers in Door is that none of them agree in *any* season. Nor do the professional weathermen ever agree. You're just living in a place

185

without any constants. And if a fellow across the road says he had 20 below on his thermometer, and you say you had 30, it's agreed. And understood. It's the Door County variable factor. Everything's variable around here.)

"Mabel, it was take-away 23 when I gots home from Husby's last night." "Harry, we don't even have a thermometer. Who knows what you was readin' where."

On the tenth of April I wake up to a gently falling snow. It's a dream, of course. But just to be sure, I walk around the kitchen making coffee with my eyes closed, before stepping out for my morning walk. Stepping out upon the earth, I turn my head back and open one eye. Yep, those are my footprints in snow, in snow, in snow. If you think back to November and count the months, it has been snowing in Door County for a hell of a long time. Door County is uniquely a land of one season: winter and what comes before. If you continue to think about this for more than two minutes in April, you may come down with a severe sense of depression. The trick is never look back in April in Door County. And looking ahead, it's . . . .

Easter Sunday! Time for Easter egg hunts . . . in the snow. Easter bonnets . . . in the snow. And the Door County version of the Easter bunny: the snowshoe hare. By 4 p.m. on Easter Sunday, the sun finally appears, hangs around for a whole hour and a half, then absconds for days in the clouds. Easter Sunday is followed by days of drizzle, the miraculous appearance of crocuses on April 15th, and an ominous overcast. A dull, depressing November kind of day, when at 8 a.m. the rain begins again, while snow still sequesters itself in those sunless spots of nature found along the sunken southern edges of roadside ditches and in those cold zones of Door County's impenetrable forests. One week after Easter brings cold rain, intermittent snowflakes and . . . yes . . . the grass around the house turning *officially* green!

"Mabel, you best drag the lawn mower outa the cellar, seein' my hernia's actin' up again." "Yer hernia, Harry, my _____!"

Ah, but it's SPRING AGAIN, and the world is mudluscious, says cummings, and come April 18th, the air is so delicious you can cup it in your hand and swallow it whole. Sparrows and robins are pecking and turning over dead leaves, looking for new life. Woodpeckers are testing the percussion qualities of trees. You just know it in your bones that at last, this is *it!* The waters of the bay (far out) are Oh so blue, the ice so thin around the shoreline that in another day or two it will be history. There's a feeling, too, while driving down the backroads that the woods, the fields, the roadside, all of nature in Door is sprucing itself up, shaking off the death of fallen branches, leaves, the whole dead dance of decay since last September. And it's being done, alas, unassisted by man with his scratchy rakes, his plastic sacks of fertilizer, leaf mulching machines, trash bags, and little bonfires of silver ash. The earth just taking care of itself in its own fashion, its own time, no help needed from you or you or you, thank you. Here come

186

the song birds now, and here comes the slow greening of trees, while flowers strengthen their colors and prepare to explode.

An early evening spring walk down the road and into the field where I find Gust Klenke's old beehives and check to see if there is any action going on. I place my ear near the entrance and hear nothing. No new buzzing in the old hive. But scattered around the entrance, on the ground, a veritable graveyard of dead bee bodies: spring cleaning going on. Soon the world will all be blossoms and clover, nectar and the honeying business of bees busy again.

On an afternoon in the middle of April I'm driving to Sheboygan to talk about *Door Way* that night . . . and I'm driving through Door under clouds, then rain, then wind, then . . . snow. Hard, cold rain mixed with snow. Returning somewhere around three in the morning, driving north on County S, I face blizzard conditions. The road is snow-packed and icy, the car swerving. My hands tightening on the steering wheel till the fingers ache. This is winter in Wisconsin. But, for crissake this is SPRING!

April 20th: more of the above. Thirty-two degrees. Sweater weather . . . the wind blowing snow off the bay. I'VE GOT TO GET OUT OF THIS PLACE! By 6:30 p.m., a sunset of such summer dimensions—blood orange, gold, pink, lavender, caught in the bare black branches of trees, and suddenly, seemingly out of nowhere since the sky is mostly blue and losing its light, but in all this color and form and intimations of summer sunsetting time, *snowflakes* filter down, jeweled . . . small particles of falling light. I have *never* seen this in Door County before (certainly not in April) and equate it to something visionary. I remain transfixed for a long, long time.

April 21st: clear, crisp air, 30 degrees, and pure light. The sky is raucous with ravens, two of them rising to the very tops of trees and laughing at me. The path to the coop is slightly frozen under my feet and makes wonderful crunching sounds with each step. It's official: The ice has gone out of the bay! (According to Winky Larson and Al Johnson, the latest it has ever gone out has been May 4th. According to Mike Till, the earliest is March 17th.) So, looking at it one way, things are definitely getting better.

So much better that in the next few days, in and out of Door County again—Door County to Chicago to Madison and back to Door—I am aware of how truly green it is beyond the Door peninsula. There's a man going out in a rowboat near Algoma. There are kids moving into a field with their kites in Kewaunee. A man in Manitowoc is fixing his fences. In Cicero, Illinois, my father is cutting the lawn (an old neighborhood pastime). A red-tailed hawk sweeps in front of me on my way to Madison. Heading back to Door, through Brown County, the air is heavy and golden with manure . . . spreaders and farmers. High above my house the hawks have arrived, circling, swooping, kettling, riding the thermals somewhat in the spirit of small children giving their bodies completely to the movements of spring.

187

"Mabel, see dem hawks?" "Where?" "They're not on 'Days of Our Lives', Mabel, you won't see 'em on there."

Rain last night has left the road, this morning of April 26th, warm and wet and filled with the thick and thin of juicy worms, extending and retrieving themselves in a wet reflection of spring. Pussy willows have opened their silver furry eyes. Hepaticas are in heat. And on Highway 42, late morning, two bikers, a young man and a young woman, have abandoned their bikes on the side of the road to embrace and kiss the warm Door day away with sighs of spring.

As April assimilates the Door winter mind completely, there are yet wild leeks to be gathered for salads and soups, the yellow flower of adder's tongue to behold, mayflies to be swatted in Sister Bay, and one's ears to remain either open or closed to the deafening sweet sounds of birdsongs, calls, screams, shouts, lilts, cackles, caws each morning. This *is* the woods so wild, the forest primeval.

"Mabel, it sounds like a goddam jungle out there this morning." "It's only spring, Harry, spring, ta da!"

May 1st: the swallows have returned, not to Capistrano, but to my birdhouses and telephone wires. They are up to their tricks again of aerial intercourse, love on the high wires. "Mabel, dem swallows sure know how to keep a good man down." "I ain't sayin' nothin', Harry," she says, enviously eyeing high-tailing and winging it on the high wire. But the return of swallows . . . *they* are spring. And the trilliums in bud, *they* are spring. And this morning, so alive, is made to be eaten raw. The afternoon temperature reaches 70 degrees, and in Sister Bay I see the first beautiful tourist woman walking around in shorts short enough to shorten any man's breath. This *certainly* is a sign of spring like no other in Door.

"Mabel, I saw a lady tourist walk into Husby's for a six-pack and she wasn't wearin' nothin' under you know can you imagine and they were like this right there, right there! and I could hardly hold my Coronet and . . ." "Stuff it, Harry."

Certainly spring has sprung . . . though not quite by Al Johnson's calendar, since it won't be till somewhere around the 20th of May when he begins tossing his goats on the roof, depending how well and how high the grass is.

And what we enter now, because of the magical sense of time and wonder, is something akin to a trance. The land speaks it. The water reflects it. The birds sing it. The trees reach for it. The flowers color it. The sun caresses it. And what this whole manifestation of wonder does is rid us of all our complexities, our masks, our fears, our winter's growth of worry and angst. Be it unrequited love, be it strife in the home, economic entanglements, physical maladies, separation from others or ourselves, this time of spring transports us, transfigures us, transforms us, and we know "it" and are whole again. Everything *can* be perfect; perfection is all around. And there is no suffering, no ill will, no hard times, and no death—especially our own. In this sweet time of earth, air, fire, and water, we are gods and know how and why we must live without reason, like children, like flowers and trees and birds and animals and earth and light and wind and water. And only once a year is this visited upon us, and we live this universe of moment within ourselves. All the rest is dying, and how sorrowfully, sadly, and with such human weakness do we forsake the moment and crawl back to the comfort we call "real" in this world. While the unreal world waits there, which the elusive and illusionary spring briefly reminds us each year . . . the seasons of paradise are all one now . . . and we shall live forever, and death shall have no dominion.

By May 3rd dandelions are growing on Al Johnson's roof, and the Great Goat Herdsman himself is up there, watering the lawn, smiling at his goat's eye view of the world.

The bats have returned above the roof of my house (how do they find my place every year?) and are swooping and swirling in a twilight speckled with insects.

And the evening of May 5th . . . Shhhhhh . . . one of the loveliest sounds of all . . . and how I do wait for it each spring and linger over its last call each fall: ah, the whippoorwill, whippoorwill, whippoorwill, whippoorwill, whippoorwill . . . That's it! Officially, winter is over in my book. For never in my life in Door have I experienced a mixture of whippoorwill and snow.

At 4 the next morning I awake to the sound of a whipper willing it beside my bedroom window once more.

"Mabel, get my shotgun. That damn whippoorwill won't give me a decent night's sleep." "Roll over, Harry, and just count all them sweet young things in their T-shirts jumping over the Sturgeon Bay bridge for the summer." "Zzzzzzzz."

Days of gentle mist and a foggy morning rain. A sense of the greening earth dabbing itself with sweet scented moisture. Warblers, oven birds, bluebirds . . . the sound of an owl. The light between the trees in the woods across the road is definitely diminishing, as the new leaves unfurl, thicken on the branches, till all the wood light will be gone, and the horizon will disappear.

There is talk of morel mushrooms magically making their way through the earth's floor in the Ephraim area—though in my neck of the woods it's too early for them yet. (Though, according to Ingert Johnson, they come out when the yellow flowers come out. "What yellow flowers, Ingert?" "Just yellow flowers," she says. I spend the next day, and the day after amidst yellow flowers and find nothing but more yellow flowers.) I dig a trench in the garden for my wife to plant potatoes. The temperature reaches 80 degrees on May 11th—the first feel of summer heat on my body since last July. Spiders are spinning. All manner of insects are trying out their legs. And ants have begun their annual invasion of the house.

189

The garden sky the next afternoon is alive with wings, wings, wings. Wings of barn swallows, wings of tree swallows, wings of bluebirds, wings of gulls, wings of hawks—all of them together at the same time! From the highest branch of the tallest maple on the roadside, a towhee calls time to *drink-your-tea,* while a catbird meows a reply, and a red-breasted grosbeak trills a Schubert song, crows crow, grackles grackle, a thrasher thrashes around a pile of leaves, and a red-headed woodpecker hits a dead tree and picks up the beat while fiddler ferns begin fiddling in the fields. Who wants to dance? Not I, says the shy garden snake slithering into the old stone fence.

Marsh marigolds manifest themselves in the marshes by the middle of May. And who can tell just when butterflies came flitting, fluttering in, unleashing their multi-colored patterned wings? All this profusion of color and wings and petals and warm light.

May meandering toward Memorial Day—D day, the first summer invasion of tourists. Mosquitoes, moths, frogs, sailboats in the bay. That's dew in the morning now, no more frost.

Then the cherry blossoms arrive just in time (followed by apple blossoms), lighting up the landscape like clusters of snowflakes held still . . .

> Many, many things
> they bring to mind—
> cherry blossoms!

wrote Basho in Japan in 1686 in his world, being *this* world, forever now.

Lady slippers, lily-of-the-valley, luna moths all in one time.

Wild asparagus, wild columbine, wild strawberries make their debut.

The earth warming in the day, the cool air from the lake moving in over it at night, masquerading the land in the gentle laying and lifting of mysterious, soft violet scarves.

The air will be drowsy with the smell of lilacs in a few days, and an unidentified man shall be found drunk in a bed of forget-me-nots so blue he's sure they belong to the eyes of a women he once loved.

May 22nd: The temperature at night drops to the 30's. The furnace goes on. All morning long the wind practices its November song. From somewhere on a back hook of the closet, I resurrect my down vest.

Everyone in town looks depressed. The day is as gray as our hearts.

In Al's there's talk of when the ice might be moving back in.

If the truth be known, spring never settles in Door county at all.

Mostly it's the way we remember and imagine things elsewhere.

Mostly around here, it's always winter on our minds.

190

Summer Gone

Summer Gone

Looking forward and back . . .

Labor Day marks the end. The slow dying time again.

But for some, May marks the beginning. Cherry blossom time. The orchards are all popcorn; the bees are doing what bees are supposed to do. The sleeping peninsula, having shed its dull, icy edges some time ago, yawns, lets loose a sparkling blue aura all around it, breathes deep an intensive green of maple, pine, birch, feels earth (and stone) upturn, speckled with wildflowers and the wings of birds and butterflies in fluttering color. The sun shines. Consistently. (Almost.)

For some it begins then.

For me it may begin with Al heaving his goats upon the roof, and my not being able to get past the crowd in the lobby to reach my reserved stool at the counter for a cup of coffee. Or Tony Demarinis opening his door, where I elbow my way in and find myself (a wasted man who has weathered another Door County winter in the absence of homemade pizza, Tony-style) suddenly coming alive again as I sink my teeth into hot, juicy, spicy, simmering tomato sauce and cheese, Italian sausage, and crunchy crust. In a few minutes flat I have swallowed the sun, breathe oregano, and speak Italian.

"How's a pizza?" smiles Tony, who always smiles. A genuine, generous, good and gracious human being.

"As good as summer. I'll be back" (every week, sometimes two or three times a week, gathering Italian sausage strength and spicy memories for the long, bleak, bland winter ahead which follows the short, hot summer just beginning).

Wilson's is another early warning signal. The return of the ice cream cone and an Ephraim sunset while licking the chocolate, black cherry, and mint chip off the fingers.

Summer is an appetite.

I think of it often, in and out of season.

It's difficult for those who live in Door County the year round to describe the mania that takes hold of this place and how we are all swept away, inundated, with both the dramatic changes in nature in this time, and a mind-boggling influx of tourists (including relatives, friends,

195

unexpected/uninvited guests) all in a brief span of less than three months, after nine months of "peace" and relative nothingness—a stillness of winter close to death, and the dreary, drizzly aftermath called April, May, and June.

Come summer it's like walking around blindfolded and suddenly having one's vision restored.

The difference between solitary confinement and freedom.

Strolling and running; walking backwards and leaping forward; closing doors, opening them; Gills Rock, Wisconsin, and New York City; day and night, black and white, down and up, then and now. Future shock.

The beginning of each summer, however, is marked too by the doubting Thomases, the business people, the cherry growers, any and all with a stake in the Door (even the man-on-the-street), who mill around gloomily speculating if it's going to be a good summer or not. Everything seems a bad omen in June.

I listen to their fearful talk, smile, say nothing.

Maybe ten years ago there was a nervousness in the Door County air because everyone in America, it seemed, was hell-bent on a European summer vacation. "It ain't gonna be as good as last year, let me tell you." Then there was the fear that the revolution, of sorts, of the late 60's would keep all urban America home, protecting or putting out the home-fires. "It ain't gonna be as good as last year, let me tell you." Enter the Hippies, who just might foul up Door's summer economy, followed by Lyndon Johnson, the Vietnam war, Nixon, Watergate, the gas crisis, Carter's catastrophic inflation bringing on ruin and deprivation, followed by Reaganomics.

In between there was always the Wisconsin Dells to wonder about ("Damn Dells keeps pullin 'em in every summer"). And if there was no fear left but fear itself, there were always the idiosyncrasies of Door County weather—too wet or too cold some summers. (According to one old timer it once snowed in Bailey's Harbor on the 4th of July.) "It ain't gonna be as good as last year, let me tell you."

No, it just keeps getting better! I want to shout by the end of June when I have to squeeze my way past a thickness of camera-clicking, goat-dazed early summer tourists, shoving and nudging my way to a spot at the counter where hopefully maybe one empty stool awaits me with just enough space to slightly open the pages of the morning paper, sip coffee with my elbow in my stomach, and read about how gas prices are reducing summer tourism all over America.

These goat-loving visitors must be reading a different newspaper, I tell myself.

The forces of summer (both natural and manmade) begin to gather by mid-June, peaking (for the first time) on the 4th of July and continually peaking on through Labor Day.

If you live in Door, you notice yourself beginning to shed a little clothing in June. Short-sleeve weather at last. And there's an outside chance that your own white winter flesh may take on a little burn and give way to tan.

Nights, though, Door's speciality in summertime, remain cool, and one finds himself with the windows wide opened, comfortably blanketed in the early hours of morning.

June, in your own mind, in your own actions, remains a place of uncertainty. The visitors (to the county, to your own house) have not quite arrived. You're still trying to shake a desolate and vague memory of winter that refuses to melt in your head.

There's the garden to think about, the earth to turn, seeds to plant. Some of the days out there are filled with warmth spreading over the tired back, as one bends over the soil with muddy hands dreaming of summer days just ahead and a garden rampant with onions, radishes, cucumbers, beans, peas . . . and oh for some juicy, fresh red tomatoes after ten months of eating store-bought ones, the color of dead light bulbs.

The trilliums have come and gone, the robins are already nesting, the roadside is dappled in the splendor of yellow and orange hawkweed, prairie rose, daisies, goat's beard, forget-me-not blue, while wild strawberries begin to inherit the earth, close-at-hand, begging to be seen and soon tasted.

The sky, too, seems intent upon being bluer than robins' eggs, the air fresher tasting than November's first snowflake on the tongue, and the water of the lakes and bays glistens in the gladness of light. One feels a desire (not quite a passion—yet) to just be out there, more and more, in the midst of it all. And no house (new and beautiful, old and quaint, condo hum and drum) can quite contain a man once summer calls.

You begin to lose track of days.

Start with the sunrise, either over Lake Michigan at Europe, Rowley's, or Moonlight Bay. Or over the fields, the farms, the quiet back roads that speak so naturally of Door.

If you're lucky enough to be deep into the country of Door, you may hear a cock crow, a robin sing, a jay screech, a crow caw, a rose breasted grosbeak lilt, or just *see* an oriole, a thrasher, a goldfinch, a cardinal, a meadowlark, a killdeer, a pine siskin, a bluebird, a waxwing, etc. Tree swallows flash an irridescent blue-green above the garden, weaving the morning sun in their own meaningful way; gulls flap inward from the lake, sometimes crying for joy in the shimmering whiteness of their angled wings.

I speak of munificence, now. The growing momentum of morning, of summer somersaulting into July . . . .

Of the 8 a.m. ferry boat run from Gills Rock to Washington Island, the coming and going of them all day long, the cars and trucks and campers lined up like there's no tomorrow, the people milling about, bikers, hikers, motorcyclers, all seeking a summer's escape to an island, many for no other reason than because it's there! (Some will return with the usual complaint: "There's nothing there." But of course, they missed it entirely.)

(And on Friday night of the Labor Day weekend, cars and campers will be lined up a mile or more down 42, and the ferry will run all through the night and the next morning before the line disappears.) Ah, summer's end. But not yet.

There's more to Gills Rock (the invisible metropolis at the Top O' The Thumb, visible only in summer) than the ferry boat connection to Washington Island, "North of the Tension Line." There's the fine potter, Thor (Larry Thoreson of Gills Rock Stoneware), the Yankee Clipper and the Bounty (excursion boats) and smoked fish for sale and the faithful fishing tug Faith II and the charter fishing boats; there's the Shoreline Restaurant-Motel, Fish Boil, gift shop, gas pump, etc. And Gills Rock (not much bigger than the top of your thumb) all goes a little crazy on a summer's day, with the traffic funneling into a one-way frenzy (hardly room to turn, to park for free, to stay). There are some tourists, I've heard tell, who found themselves Shanghaied on a ferry to the Island all because they were in the wrong line.

And this is only the *tip* of the ice . . . I mean, peninsula, in the peak of the hot season.

Working my way toward Ellison Bay now, a mid-morning summer's day, stuck behind the incredible swaying hulk of a Winnebago blocking my view, O woe is me, from all the fields green and ripening into hay . . . wrathful little Winnebago kids sticking their tongues out at me . . . gotta pass this motha before he ruins my whole summer day. Into the local post office then, filled with strangers buying stamps for Wish-You-Were-Here post cards while I wait in line wishing they were there.

Into Newman's Pioneer Store for my morning paper . . . squeezing, stretching my arm past three bunches of rotund strangers who have commandeered the counter with one piece of fruit in each hand, their eyes on the antiqued walls and ceiling, gawking like this sure ain't a Jewel supermarket in Chicago. "Excuse me, excuse me, that's my hand. All I want is my *Trib* and a daily ration of good cigars. No, no, don't say it!"

"What do you people do around here all winter?"

We manufacture T-shirts that say WHERE THE HELL IS ELLISON DAY ANYWAY?

Outside again, across the street, people are sulking around the two phone booths, and the phones, as usual, are mostly not working in summer—or any other season of the year. (Someday I must write that saga: "Telling it to General Tel and Tel!")

Figure it this way, I console a man about to take a borrowed hammer from Kenny's bustling Gobel Mobil filling station to convince the operator that he can't hear his party and he's already paid through the nose twice, but she can't hear his final futile plea, and now the operator's voice is fading, and the man is about to cry (or kill his first telephone) . . . figure you came here to Door to get away from it all, I tell him, and the phone company is merely obliging.

Outside Shirley Till's Olde Ellison Bay Shop, Mike Till, designer-in-residence, sets his tourist tempting cigar store-type Indian in place, whispering in his ear: "Scalp any little bastard who tries to pull your braids, tweak your nose, poke your eyes, or sit in your lap!"

The Ellison Bay tennis courts are hopping with players, while bathers are already beginning to gather at the beach. In three more hours—from 1 till 5 o'clock—the sand will be covered with mostly bare bodies—small, medium, and extra large—the water filled with waders, floaters, splashers, jumpers, divers, swimmers, screamers, and a few dangerous motor boats always edging their way in toward the beach to dock, too close for comfort for the little bathers especially, polluting the beach water with lovely little rainbow slick calling cards.

On top of Hanson's panoramic Ellison Bay hill, some serious visiting photographers are at hand (they are always at hand at this vista) carefully, conscientiously, religiously focusing their Kodak Instamatics at the overwhelming view of hill, pond, bay, cliff, water, horizon, cloud, sky, determined to get it all in. You might as well take a picture of the bottom of your shoe, I think to myself, for all the reality you think you're going to capture in that shot.

The sun is maybe 10:30 o'clock high by now, losing some of its early morning softness, moving into a stark, highnoon yellow-white. I proceed, with summer abandon, down 42, past Wink Larson's Orchards, nearing the late Doc Farmer's place, on my normal Sister Bay morning run, though not so normal in summer with so many indeterminate factors (hordes of summer visitors) likely to play havoc with my daily routine.

Like the guy in front of me, from Iowa, who has just hit the brakes, pulled to the side of the road, while wife, children, aunts, uncles, grandma and grandpa emerge to stand before a red ripe cherry orchard and have their picture taken.

Nearing the hill (driving south) that marks my final descent (plunge) into Sister Bay in the heat of a summer's day, I take note that Caleb Johnson is at it again, manicuring the landscape around his house this day, as every day, every season but winter (when he probably arranges the snow to look better) in a *Better Homes and Gardens* picture of perfection that would drive me mad, but seems to give Caleb peace and reason for being (retired) in Door County, so who am I to judge? I just blow my horn at him in passing, but the horn never works, so I wave my hand, but he never notices because he's forever facing the earth, pulling an errant weed that should know better than rear its ugly leaf on Caleb Johnson's smooth turf.

The car and driver roll, then, into downtown Sister Bay, still a bare minimum of traffic on the "outskirts" (the hill to where Clean Piece Wally Mickelson held court in Lundh's Used Car lot) and suddenly (somewhere around the marina and the Bakery of Sister Bay) I enter a conglomeration of parked cars and inch-by-inch moving traffic that bears a close resemblance to rush hour traffic in Milwaukee or Chicago.

The mania begins: this can't be Sister Bay where the hell are all these people coming from?

The panic continues: my body is in sore need of its regular morning fix of caffeine, ala Al Johnson's, and I can barely see the goats on the roof from this vantage point of bumper traffic, though, of course, some of the hold-up in movement this (most, from now on) summer morning is the gaper's block in front of the world's most renowned grass roof, with people packed in both lines of traffic, smiling, pointing, staring. (And we all know what they're saying.)

To that classic used, abused, tired touristic profundity: WHAT DO PEOPLE DO AROUND HERE ALL WINTER? we now add a second worn and wondrous insight: LOOK AT THE GOATS ON THE ROOF!

I make a mental note for Mike Till to put out a whole band of Indians—on his roof—while continuing to inch my way past Al's, hot on a search for a parking space, which I eventually discover somewhere behind the Sister Bay Post Office between a picnic bench and a cedar tree.

Walking toward the main stream of Sister Bay life, I figure I might call my agent in New York and propose a novel called THE GOATS OF SUMMER, and while climbing over parked cars and two lanes of start-and-stop traffic to get at the phones across the street, I find a small and sullen crowd gathered around the two doorless phone booths (removed, compliments of General Tel and Tel) with both booths occupied by callers screaming over the din of traffic, less than 5 feet away) and the push of waiting tourists anxious to get to the phones and scream next.

In need of a coffee fix, I check Johnny's Cottage Restaurant, but they are packing them in there. No chance for a cup of coffee and Flossie Elquist's homemade pie.

Gotta get going. Gotta get to Al's. Moving into the flow of streetwalkers now, all headed for either Krist's or Al's, I am carried along swiftly and then abruptly deposited among the throngs of goat worshippers, shutter flippers, snap shooters, photo freaks all trying to record for posterity (and that handful of folks back home who have never seen a goat on a roof in Door County in summer) *their* private vision.

"Look at the . . . "

Yeah, yeah, lady, I just want a cup of coffee. Excuse me, please. Pardon me. Oh, I'm sorry . . . excuse me . . .

The Great Wall of China you can at least walk, while the great wall of goat-worshippers remains solid. I push and shove my way amongst the legion of admirers while they gather and look and wait to be nearer to Al Johnson's famous Swedish pancakes and Ingert Johnson's beautiful boutique.

Bad omen: the tour buses are in; the street, the lot is full of them; people are walking around with these happy yellow badges proclaiming I GOT AWAY FROM IT ALL and their names while going ga-ga over the goats and waiting to be served their Swedish pancakes. The wait, at this moment in time, is something like three days, by any reasonable estimate, in any reasonable restaurant. But this is not a reasonable scene as Al, in his customary whirlwind, clears tables faster than Houdini and can actually keep ahead of the buses. Yet all of this matters nought to me, struggling to squeeze my way past the hostess and the cashier to see if there is any possibility for an open stool at the counter. Perhaps an I GOT AWAY FROM IT ALL person passed away and really got away from it all.

Not a chance.

The inevitable moment of July Door County truth has been reached. "They" are here. The pinnacle of summer has arrived and will be with us (me) till the day after Labor Day, and there is no more room at the inn. In resignation I turn (stepping on toes, and stepped upon), push, squeeze, squirm my way back to some living breathing space outside (usually in front of Casperson's Funeral Home), ending up at Kenneavy's Kitchen of Sister Bay, outside or inside, licking my wounds, physical and psychic, with a chocolate donut and a cup of coffee. Goatdom be damned. Once again my routine is destroyed. My seat at Al's usurped. My newspaper unread.

Moments later I drift a bit in downtown Sister Bay, stopping at Krist's, where the checkout lines are comparable to the lines of traffic outside, and where the Checkout Queen, Eleanor Bowers, manages to stay on top of it all and sometimes smile.

And then across the street again—whenever there's a break in the traffic—to pay Helen Carlson a visit at the library, to pay another installment on the copying machine (which, by any account, belongs to me after four or five years of maybe 4,000 pages at 10¢ a sheet), followed by maybe a little shopping at the Cove, Passtimes, Jungwirth's, and Bunda's. Retrieving my car, stopping off to see Lyle at the Sister Bay Co-op to argue over the price of everything; making another weekly appointment for an overhaul with the manic mechanic and laughing man, Gene Olson of Olson's to patch up my 90,000 mile engine one more time ("You think it'll last now, Gene?" A dead serious expression on his face: "Sure . . . about another week," followed by his laughter—sounding something like a cross between a machine gun and a cackle—followed by a joke, unprintable); then maybe another deposit/withdrawal visit at the local bank where the congenial lady tellers—Sweet Lucy and Smiling Ruth—somehow maintain a friendly disposition through the terrors of tourist banking, though if the truth were known I suspect they take turns going into the depths of the vault box room to let out an occasion scream . . . which, I have been informed, the hostess of the Hotel Du Nord is wont to do on a summer's evening after the 50th person has asked her for the 150th time: "Is our table ready yet? You said about an hour, an hour and a half ago!" Exit calm hostess to the interior of the kitchen for a long loud, "AAAAAHHHHhhhhhhhh!" Re-enter hostess with a smile: "Just as soon as the next table of four opens."

Noon. Heading home. To avoid the summer madness on the main drag, I opt for the pure sanity of the backroads where I am amazed, as always, to find the innocence of the county relatively intact. Amazed how so few of the summer tourists ever venture beyond their lifeline, highways 42 or 57. Amazed to realize once more how so few of them really know what this county is all about. And I think I'll keep it a secret, finding the true pulse of this county on these backroads which, if one is really in touch with the inner geography of things, lead everywhere to the true source of this county's magic.

Lunch is brief, a momentary pleasure, often fresh produce from the garden and little more . . . Swiss chard, spinach, lettuce, radishes. Whatever's in season. Strawberries. Whatever's there—eat, enjoy. Time to sit down. And time to run. For it is not the body that demands nourishment so much in the season of summer as the spirit.

Summer is also a thirst. The sun calls: boating, sailing, water skiing, fishing, golfing, tennis, biking, hiking, kiting, gardening, sunning, swimming. To be out there *alive,* taking it all in. If winter diminishes us, turns us inward and makes philosophers of us all, summer expands our vision, releases us, makes gods of us all.

No time to eat. Gotta run! Gotta go! To do it all now, *everything*, while it lasts. Both the tourist, with his precious two weeks, and the Door County resident, well aware of the inevitable onrush of fall/winter, unconsciously adhere to that old Far Eastern dictum: the time is now.

The sun is high. The temperature is rising. And if there is one thing about this county that raises the beauty of the landscape to the ethereal, that baptizes it in a translucency of light that lends grace to the beholder—it is water. Call it a peninsula, call it an island. Bays, lakes, creeks, canals, marshes, a river—it is a floating world anyway you look at it. And in summer, of all seasons, we truly enter the setting and become one.

Whether a man or woman stand on a beach and merely watch a sunrise or sunset; whether one crosses by ferry to Washington Island; whether you fish it, boat it, scuba dive it, ski it, canoe it, sail it, swim it, or fly above it, it is the water, always the water that calls whatever the spirit within us to come and commune in this most sacred and primeval of all elements.

And so in summer, we live in water. Even the welcoming rain is different here, purifying, smelling of clean sky, cedar woods, fresh earth. The lightning storms, dramatic. Thunder, magnificent. And rainbows (sometimes two at a time, as a late afternoon in August this year) magical.

There is *nothing* like Europe Bay beach, Newport beach, Whitefish Bay, the sand beaches on Washington and Rock Islands . . . the cool clear water on a hot summer afternoon.

So you go there, and dissolve, or to the village and town beaches on the bays. Or you find your own private place to be at one with the water, anywhere, anyway you choose, even naked to the waters—at the nude bathing beach (which shall remain secret) or making your own.

The sand, the sun, the water. Put them all together they spell summer.

Then a leisurely drive home around 5 o'clock, the sand still clinging to the toes and elbows, a grittiness to the warm, reddening skin, the eyes brighter, a comfort to the body, settling into itself, a coolness as if somehow the clear water of the lake flowed gently beneath the flesh.

In the late afternoon, the fields seem at rest in the summer sun. There is nothing going on but bees, birds, butterflies, a warm breeze and golden light. A biker glides by. And if it is August on Townline Road, Art Simpson is filling his roadside vegetable stand with the most unusual offer to be found anywhere—but Townline Road in Door County. Credit it to that rare, old fashioned quality so little seen among people today, the art of giving and sharing:

FREE, the sign reads. HELP YOURSELF TO THE ITEMS ON THIS TABLE WHICH ARE EXCESS FROM OUR GARDEN. YOU CAN'T BEAT OUR PRICES.

But if there is a slight sense of peace in such a summer afternoon, there is also an anxiety accompanying any summer's morning/afternoon/night that anyone fortunate/unfortunate to own even the slightest piece of Door County earth will recognize. I speak of the *visitors* descending *en masse*. Relatives, friends, friends of friends, passers-by, and total strangers.

They are in your mailbox: "We'll be up the 4th of July weekend. Find us a nice place to stay. Nothing too fancy or expensive. Just so it's clean and reasonable and on the water."

They are on the phone, forever on the phone: "How you been, old buddy? I didn't know you lived in Door County! Yeah, what's-his-name told us. We're over here camping in Peninsula Park and thought we'd drop by tonight. Yeah, just me, the new wife, her three kids, my two from the first marriage, and guess what? I'm a father again! We'll see you around 5 . . . ."

And the phone never stops ringing, July, August, on into September. Maybe it's a long lost relative on the phone: "Sure . . . don't you remember me? I'm your uncle, for crissake! I'm over here in Effram or someplace with Aunt Zelda, my twin German shepherds, Rip and Maul, three cats, and a parakeet. How do we find your place?"

The first summer here, you graciously welcome one and all. The second, you mostly smile and nod. The third, you learn the art of postponement—not today, maybe tomorrow or Saturday. The fourth, you begin telling them how crowded Door County is in summer and reroute them to the Dells. And by the fifth summer, you maybe say to your long lost relative:

Uncle who? I have no uncles (aunts, cousins, brothers, sisters, nieces, nephews, distant friends). How do you find my place? Easy. You take County A to F, pull a right, hook another sharp right on Q about a mile down, grab ZZ, you'll see the sign, to the stoplight, make a left, then go down Airport Road to E. I'm maybe a mile down the road from there. Look forward to seeing you, real soon.

Riiinnnnngggggggg . . .

Says the wife: "It's your mother's neighbor . . . or cousin's boss' daughter . . . or former editor's half-brother's stepson and his spaced out girlfriend of sixteen on a cross-country trek in a van, looking for some free green space to crash till whenever/wherever the spirit moves them next."

I'm not home! I don't live here anymore. The place has been sold and turned into a rural clinic for the treatment of contagious diseases, and you are the director in charge of admissions. I DON'T WANT TO ANSWER THAT GODDAM PHONE AGAIN TILL FEBRUARY! THEN LET THEM COME. THAT'S THE TRUE TEST OF FRIENDSHIP. WILL THEY LOVE ME IN DOOR COUNTY IN WINTER AS MUCH AS THEY LOVE ME IN SUMMER AND FALL?

Yet, if the truth be known, I often enjoy playing tour guide, sharing this setting with friends and strangers who are seeing Door County for the first time. There's an undefinable pleasure in pointing out the people and the places you've known so well, for so long, and discovering it all again with others, suddenly fresh and new now under another summer's sun.

And if the truth be known, one comes to realize his own special vision of the county can never truly be shared. There are some guests who will *never* understand why you live in the woods ("Why don't you cut some of those damn trees down?"); visitors who will always find the beaches of Lake Michigan too cold; friends who see no difference between a trillium and a daisy and frankly don't give a damn.

"How can you *stand* it here, it's so quiet!"

Then go. Get out of here. Leave me be.

And if the truth really be known, there is much to be said for the old Chinese saying that both fish and guests begin to smell after three days (in some instances, three hours).

You come, in time, to respect your own selfishness. Door County, especially in summer, is mine. Come as you are, when you will—but don't tread on me.

In the evenings, especially. The lateness of light in a metallic blue-black sky. The rarity of summering nights in Door. Beginning, perhaps, with an elegant dinner at the Hotel Du Nord before a concert at Birch Creek Farm, the Peninsula Music Festival, or an evening at the Peninsula Players in Fish Creek.

Night picks up where the momentum of morning left off, helter-skeltering a person into countless excitements, a summer's deliriousness, a wanting to taste, touch, feel, see everything.

A Drive-In movie at the Skyway: a Shoreline (or Viking, or White Gull Inn) Fish boil; a sunset off Gills Rock; a moonrise over Europe Bay; a visit with Uncle Tom Collis the pancake man, all dressed in white, closing up the shop, heading down the road to his new home; Go-Karts in Sister Bay; or go buy and fly a kite with Kitemaster Toby Schlick in Fish Creek next to Thumb Fun; an ice cream cone at Wilson's (where for the first time in the recorded history of Ephraim ice cream seekers you've got to take a number and wait till all the ice cream cows come home for your cone and/or wait till wait in line for a mysterious hostess to find you an empty booth, all of which is mass confusion, longer waiting than this body can tolerate, so I either wait in Wilson's and fume, because it's a summer's night tradition I can't shake, or learn to do the Door-Deli in Sister Bay instead for the biggest cone to be created anywhere; maybe a beer at Husby's; a walk through the Walkway . . . "Hello, Gary," of the Eight of Pentacles, "Hello, Grutzmachers" of Passtimes Books, Hello, Sports of All Sorts; and though I could go for a plate of Al Johnson's fried perch or a beef sandwich, the goats will be sleeping, the ducks long gone south, and the moon but a memory before I could ever work my way through that crowd.

How about a soft-cream (chocolate) at the Patio Drive-In? Fine. Or a cocktail at Gordon Lodge, *the* place to drink to the sunset. Or a movie, yes, a movie. Or course, a movie . . . and all summer night's long mania for movies at Andy Redmann's Lake Cinema in Baileys Harbor. Or there's Omnibus; a sub at Digger's; a great hamburger and real french fries at the Alibi Sandwiche Shop; all of Fish Creek at night.

Or all of Baileys Harbor all night long, but especially if it's July and the Birch Creek Farm jazz people (faculty and students) are in town, and *the* place to tune into them (after concert, after hours) with margaritas or what-your-pleasure, is the Common House in Baileys where I've spent many a starspangled night listening to the finest jazz this side of Chicago, St. Louis, or New Orleans, and much of it under the quiet, rocking, driving presence of jazz faculty leader and bass guitar player, Gene Aitken and a superb old sax man, Ben Baldewicz, plus a scraggily bearded guitar player, Fred Hamilton who makes smoke with the strings, and two fabulous young horn players (nameless), one curly-headed trumpet player who straightened his own hair on the high notes, and one dark-haired, mustacioed master of the flugelhorn who, when he was not playing, lapsed with closed eyes into a smiling, swaying dream state, caressing his musical instrument as if it were the most beautiful woman in the world and he loved her/it because together they made music, they made jazz, and they (all of them together) made a summer's night miraculous, as memorable as the margaritas which flowed with the music, or the visiting poet, Dave Etter, who was sure he was visiting another session with Miles Davis, Gerry Mulligan, et. al., or the visiting editor/friend, Ralph Rausch, who matter-of-factly pointed out as we drifted past Al Johnson's later in the heat of the night: "Hey, there's a dead goat on Al's roof."

And the beat goes on and on and on, on a summer's night that seems to never end, all the nights the same yet each unique in certain delights, be it the cool wind moving through the dark pines, the shadowed flight or call of the bat, the nighthawk, the whippoorwill . . . crickets, mosquitoes, frogs, moths, coons, skunks; the deer in your headlights on the side of the road; the lights of a freighter passing through Death's Door; or Gust Klenke, the honey man, walking to the store in the dark with his dog. All the quiet motion. The county asleep in the stillness of the midnight hour.

Looking forward and back . . . Here now. And gone.

The ending amidst us though we never quite see it. Refuse to recognize the signs.

The beginning of the end is a presence sometimes as early as mid July, up in the very tops of maple trees. One branch, only one . . . sometimes the very smallest . . . the green already turning to gold and red.

Still we revel, blindly, through August, the month that pulls the quickest disappearing act in the year.

For some it's all over when they begin to see the goldenrod in the field. For some it's all over when the sun just isn't hitting the same angle on the beach in August the way it did in July, and the water seems suddenly colder.

For most summer people and visitors it's Labor Day and Labor Day only that signals: The End. And the cars and trailers and vans, stretching from here to the Illinois state line beat a slow and sad retreat home, determined to be born again in Door County come next summer.

And for some it isn't all over till the last Illinois license plate crosses the Sturgeon Bay bridge, south, at 6 a.m. or so on the day after Labor Day.

For me it's all over at 10:30 a.m. that same day after Labor Day morning when I stroll directly to the counter of Al Johnson's, nod hello to Al and some of the regulars, open my newspaper, see a smiling waitress named Jill, or Denise, or Annika pour a cup of hot black coffee before me and ask:

"Where you been all summer?"

Around.

The Season of Looking Back

The Season of Looking Back

It's the one season in Door, even in the midst of it, we are always looking back upon. Each September reminds us of every September in our life, and it is always a long, long way from May to September. There is an immediancy to the time bordering upon a threat: it seems to grab us by the throat to say: What's gone is gone. What lies ahead is no surprise. So be it.

Labor Day brings the first chilly wind out of the north to sweep all the tourists south, back home to where they came from. It clears the heads of natives and outsiders as well with a freshness, a new start. The setting is itself again. As my late friend Chet Elquist used to say, "It's nice to have the county to ourselves again." In this way, *only*, is the old once again new.

What holds us most in those early days of September is how summer still lingers here and there: a warm morning through the countryside—just like July, you'd swear; a day of such absolute stillness you *know* you're part of every birch and maple, every milkweed plant . . . the same old rhythm of it all; a night of such a miracle of moon you feel free to run across a field, touch it, put both your arms around it and carry it home for keeps.

But there are gentle reminders that fall is fickleness at best. The waters of the bays may still look most inviting, but you really don't venture in for a swim anymore. Oh, maybe a day or two soon after Labor Day, when your head is still wrapped in summer, and your body retains an August warmth. You meet the waters of Europe Bay full force, delighting in the privacy of a beach you can now call your own once more. ("Come on in! You see, it's warm. It's summer still.") Only the next afternoon you notice you've gone in only knee-deep. And a day or so later, you don't get your feet wet at all. (How does the body know the time is ended?) Better now to walk the beach alone. Take pleasure in the seeing, the sound of water whispering in sand, stone, rock and shore.

Summer calls to enter, to come inside—the water, the woods, the earth, the fields, the day, the night. Autumn says, "Look, but don't get too friendly. I am not what I seem to be.

"I am the color of flowers cool and fading. I am birds who have all suddenly turned gray. I am chipmunks and squirrels and mice foraging. I am insects disappearing—webs unravelled, flies caught dizzily dancing behind warm panes of glass, caterpillars transformed to butterflies, I am changing, moving, dying . . .

"I am all this and yet more."

Autumn notes, sight, sound, smell: leaves changing color, leaves sounding their death rattle in the wind, leaves rotting in the rain. Putrefaction of the roadside, the fields, the forest floor.

Contrast: death in the midst of fields still shimmering in the light of goldenrod, mullein, and the luminous lavender of wild aster, one of the last flowers to go.

Contrast: maple trees glowing against the ominous gray clouds, gray wind, gray rain. Days flipping back and forth . . . "like" summer, "like" fall . . . but which one, *really* . . . and why now, in late September, the rumblings of a good old summer thunderstorm coming through the back door?

And just what is that fear that seems to settle in and chill these bones?

A time for the air to define itself in a mist, a haze in the lowlands of the morning and evening fields, swamps, and shores. Silver evaporating in sunlight. Silver polished by the moon. Either the warm earth and the cool air, or the cool air and the warm earth. A dialogue of moisture, and farewells. A season, again, unsure of itself, but assuredly turning away from us.

The windows of the house grow foggy with condensation.

Darkness comes early.

Shaggy mane mushrooms are up.

The furnace goes on.

It's time for baking bread.

Kohlrabi, cabbages, carrots, beets, rooted firmly to the earth. Red and white potatoes hidden in their dark pockets of soil. Acorn squash in armor plate. Pumpkins bursting their confines, gorged in color and shape of the distant September sun. Grapes in gobs, purple and violet, hang ready, though still tart to the taste.

The garden thins under the threat of frost. Green grow the tomatoes (by tons) in all of Door through September . . . the season for tomatoes always too short. So one savors the red of the juiciest, ripest August tomato and plays games with the season's cool sun moving further and further away.

Time now for all the paraphernalia of protection: rugs, rags, bedspreads, old blankets, plastic, bushel baskets to cover the tomatoes at night, to keep faith in the morning's sun. Maybe, *maybe* another sweet red delicious juicy-tasting tomato that weeps when you cut into it. Maybe, just maybe one or a dozen more before the killer frost does them all in for good.

Die-hard gardeners, unable to resign themselves to waste, will pick the tomatoes green, cook them, preserve them, keep them in that way. Still others will pursue one of a hundred old wive's tales: "You pick them green, and you wrap each tomato in newspaper, store them in the cellar or garage where they will slowly begin to ripen. And when you have a taste for a good tomato, you unwrap one, eat it, and it's just as good and juicy as a summer ripe tomato off the vine."

To which I reply, B.S. Green tomatoes wrapped in newspaper taste like green tomatoes wrapped in newspaper. They taste like what the stores in these parts pass off for tomatoes all winter. They taste like green, slightly yellowed rubber. They taste like pharmaceutical cotton. They taste like dishwater with seeds. They taste like green tomatoes that grew too large too late to be touched by Door County's summer sun.

Only the sunflowers understand it's September. They've lost track of the sun, shed their fire, and mourn the time, leaning and bent, their heads hung low like bearded old men, their faces all gone to seed.

And what is that fear again that shadows the heart on an autumn's eve? The whippoorwill's call grows distant. Bats sweep the twilight scavenging for whatever remains. A few stray moths at midnight, frantic at the screen near my reading lamp, give their autumn leaf wings rest for a moment, their eyes two pin-pricks of fire.

But oh, come October . . . and still looking back.

In the city of my youth, in the neighborhood, in Chicago, I loved this falling month most of all. Loved the smell of burning leaves along all the gutters of my neighborhood streets. Loved the gray October days in downtown Chicago. Loved the ride there on the El, the World Series time, the people of the Loop going about their business: the newsies, the cops, the clerks, the waitresses, the panhandlers. Grant Park, Michigan Avenue, the river, the lake, the museums, the Art Institute, the Library, the book-stores—all of it caught in that peculiar city-light of October, the wind and the skyscraper sun.

"An October city," Nelson Algren called it. "An October sort of city even in spring. With somebody's washing always whipping, in smoky October colors off the third-floor rear by that same wind that drives the yellowing comic strips down all the gutters that lead away from home."

And here, "away from home," here in Door in October, though I remember with fondness the grayness of Chicago, it's the brightness of sky, of sun, a preciousness of autumn light I've come to see and know and love and call October. Five glorious days of it this year, this October. Five in a row . . . "The light! The light! The light!" I read from my notes. The light held in the blazing sugar maple trees. The yellow light glowing in the spade-shaped birch leaf, luminous, even in falling, even in rain, spangling the roadside and forest floor in a glistening tapestry of pieces of an old setting sun.

Then the tops of all the trees slowly opened by the wind . . . a veritable rain of leaves, of light drifting both through a wider landscape unveiling old horizons, and down the branches to the lower leaves, the trunk, the ground.

We breathe light in these times, and the fields, burnished, brassy, welcome us with the shapes of plants, once green, caught still . . . with seeds, thorns, the open hollow sound of milkweed pods in wind, like wings of stationary birds . . . and the drifting down of milkweed seed, the stuff of dreams.

Apples. Thanks to Eve they haunt us yet. Echoes of the Fall to tempt the taste of any man. Delicious, Cortland, Jonathon, McIntosh, Greening . . . even an apple some poet dubbed "Snow." Wild apple trees along the road. A huge barrel of apples outside Larson's Orchards near Ellison Bay—Help yourself. Free. Compliments of Door County's die-hard Democrat, Winky Larson.

If summer tells the story of cherries in these parts, autumn is an allegory to apples up and down the peninsula. Apple juice, apple cider, apple pie, apple slices, apple sauce, apple cobbler, apple butter, apple dumplings. Apples to put in a child's lunch, to put on the teacher's desk, to keep the doctor away. Apples to polish on the sleeve of your shirt. Apples to dunk for. Taffy apples. Apples to sink your teeth into with a snapping sound, tast the white meat, the juice, split the seeds and toss the core away. Apple of my eye. Apples, "keepers" like Cortlands to store in the cellar and leisurely draw upon deep into winter, to remember the taste of fall once again, to linger by a fire of apple wood.

> Remember Johnny Appleseed
> All ye who love the apple;
> He served his kind by Word and Deed,
> In God's grand greenwood chapel.
> —William Henry Venable

Fall in the towns and villages of Door? When Tony Demarinis posts a sign in the window that the end of October will be the end of pizza for another year. When restaurants such as Johnny's Cottage go on half-time. When the lights go out for good at Andy Redmann's Lake Cinema and all the film freaks go cold turkey. When Ephraim's dock and harbor is suddenly barren of all the bobbing white boats. When yellow schoolbuses crawl along the back roads once more. When Al Johnson's Swedish Restaurant is crowded mostly on weekends. When Lucy Sohns of the Ellison Bay branch of the Bank of Sturgeon Bay says, "Have some free coffee and donuts. This is our last day."

It's all over. Fini. THE END? But no, not just yet.

If the Indians found a brief and second summer in autumn, so did Sister Bay.

Enter a madness beyond measure: Fall Festival in Sister Bay. Summer, Part II. When all the people we thought we left behind, beyond, far over and past the Sturgeon Bay bridge return for encores. In droves . . . cars, buses, trailers, campers, pickups, planes, motorcycles, mo-peds, U-Hauls and 10-speed bikes. For what? For Fall Festival. Something the local businessmen drummed up years ago as a kind of private celebration in thanks for a successful summer season of mucho tourism. Some bratwurst, some beer, a few rides, a little music, a little home-style parade, an authentic local production of a big time Broadway musical. Not Munich's Octoberfest exactly, but small town enough for here, every fall when the leaves were at their color best, somewhere around the second week in October. And so it went. And so it goes. And so, once again, we witness innocence turn slowly/quickly into a bit of a monster, something like what's become of Thanksgiving and Christmas. You begin with a turkey or a bright star and before you know it you've got an extravaganza on your hands.

In the immortal words of Al Johnson (who can sometimes be seen on his own roof in Fall Fest time, holding and hugging his goats, protecting them from parades and falling ping pong balls): "It's outa hand! Somebody's gonna get killed."

(I think he was referring to the quaint custom of a helicopter flying a few feet over the main drag of downtown Sister Bay dropping thousands of ping pong balls—some of them redeemable at the local merchants—while tots, children, teenagers, mothers, fathers, aunts, uncles, grandmas, grandpas, visiting senior citizens, rekindle their animal instincts in a mass assault of pushing, shoving, shouting, lurching, grabbing, gouging, stepping, stomping, diving, blocking, stealing, snatching, flattening—usually tots and children—each other in hot pursuit of the ubiquitous magic ping pong ball that just might be their ticket to heaven—or a free hamburger.)

Fun at the Fall Festival? You bet your life. You certainly do.

Each year I vow never to return to Sister Bay again under such circumstance, and each year I somehow get caught up in some of the madness—just to see if it's *still happening,* I tell myself.

There's the Cake Walk and dance in the village hall on Friday night, the carnival rides for kids and all, all weekend. The craftspeople peddling their wares from booths—everything from log splitters to silver jewelry to downhome kitchen kitsch, like owls made of neon yarn you couldn't imagine anyone wanting or buying—but they do. And then there's the parade come Saturday—ah, the parade—and the church of your choice on Sunday.

I love a parade. All the world does. They start sometime in May around here, in every village, hamlet, town of Door for one "celebration" or another—Jacksonport has its Maifest, Ellison Bay its Olde Ellison Bay Days, Ephraim its Fyr-Bal (one town has even begun one now in winter); the biggest and the best is usually the 4th of July parade in Baileys Harbor.

But the real beauty of them all (and if you look real close, you'll see) is it's pretty much the same damn parade with most of the major participants taking a few days breather before they go marching up and down the peninsula once more.

Homemade parades, I call them. One tractor after another with an occasional pickup truck in between. Hard candy tossed to the kids. Makeshift floats of hay wagons decorated in the living branches of cherry, apple, birch and maple trees. Some antique cars of the local buffs, stored in their barns all year. A lumber truck. A fire engine. Signs here and there on most of the vehicles advertising services and merchandise of the local kind. Sometimes a politician or two. Sometimes a King and Queen of the festivity, or even a Chief. Good old Zero, Door County's resident clown, handshaking the kids, hugging the adults, fooling with us all. Uncle Sam on stilts. One sort-of-local high school marching band. A couple of horses doing their stuff. The sound of that old steam threshing machine with Tiny om-pa-pahing on the tuba, and the polka stomping music setting our feet to dancing. Some kids on crepe-papered bikes picking up the pieces at the end, cause hell, who wants any parade to end? And why can't we be in it too? And always a few stray dogs representing each town. And finally Baldy the Sheriff in the police car (either at the head or the end of a parade) calling to his friends, joking with them through the bullhorn.

Come Fall Festival, here comes the parade again, about the same as before. Some of the local folks are certainly recognizable: "There's Johnny Bean, my bus driver, driving his dump truck!" one kid yells. "Here comes the Haunted House hearse and Dracula from Thumb Fun!" "Hey look," says one tourist to another, "they're throwing apples from that float down there." "Yeah," says the other, "I hear they got a bumper crop this year."

Having OD'ed on parades and tourists for the year, I push my way toward the relative sanity/sanctuary of the Sister Bay library to leaf through old and new magazines, make another payment on my copying machine, and small talk away the final momentous moments of the parade with the librarian, Helen Carlson. Only to discover she's *listening* to it on WDOR radio! The Sister Bay Fall Festival parade, narrated by . . . well, who else? And how could I ever forget that voice? Yep, the inimitable, unmistakeable, 'hereeees Wally!" (Mickelson) giving a float by friend by float description, highlighted by his incredible laugh, "heh, heh, heh!"

I toss in the magazines, the books, the towel. It's no use, I can't escape. I'm a prisoner of the parade till the final float creeps by, the last dog barks, the crowds, the cars, all of it thins out. I try a little popcorn. A bratwurst here, a beer there. I run into Evie and Harvey Olson from up my way who confess they're caught up in it all too: "Just having a ball looking at the people," Evie says. The weather's turned cold. We stand and talk and stare. Harvey mentions how hard the wind is beginning to flow, looks up into the sky and says: "The gulls are flying backwards."

Backwards indeed, into fall, that penultimate time when the season of a man's life is tinged with regret and intimations of The End, in all its guises, be it winter or the final breath.

So the gulls are flying backwards, the ducks are waddling around

Casperson's Funeral Home and Al's pond with a vision of ice in their eyes, the Canada geese (first sighting, October 1, this year) are honking overhead and south again in their own inimitable pattern from and to the past, while the tourists prepare to depart en masse on the final day of Fall Festival leaving the rest of us here to cope with it "all," with what's left or dying in whatever time is left, whatever mood, sense of loss, the landscape leaves us.

October: cold, gray, overcast days . . . wind storms to strip the trees bare . . . where has everyone gone? . . . nobody's home . . . a single robin spotted on the road. The sun, when it does appear, shines in a most miraculous way.

I am driving the sunny Sunday back roads of the peninsula's center in autumn's dying days, passing the Zion Methodist Church, 9 a.m. worship service, Pastor Joseph Burke. The setting is so pure Americana I have to rub my eyes. It's all the quiet countryside and innocent white frame church steeple scenes we've ever known or seen to be New England here in the heart of the Midwest: perfect white church, perfect blue roof and blue sky touched with perfect puffs of clouds. It's a picture postcard scene sold in all the local giftshops. It's a calendar photograph depicting the month of October hanging on our kitchen walls. It's 100 proof Door County. Pure fantasy. It's what this countryside was, a long, long time ago. Only it's here and now, as well as then, all of it very real and true.

I park the car to verify the scene, to orient myself.

There are nine cars in the parking lot. The maple trees along the road blaze in red and gold against the blue sky, the white church, the distant farms and fields. A slight wind stirs the trees, spreads the llight, coaxes the clouds along.

I pause before the closed doors of the country church, hear a muffled hymn of the morning worshippers, but do not go in. The hymn for me is here outside, the perfect moment of this place.

In the small graveyard just beyond, I read the townspeople's names, and recall a fragment of a Dave Etter poem: "I return now/to muse among/these gravestones/The proud names/bang in my ears/like screen doors/ . . ."

Looking back . . . doors closing . . . banging shut . . . falling . . . .

The first snow showers . . .

The change in time, pushing the hour back to where? to when?

Darkness grows early and defines the whole day.

The spotters are on my road again at night, checking the movement of deer in the woods. The shots ring out in November; Thanksgiving . . . the killing of the deer.

The road crew weaves the windy fields with a rhythm of faded snow-fences, marked with a broken yet perfect huge white D.

"In moments of tense depression, natural things, particularly fences, appear more beautiful—heart-breakingly so," wrote the poet Roethke.

217

The roof of Al Johnson's restaurant reveals three red-ribboned wooden reindeer.

Just when does fall end?

The first real snow falls and we watch in astonishment, the road, the fields, the woods, and finally the September of ourselves disappear. We pull the door closed behind us. With a click.

We begin to forget.

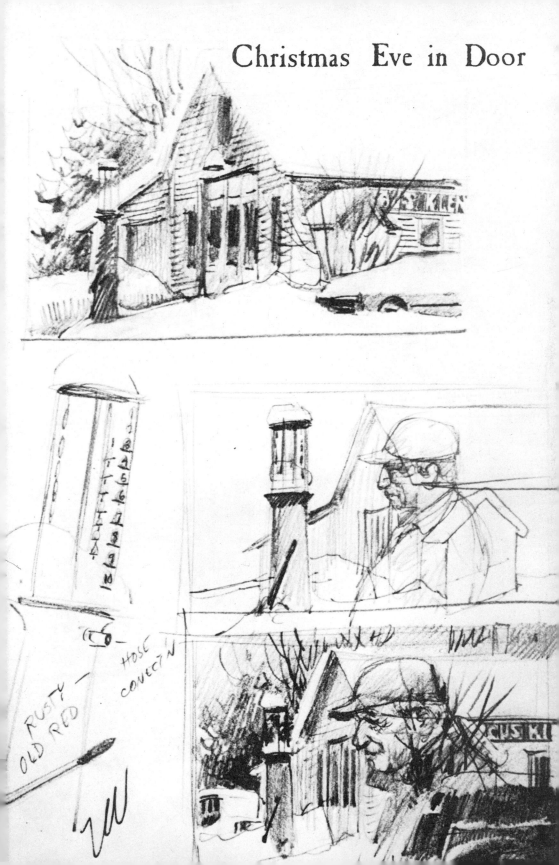

Christmas Eve in Door

It's a different time in many ways: the absence of snow for one, the fact this is my first Christmas Eve in Door after years of living here.

My Christmases have all been Chicago Christmases: shopping in the Loop, the neighborhood, the suburban plazas, and Chicago's Magnificent Mile. Christmas Eve at my parents: French fried shrimp from a local deli, homemade bakery, aunts, uncles, cousins, neighbors, the opening of gifts, and in my early days, midnight mass.

Christmas Day with my in-laws in their neighborhood, right next door to mine. The early morning opening of gifts, Grandma's traditional Christmas dinner, goose or duck or turkey or some Czech dish, followed by an afternoon and an evening of slumbering in cozy armchairs, recovering.

If the truth be known, I could have gone back and partially experienced such traditions once again.

If the truth be known, a death in the family has altered things a bit. For a change of scene, sometimes necessary in such situations, Christmas was to be moved to another location, the burden of memories eased. I remained behind, getting on with my work, holding the fort: one house, a chicken coop, two aquariums thick with tropical fish, one parakeet, one dog, and about 1,500 house plants, each with special needs.

If the truth be known, for years now the specialness of this season has meant less and less to me. Christmas was best as a child, and then as a father of small children. Now I find it impossible to muster the expected enthusiasm.

The commerce of Christ grows more and more repulsive. A time of giving? A time of greed. And as for a new year, I've never known one that was distinct from the old or what lies ahead. It's all the same piece of cloth. Numbering helps, I guess, though I prefer the timeclock of seasons, of day turning into night.

Nor is it a case of "losing the spirit"; a writer's work, if it is to have any meaning at all, is to constantly find it, redefine it, and make it known in whatever way, Christmas or no Christmas. Even as I am now engaged in doing, alone, this very afternoon of Christmas Eve in Door.

If the truth be known, I relish solitude a good part of the time, living in my head, creating all kinds of worlds there. I need but the slightest reality to set me off: a face, a gesture, a city, a glimpse of the natural countryside.

Even just a memory will do.

An early afternoon phone call from my wife and kids indicates that all is well in their place, leads me to wonder alone about my Christmas here.

4 p.m. I am finished with the words, the people, the places I have been imagining on paper for the day. I turn down the heat in the coop where I work, study a morning's watercolor that has dried, close up shop and trudge into the house through a sharp wind and cold rain.

I turn on the kitchen lights in an empty house, the dog shaking herself free from an afternoon slumber. This will be a Christmas Eve of my own making: an extra treat for the dog, more seed for the late afternoon birds at the feeder, and maybe some apple pie for myself, later tonight, I decide, turning on the oven and putting it in.

Then a walk down the road, where I inevitably find myself for no reason in all times of the year, all hours, whatever the weather. The wind blows steadily from the north, a desolate wail strumming through the bare branches.

I pass the garden first, a few cornstalks and sunflowers still standing, the strange but welcome sight of the overturned earth in December without the touch of snow. Far down the next field the empty house of an old friend, Charley Root, still haunts me. His Christmas Eves past—what were they like? And that last and lonely Christmas of his, six years ago now, when I returned from Chicago with gifts and food for him, only to learn he had died in the brief time I had been gone: there was snow in this field that Christmas, and a vast emptiness from my road to his door that still remains each time I pass his darkened house.

I move down the road toward the white farmhouse of Carl and Helen Carlson, so perfect in its setting: early Americana, pure Wisconsin. The smell of woodsmoke from their chimney, the kitchen windows brightly lit, a Christmas tree out front in all its color.

I turn around and head for home, the wind blowing a little harder, the rain falling a little faster. The sky hanging low, a furry gray deepening into night. I can smell the apple pie.

I light the Christmas tree, put on some carols sung in Italian, feed the dog, the fish, the bird, making believe it's Christmas Eve.

For dinner? Well, there's that apple pie with some sharp cheddar, but that's for later. I could make some huevos rancheros or some fried rice or any number of dishes to soothe a December appetite—anything but French fried shrimp, cole slaw, hot and cold potato salad from a deli in the old neighborhood.

Pizza? I just happen to have one of my favorites in the freezer, a large cheese and sausage, carefully, creatively crafted in Door in the finest Italian tradition by Vito (Tony) Demarinis: oregano, fennel, provolone, mozzarella, memorable aromas of the old neighborhood, and a remembrance of Tony's pizzas past—summer after summer—his warmth

224

and good nature, appropriate indeed on Christmas Eve.

I take the pie out, put the pizza in, take the pizza back out, deciding at the last minute on a few extras: fresh mushrooms, green pepper, onion, a sort of red chili pepper, memories of good times and good friends in the Southwest. And as the aroma of Tony's pizza baking fills the entire house, I build an unforgettable salad and open a cold beer.

The phone rings. No one there. Then a crackling, a distant voice, my own voice echoing into the receiver, then the unmistakable voice of an old college friend, Richard Alger, calling from West Yorkshire, England. It's been fifteen years since I visited him over there, though we do correspond, though he does call whenever the mood and possibly the homemade brew is upon him. I'm forever surprised, gratified, over the length and depth of friendship. (Christmas Day will bring a call from the LewAllens and a houseful of friends in New Mexico.) I'm forever amazed how voices can bridge an entire ocean in moments.

Everything so far this afternoon heightens the prospect of an evening to be celebrated alone. I can read, I can listen to some good music, watch some TV, start on that apple pie . . . the possibilities of a long and peaceful night seem endless. Yet a restlessness persists, the urge to do something else *first,* and *then* let there be music and wine and apple pie and the dwindling hours of night.

Aside from my love of walking, my restless nature of getting up and going somewhere, I can instantly dream up any excuse imaginable to get in the car and just drive the county roads. There's a peace for me there I cannot explain, though I am aware that much of my writing is done this way. And why not now, on Christmas Eve in Door?

I fill a thermos with coffee, pack plenty of pipe tobacco, close the house, and head out on a kind of makeshift Santa Claus mission of my own, bearing gifts for no one, just a joy of self, of the moment, of the countryside, a spontaneous plunge into a Door Christmas Eve of my own discovery.

The car coughes and sputters in the December air, windshield wipers squeaking, tires humming on the wet pavement, vaguely reminiscent of a mild rainy evening in fall.

Down Timberline, past the darkened houses of Matt Daubner and Mike Till . . . night, night, night of no Christmas light. Things pick up approaching the road to Northport: colored lights on some houses, more splashes of them here and there while moving toward Gills Rock . . . stone cold dead, abandoned, no sign of a Christmas Eve ferry to Washington Island, no sign of Christmas save down on the dock where I park, where the white-capped waters of the bay lick the pier deliciously with ice, where three fishing tubs swing gently on lines in their slip, one of them with a Christmasy green hull and named "Faith II."

Back in the car heading south down 42 now, a familiar stretch of Gills

Rock houses first, clustered around the top of the thumb, giving way to farms and rural countryside. For once there is no light in Phil Phillipon's studio; Christmas Eve in the bright living room, I suspect.

Rounding the curve, past the Fitzgeralds, the Hartman house, the Coopers, all the windows ablaze, Sid Telfer Sr. and Inez tucked there in the woods, the old Ellison Bay Schoolhouse, the Clearing gate open for a winter's welcome. Then a left past the Post Office, past Gust Klenke's house, the trunk of his Buick Beemobile wide open, appropriately enough. I would not be surprised to see Gust bent over, rummaging in there in the dark, looking for some long forgotten part.

And on the corner, his worn and fading white garage—propane tanks, old stoves, power mowers, odds and ends in rusted glory, and one gas pump—all of it aglow in colored Christmas lights. Gust's holiday greeting, in a way: "From My House of Everything Imaginable To Yours." A curious old-fashioned Christmas card, almost surreal, come to life. Real, though, and unexplainably beautiful. (Those lights will shine, very likely, all through this night, and the next, and on to spring.)

In the heart of Ellison Bay, I am briefly surprised to see Newman's Pioneer Store open on Christmas Eve. But then again, there has never been a night, a time, or a need when the old Pioneer Store let me down. For this, many of us are thankful. A loaf of bread, a dozen eggs, some good cigars. Newman's is open. And there's Lester or Carol or the two of them at the old wooden counter quietly playing cribbage, quietly minding the store.

"I thought you might be closed tonight."

"People have been calling," she replies.

I buy some bacon to go along with a Christmas morning breakfast of Uncle Tom's pancakes I've planned.

"I counted five cars between here and Fish Creek tonight, when I left the store there," she says. "That's quite a contrast to this summer when I counted over 300," she laughs.

Upon leaving I nod to Lester, who has come in from the back with an armful of logs for the old stove that stands in the middle of the store, a warm and glowing reminder of country stores past—and present.

Getting back into the car, I wave to Harvey ("Sheriff") Olson just crossing the road on a Pioneer Store Christmas Eve shopping errand of his own.

The drive from Ellison Bay south is relatively unmarked by Christmas except for the decorations of the Hanson house on top of the hill, and then, approaching Sister Bay, the white steeple of Zion Lutheran Church that lights the sky in all seasons, but seems especially bright for now.

The main drag of Sister Bay is a study in stillness. Not a car. Not a soul. Only the beautifully lighted trees on the telephone poles. The wind. The shining white pavement.

The goats have left the sod roof of Al Johnson's for Bethlehem, leaving t' ee tiny wooden reindeer with quizzical faces to watch the Sister Bay night. When the lights are out in Husby's, there must be something stirring.

I proceed, with caution, toward Ephraim. The rain has let up, somewhat. I pour some coffee, light up, turn on the radio . . . but the rock music is somehow all wrong for now. I go with the silence of the night, the wind, the tires still humming on wet pavement.

In the distance, just before the turn, I see a vertical string of colored Christmas light rising to the heavens and topped with a bright burning star. Amos Rasmussen's flagpole. I smile. There's a star, too, hanging over the old Anderson store, and another on the Ephraim Village Hall, where two big, red bells toll soundlessly in the wind.

And just up the hill, on a Christmas Eve, a winter of no ice cream at Wilson's, the stained glass windows of the Moravian Church, a scene reminiscent again of an early American Christmas, where the white-bright church steeples of Ephraim hover over a traditional Christ s Eve, the stained glass aglow, while a steady stream of worshippers, in cars, moves up the hill for the evening's service. Soon carols will calm the mind and the churning waters of the harbor on this holy night.

I could go back at this point, but instead I continue toward Fish Creek, the road very dark once again. Christmas has pulled back, pulled into the villages and farms far from the road, leaving woods and fields and darkened summer houses till Fish Creek itself appears, where people are gathering at the Catholic Church and a single, magnificent Christmas decoration hangs above the street like a canopy of red and green and gold light. Beyond it is darkness, desolation. Fish Creek is gone till spring.

As I return toward Ephraim, unsure just what direction I might steer next, a light in the sky catches my eye. The star? No. Absurd in this overcast night. A beacon, though. A light of the East . . . and the West, North, South. The light of the Ephraim airport scanning the skyline, circling the low heavens, bouncing over an impenetrable layer of clouds. I follow it only to find an abandoned airstrip, a night of no departures and no arrivals, an empty phone booth, seven deserted cars and one plane, touched in Christmas red.

The tiny blue-white lights of Ephraim sparkle across the bay, a beautiful scene in all seasons, from the distance of the park hill, from the road winding past the beach. I veer to the right, up, past the Moravians singing their Eve of Christmas away, turning, climbing County Q east toward highway 57, then suddenly south, further still into Baileys Harbor.

Past Roy Lukes' place, a small light in the window, past the birdhouse of Otto Zahn, strangely alive in waving shadows of trees this blustery night, and into the heart of Baileys Harbor, both sides of the street braided in tiny Christmas trees and light. Empty, the entire town, but for the Immanuel Lutheran Church and a street filled with cars.

Onto my favorite backroads now, all the way home: turning at Paul's

Glass Bar, County EE, then a right onto County F, and further ahead, leaving F to snake my way down Townline Road. I like the cathedral of maples right down the first part of F. I like the way the whole land opens to a western and northern horizon. Even tonight, in the darkness and rain, there is somehow more sky, more light from this vantage point. Slowing down, I roll the window and look for stars, only to startle something white, a gull, with a burst of wings erupting from a field, taking flight over the beaming headlights of the car. I have never thought of gulls inland, in the night, before.

Moving along Townline, I pass Freddie Kodanko's house and wonder about him and Christmas Eve. Is the polka music playing? Does he dance alone around the tree? Is there a tree? Are his cats watching?

Then past Chet Elquist's, an old and good friend, gone now, how many Christmases already? The warm times shared with him and Florence in all seasons. Laughter, drink, fishing stories and good food. I slow down past the picture window and catch a glimpse of Flossie, alone in the dim living room looking out upon the darkness, seeing, perhaps, only the lights of a solitary car drifting by.

Crossing County Q, nearing 42, passing a house that will always be Bill Beckstrom's place to me. A memory of a finely crafted home, a comfortable living room and stone fireplace, Bill slouched in a chair, pulling on a cigarette, running a hand through his gray hair, talking plants or books or ideas with a friend, or reading alone, or lost in a labyrinth of music, a Dvorak symphony, where his living was best and nearly perfect.

East toward Sister Bay now, then bypassing it around the information booth. Picking up 57 again past the Patio Drive-In, cutting off onto Orchard to turn left on Old Stage just head. From here to Ellison Bay, home free.

Again the darkness, the wind, the landscape nothing more than what it is, textured in rain and shadow, silhouetted in barns and farmhouses, and an occasional rectangle of light floating in a distant window. The night before Christmas is nowhere in sight till the Ingwersen's place, a Christmas card painting in light—golden, white, splotches of Christmas color red/green/blue—and Phyllis and Jim walking outside in the midst of it all toward their front door.

Old Stage curving now, north mostly. A long stretch of night and no Christmas. The farms spreading further apart now. The mind wanders, loses sight. I reflect on all the Christmases I have never known but hope to someday see: Christmas in Rome, in Eastern Europe, in Mexico, in Santa Fe. I recall a midnight mass described to me on the Santa Domingo reservation, and how the rites of both cultures, Native American and Christian, come together on this night. The candles burning, the hymns, the chants, the crucifix, the Christ Child . . . "then down the aisle," as my friend described, "Indians, the dancers, dressed in buffalo heads."

That image so overwhelms me that when I look for the familiar outside, I realize that nothing seems the same to me, that for the first time, and here of all places, I am lost. Did I turn off Old Stage for some reason?

I follow the road and find myself on Water's End—Lake Michigan, where a solitary fishing tug, "Hope," no less, rests this night of all nights.

Images of the Southwest still flash through my mind . . . I think of yet another man, one of the poorest men in Door I know: the old migrant, Ignacio Gonzales, picturing him cramped in his small trailer tonight, wondering how his Eve might be. Rabbit and pinto beans? A small tree? Or maybe nothing more than sleep. I ply the backroads once again, just to know he is somewhere there, and safe.

From Waters End to 42, then back to Z . . . where is he anyway? Darkness, darkness everywhere. Cats' eyes glowing in the darkest ditch. And then a cluster of buildings which might reveal Ignacio's place. And then . . . yes, of course, there . . . his tiny trailer—but a sight I am not prepared for: Ignacio's trailer, his small world, decked out in Christmas lights! A light in the little window. The shadow of him safe inside. This, perhaps, my greatest joy tonight.

All roads lead, eventually, to Ellison Bay from here, including Mink River Road which takes me past the house of old Oscar Dysterud, moving slowly through the living room this night, past Gust Klenke's garage once again, the blue-white neon clock glowing in the window forever, it seems, 8:45 . . . more or less.

The pavement almost dry from the wind by now. But no clearing. No moon. No stars. Just an ever deepening night. The only snow to be seen, patches of it from weeks ago, still clinging to the roadside ditch past the Hartman place and Johnny Fitzgerald.

Approaching Timberline, a string of colored Christmas lights brightens the front porch of Loco's (Robert Cuellar) place. A light, always on, at Uncle Tom's old Newport School. Turning left . . . darkness . . . turning right . . . home.

I make coffee, cut the apple pie, slice some cheddar cheese, light the Christmas tree, put on three albums of classical guitar, sip wine, and open a present I have given to myself: *The Letters of D. H. Lawrence.* "The great thing is to love—therein lies the excitement, the fundamental vibration of the life force."

I read in and around a stack of other books, listen to a Dylan Thomas recording of "A Child's Christmas in Wales," answer the phone (good friends, the Rausches, extending their greetings from Western Springs, Illinois), then turn on the TV to catch John Paul the II's mass from Rome (for old time's sake), to see St. Peter's Basilica once again, to hear the Latin, the music, to witness the splendor of a ritual I once celebrated as a child, a ritual which intrigues me still in different ways.

I think of my family in other places. I think of friends spread out in so many directions. I think of my own journey in place this Christmas Eve in Door.

I think not so much of Christmas as *spirit,* alive in all men, in all seasons, in all places, and how it flickers in the darkest recesses imaginable. I think of my gift, my work: to find the people, the place, the time, the words and forms to say these things for all, yet make them mine.

Call it Christmas. Call it spirit. Call it love. Call it light.

In the midnight hours I read a Hopi incantation, and turn to sleep:

> The day has risen.
> Go I to behold the dawn.
> Go behold the dawn!
> The white-rising!
> The yellow rising!
> It has become light.

And on Christmas morning, on the road, a clarity of sky, a gift of sun.